To my
daughter

May the blessing of this Holy
Week be upon both of you.

Ethan
2017.

HOLY WEEK CONTEMPLATIONS

Holy Week
Contemplations

by

His Holiness Pope Shenouda III

ST SHENOUDA'S MONASTERY
SYDNEY, AUSTRALIA
2013

HOLY WEEK CONTEMPLATIONS

ST SHENOUDA MONASTERY
Putty Rd, Putty, NSW
Sydney, Australia

www.stshenoudamonastery.org.au

ISBN 13: 978-0-9873400-2-3

Cover Design:
Hani Ghaly,
Begoury Graphics
begourygraphics@gmail.com

Contents

PREFACE

These books first appeared in the late sixties and have since been reprinted many times. They have been combined into one book to make them more contained. Perhaps contemplations on the Holy Week of Pascha needs many more books as it is the holiest week in the year, filled with wonderful spiritual memories which are impossible to gather in one book. Contemplations on the Holy Week of Pascha are suitable at any time of the year, as the suffering of our Lord Jesus Christ is the foundation of our Christian faith. We remember the suffering of our Lord Jesus Christ every day in the sixth hour prayer of the Agpya. Therefore, we present these contemplations in your hands and, I also pray, deep in your heart.

This book is a collection of the following five books:

1. Contemplations on Holy Week

2. Contemplations on the Holy Week Praises (To You is the Power and the Glory)

3. Contemplations on Covenant Thursday

4. Contemplations on Good Friday

5. Contemplations on the Words of Christ on the Cross

Pope Shenouda III

THE IMPORTANCE OF
HOLY WEEK

The Holy Pascha Week is the holiest and most spiritual week of the entire year. It is a week filled with many holy memories in the most critical stage of the period of salvation and the most important chapter in the story of salvation. The Church has selected special readings from both the Old and New Testaments. All the readings are filled with passion and emotions which effectively reveal the relationship between God and mankind. Also the Church has selected a group of spiritual hymns and contemplations.

This week is called Passion Week, Pascha Week or Holy Week. In the English language it is called Holy Week and each day of this week is the holiest of the year. For example, Thursday is called "Holy Thursday", Friday is called "Holy Friday" and so on.

This week is dedicated completely to worship and people refrain from work and they gather in Churches for prayer and meditation. People used to take time off work to devote themselves to the Lord and the Holy commemorations. They attend Church, pray and listen to the hymns and the readings.

Many people take time of work to go on a holiday or attend a wedding etc, but what can be more beautiful than taking time off to spend with God in Church. The Christian Kings and Emperors used to grant people this week off as a holiday. In the past, Christian Kings and Emperors used to give government employees a holiday to attend worship at Church during this week. It is said that Emperor Theodosius the Great used to allow captives and prisoners to attend Holy Week with the rest of the believers. This gave them the chance to rebuild their relationship with God and reform.

Also the Masters used to give their slaves the week off for worship. The Ten Commandments says, "But the seventh day is the Sabbath of the Lord your God. In it you shall do no work; you, nor your son, nor your daughter, nor your manservant, nor your maidservant, nor your cattle, nor your stranger who is within your gates." (Exodus 20:10).

Indeed your servants and the rest of the nation have the right to worship God like you and should participate in the sanctity of these days. They have the right to take time off work to worship the Lord. So all worship together and deeply enjoy the significance of this week. During the days of slavery, the Apostles arranged in their laws that slaves should take this week off work for worship and also a further week after Easter.

Do you give your employees time off during Pascha Week? Since an employer takes time off during this week to worship then they have no need for their employees.

The signs of sorrow and grief are very visible in the Church. The pillars of the Church are wrapped in black veils; the icons are also wrapped in black as are the pulpit and the Church walls. The hymns are sung in the sorrowful tunes and the readings correspond with the journey and events of the week. The believers avoid any visible signs of joy or happiness.

Women do not wear jewellery or make up and any kind of celebrations are cancelled during this week. The whole Church is in mourning for the passion of Christ which will be explained later. Do we join in with this sorrow during Pascha Week? Or at least keep the holiness of the events? Or do we spend time amusing ourselves in fun, pleasure and entertainment and living a totally different life outside the Church?

The Church lives a high level of asceticism. Some hermits abstain from food altogether for the whole week or abstain for three days then eat one meal and then continue abstinence for another three days. Many believers also abstain from food from Thursday night right through until after the Easter service, many of them only eating bread and salt during this time. If they were unable to abstain completely, they would then eat bread with herbs as it was not suitable to eat sweets whilst remembering the sufferings of our Lord Jesus Christ for their sake. Also they used to not eat any cooked meals as they did not want to waste time preparing the food, they preferred to keep their minds and hearts on Christ and His suffering.

During this week the only sacraments which are practiced are the Sacrament of Confession and the Sacrament of Priesthood. During Holy Week the Sacraments of Baptism and the Holy Myron are not practiced. Also the Raising of Incense and the Holy Liturgy are not held except on Covenant Thursday and Joyous Saturday. And of course it is impossible to practice the Sacrament of Holy Matrimony. The Sacrament of the Unction of the Sick is carried out on friday, the Seal of the Fast, just before the start of Holy Week.

No funeral services are held during this week. In the event of someone passing away, there is no raising of incense, but the body is taken to the Church to attend the Pascha prayers and the absolution is read, as well as special prayers.

During Holy Week we do not pray from the Agpya. The Agpya prayers are replaced by the Pascha praises. This is because the Agpya prayers represent many events in the life of Christ, but during this week we are focusing only on the suffering of Christ. For instance, in the Morning Prayer we remember the birth of Christ, in the Midnight Prayer we remember the second coming and in the Third Hour Prayer we remember the descent of the Holy Spirit on the disciples. However, during this week, we want to focus only on the suffering of our Lord Jesus Christ.

Even the Sixth Hour Prayer, which reminds us of Christ's Crucifixion and the Ninth Hour Prayer where we are reminded of His death are not prayed during Holy Week. These prayers are postponed until Good Friday so that we can follow Christ's journey in chronological order. As for the Psalms, we select from them what is suitable for this week. The remaining Psalms from the Agpya which have any meaning other than the suffering of Christ and the events of this week are omitted.

WHY THIS WEEK IS CALLED PASCHA WEEK?

The word Pascha means "Passover" which is taken from Exodus 12:18 when God said, "When I see the blood, I will pass over you." In the first Passover the Israelites were saved by the blood. Our Lord Jesus Christ is referred to as the Passover as it is said, "For indeed Christ, our Passover, was sacrificed for us" (I Corinthians 5:7).

Throughout this Holy week we remember the sufferings of our Lord Jesus Christ, who offered Himself as a Passover. This happened so that when the Father saw the blood of the Passover, He would redeem us from the sword of death so as not to perish. We also remember that His blood was shed for our sake. There is no salvation except through His blood, as it happened at the first Passover (Exodus 12).

THESE DAYS ARE HOLY DAYS

Not only are the Pascha days holy days they are the holiest days of the year. What do we mean when we say the Pascha days are holy days? All the days of our lives are considered holy days. Each day we pray the Prayer of Thanksgiving saying; "Keep us in peace this blessed day and all the days of our life." We say this every day because our Lord Jesus Christ has given us life through His blood. Hence, through His blood, our life is sanctified. However, there is no denying that there are days that are holier than others.

Perhaps the first example of this is the sanctification of the Lord's day every week. This is mentioned in the Holy Bible in the story of Creation, "Remember the Sabbath day, to keep it holy." (Exodus 21:2), "observe the Sabbath day to keep it Holy." (Deuteronomy 5:12).

It is the day of the Lord, a holy day, a day that is blessed and sanctified by the Lord and He asked us to also make it holy. In Greek it is called "kericaki", which means the Lord's day. It is a day dedicated to the Lord in which we do not work as He commanded us. We also do not work on any of the other holy days which the Lord referred to (Leviticus 23).

These days are more holy than other days. Our whole lives are holy; however the days of the Lord are extremely holy. This is because they are dedicated to the Lord. There are moments which have their own unique kind of holiness for spiritual reasons. Despite the fact that our life is holy, the times of prayer, meditation, visions and revelations has its own unique holiness.

And there are Holy days in everyone's life. The day that the Lord appeared to Saul (Acts 9), was a day of special holiness. And the day which Saint John the Beloved saw his vision and wrote the Book of Revelation was also a day of special holiness. Also the days of fasts and feasts are days that have their own special holiness, unlike any other day.

If the days of Lent are the holiest days of the year and the Pascha week is in Lent, then we can say that Pascha week is the holiest week of the year. The holy Lent contains the highest level of asceticism, more than any other fast. Therefore, the level of worship during Holy Week, when the believers gather together in the Church, raising their prayers in one spirit, listening to the selected readings from the Old and New Testaments, as well as the deep praises with their deep spiritual impact, is very holy indeed.

The spiritual memories of this week are very powerful, as we follow Christ step by step, as we sing the Pascha praises, "To You is the Power, the Glory and the Honour forever, Amen, Emmanuel our God and our King."

The spiritual meaning of this week has its own unique depth.

Believers are dedicated, serious, meticulous and more submissive to God, giving all their time to Him. Although it is ideal to dedicate all your time to Him during this week, if you are unable to dedicate your full time to Christ our Lord, then try as much as you can to devote some time at least.

It is a week which we enter into fellowship of Christ's sufferings. We put before us all His sufferings, with a contrite heart and true repentance in order to prepare ourselves for Holy Communion on Covenant Thursday. It was on this day that the Lord made His covenant with his pure disciples and established this great mystery (the Sacrament of Holy Communion). Now we need to ask, how did this Holy Week start?

How did this week start?

The sufferings of Christ started as early as when King Herod planned to kill Him when he ordered the killing of the children of Bethlehem. King Herod thought that our Lord Jesus Christ was among those who were killed but in fact the Holy Family escaped to Egypt before this was achieved.

Our Lord's earthly service was filled with suffering from the very beginning. For instance, there was the controversy of the Scribes and the Pharisees fighting against Him and the jealousy towards Christ when they witnessed the people's interest in Him.

How many times did they try to kill Him and they could not? This is because His hour had not yet come. And when did this hour come? It came when He gave Himself up to redeem the world. The thread of the controversy against Him began when they seriously considered killing Him on Sunday, and they paid the price to Judah on Wednesday and arrested the Lord on Thursday night (Friday eve). Together we will try to continue with this story to see how this controversy started:

I Christ's popularity caused the Jewish leaders to be envious. Our Lord Jesus Christ was very popular and much loved among the people. Thousands of people crowded around Him and were amazed by His teachings and His miracles, but the Jewish leaders envied Him. They tried to turn the crowds against Him by saying that His miracles were not from God. They said, "This fellow does not cast out demons except by Beelzebub, the ruler of the demons." (Matthew 12:24). They also told the people that Christ makes the Law invalid, but they failed in their plans and the people still loved and followed Jesus.

2 Then He raised Lazarus on Saturday. It was a profound miracle. It was different from the miracle of raising the daughter of Jairus and raising the son of the widow of Nain, when he was in his coffin, because four days had passed since his death (John 11:39) and it was said about him that, "there would be a stench." (John 11:39). This miracle had a great impact and many people believed in Him.

3 Before raising Lazarus He opened the eyes of the blind man. This was the first time such a miracle occurred, "Since the world began it has been unheard of that anyone opened the eyes of one who was born blind" (John 9:32).

So the Jewish leaders started to use the authorities and they cast Him out, "For the Jews had agreed already that if anyone confessed that He was Christ, he would be put out of the synagogue." (John 9:22).

At the death of Lazarus, people remembered this miracle, "and some of them said, 'Could not this Man, who opened the eyes of the blind, also have kept this man form dying?'" (John 11: 37).

4 After the miracle of raising Lazarus, they gathered a council against Christ. Then the chief priests and the Pharisees gathered a council and said, "What shall we do? For this Man works many signs. If we let Him alone like this, everyone will believe in Him,

and the Romans will come and take away both our place and nation." And Caiaphas, being high priest that year, said to them, "You know nothing at all, nor do you consider that it is expedient for us that one man should die for the people, and not that the whole nation should perish." (John11:46-50).

It is clear that this was a false accusation because the miracles of Christ did not result in the destruction of the nation nor affect the Roman rule. So the raising of Lazarus and it's effects pushed the Jewish leaders to hold a council. After the council it was said, "Then, from that day on, they plotted to put Him to death". Also, they tried to kill Lazarus.

5 Sunday came and the Jewish leaders became agitated and wanted to kill Him. The way the people greeted Him as a King aggravated them even more. The People cried out: "Blessed is He who comes in the name of the Lord! The King of Israel!" (John 12: 13). So the Jewish leaders felt that they had lost their authority. This became clear as they, out of envy, insisted on killing him. And the Pharisees therefore said among themselves, 'You see that you are accomplishing nothing. Look, the world has gone after Him!" (John 12:19).

6 What about those people who loved Christ? How could they face the crowds who shouted, "Crucify Him?" Where before they called Him 'The King of Israel?" This is because Christ refused the earthly kingdom, as He said "My Kingdom is not of this world." (John 18:36).

Thus, the people had great hopes on the coming of the Kingdom of Christ as they chanted on Palm Sunday, Hosanna! The Jewish leaders were successful in influencing these people to gain them on their side.

7 But The Lord Jesus Christ felt that His hour was near and He began to practice His authority in order to fulfill His death

that He wanted.　So He purified the temple and scolded the Jewish Leaders.

CONTEMPLATIONS ON THE SUFFERING OF CHRIST

The most useful thing in our spiritual life is for us to reflect on suffering, and in particular the sufferings of Christ. Meditation in suffering lifts up the spirit. It lifts the spirit above the level of worldly desires. Therefore, when one is in the state of suffering, usually his/her spirit is stronger, spiritually deeper and often detached from the love of the world.

When we are in the state of joy we may feel cheerful and happy that the world is on our side but during times of suffering and pain we feel that the love of the world has disappeared from our hearts.

Therefore, it is easier for the sick person to draw closer to God. When a person is sick and experiencing suffering and pain they can accept to hear about and talk about God, loves to pray and asks people to pray for them and the word of God is always on their lips, more than in the case of good health.

Likewise, the person who is experiencing hardship and sadness or any sort of graveness, their heart is usually far from the lusts of the world and materialistic things. Perhaps the Lord allows such suffering because it may be beneficial to our spirit if handled wisely. Those who visit tombstones benefit from just looking at images of death and remember lost friends and loved ones; this gives them a deeper understanding and a deeper spiritual life.

There are many stories of Saints who benefited greatly from death. Saint Anthony the Great benefited spiritually from the death of his father. Also, he lived the first few years of his monastic life in a grave. Saint Macarious the Great used to keep a skull in his cell and would rest on it while sleeping.

Just the mention of death can be of benefit to the heart of a wise man. What about the mention of Christ's death and His suffering? Therefore during Holy Week, believers are more spiritually deep. Suffering is the most significant contemplation that we must meditate on in the life of our Lord Jesus Christ.

The Cross is our Christian motto, a symbol of suffering. The Cross encompasses the depth of the physical suffering (pain) of Christ. It impacts our souls more than any other event in the glorious life of our Lord. There is no doubt that every event in the life of our Lord Jesus Christ impacts us, but the image of the Cross is the most influential one.

It was said that when Gandhi, the well known Indian leader, stood before the image of the crucifixion, he was deeply moved by it in spite of being a Hindu.

The Angel of Resurrection focused on the sentence, "The Crucified", so he said to the women, "Do not be afraid, for I know that you seek Jesus who was crucified. He is not here for He is risen." (Matthew 28:5-6). He called Him "crucified" even after His resurrection and He continued to be called "the crucified", as St Paul said, "For indeed Christ our Passover was sacrificed for us." (I Corinthians 5-7). Also, St. John said about Him, "And in the midst of the elders, stood a Lamb as though it had been slain." (Revelation 5:6). St. John also said that he heard the, "Voice of many angels saying, 'Worthy is the Lamb who was slain to receive power and riches and wisdom. And strength and honour and glory and blessing.'" (Revelation 5:12). Thus, we see that the Bible focused on Christ's suffering even in the Book of Revelation. This shows us that Christ's suffering is not only the earthly subject of contemplation, but also the heavenly.

All His suffering is recorded in the Bible, not only the events of the Cross, but many other events in His life on earth. His suffering was not only one week, but throughout His ministry and even since His birth. Divine inspiration summarised the life of our Lord in the flesh in the following deep, focused sentence which described Him as, "A Man of sorrows and acquainted with grief." (Isaiah 53:3).

He was born during the coldest days of winter, in a very cold place which was the manger, as there was no place for them (Luke 2:7). King Herod made every effort to kill Him, so he had all the children of Bethlehem killed that He might be among them! So the Holy family had to flee to Egypt with Him. Then they returned, "After those who sought the young Child's life were dead." (Matthew 2:20).

The Lord Jesus Christ spent His early childhood and His youth unknown in a house of a poor carpenter. The world knows little of this period in time. Christ lived as a poor person, bearing the narrow road for our sake. He did not walk the wide road, but had a life full of suffering, both emotionally and physically. He did not have a house or money. When tax collectors came to collect the taxes He had nothing to give.

He experienced hardship, hunger and thirst. An example of this was when He said that He was tired after a long journey to save the Samaritan woman. The Holy Bible says, "Jesus therefore, being wearied from His journey, sat thus by the well, it was about the sixth hour". (John 4: 6).

Just as Christ experienced hardships He also hungered, but when we say hungered we do not mean the usual hunger as if one was delayed an hour or so from eating. When it was said that Christ was hungry on the mountain, it is that hunger that is above what humans can tolerate from the abstinence of food. It was said that "afterward He was hungry," (Matthew 4:2), at last after forty days of fasting! When it was said that He was thirsty on the Cross, it was describing an intolerable thirst; after all the fluid was lost from His body.

The hunger and thirst He felt at the well of the Samaritan woman was not of the hunger and thirst of food and water. The Holy Bible does not mention that He ate food or drank water. Christ said, "My food is to do the will of Him who sent me." (John 4:34).

Christ experienced the pain of rejection in His ministry. "He came to His own, and His own did not receive Him." (John 1:11).

"And the light shines in the darkness, and the darkness did not comprehend it." (JohnI:5). It is painful to know that the light came into the world and men loved the darkness rather than the light because their deeds were evil. (John 3:19). In the Lord the prophecy of the Psalm was fulfilled, "Those also who render evil for good, They are my adversaries, because I follow what is good." (Psalm 38:20).

All His life He treated people with love, but He did not find love in return. He did not find love which was equal to His love or even good treatment which was similar to His good treatment of others. This is clearly seen in the verse, "The Son of man has nowhere to lay His head." (Matthew 8:20). As we read this verse and consider it from a physical viewpoint, we should also understand it from the emotional side.

The Lord Jesus Christ lived among ungrateful, denying people, denying His love and denying His good works. Once He went to His own country Bethlehem, and they rejected Him. They did not believe Him, but they scorned Him and treated Him with contempt saying; "When He had come to His own country, He taught them in their synagogue, so that they were astonished and said, "Where did this Man get this wisdom and these mighty works? Is this not the carpenter's son? Is not His mother called Mary? And His brothers James, Joses, Simon, and Judas? And His sisters, are they not all with us? Where then did this Man get all these things?" So they were offended at Him. But Jesus said to them, "A prophet is not without honour except in his own country and in his own house." Now He did not do many mighty works there because of their unbelief." (Matthew 13:54-57). So the Lord said to them, "A prophet is not without honour except in his own country, among his own relatives and in his own house".

Then He went to a city of Samaria and its door was closed in his face. The disciples were not happy about this, but He bore with Samaria in great love and patience until he was able to enter and work for its salvation. And when He saw the fruit of His work in Samaria

He said to His disciples, "I sent you to reap that for which you have not laboured; others have labored, and you have entered into their labors." (John 4:38). Truly the work for the salvation of souls needs much hard work, suffering, tolerance and longsuffering.

Sometimes, He sees the doors of our hearts closed so He stands there and knocks. It may take a long time, until His head is wet with dew, and His locks of hair with drops of the night. (Song of Songs 5:2). Here the Lord teaches us that in order to earn the love of the people we need to acquire endurance, patience and longsuffering.

Sometimes the hearts of people are hard and stiff and cannot be entered quickly or easily. So if you have tried hard to earn the hearts of people and couldn't, do not be upset, or if you have entered a person's heart and did not find the same level of love, do not be sad as this happened to Christ and He is the source of love and He continued treating people with love.

But while He was among people He "went about doing good." (Acts 10:38). "And Jesus went about all Galilee, teaching in their synagogues, preaching the gospel of the kingdom, and healing all kinds of sickness and all kinds of disease among the people." (Matthew 4:23). Who of those people did not receive from the love of Christ? Each and every one received it, even those who rejected Him, even those who later cried "Crucify Him, crucify Him." He spread His love to all, but was criticised by the Jewish leaders. When He felt pity for the tax collector and wanted to save his soul, they criticized Him saying, "He has gone to be a guest with a man who is a sinner". (Luke 19:7). So Christ answered and said; "Today salvation has come to this house, because he also is a son of Abraham." (Luke 19:9).

The Lord endured those who criticised Him, and continued to try and gain them. How many times did He do good and was criticised for it? This was seen in His love for the tax collectors (Luke 18:9-14) and the Samaritans (Luke 10:30-35). He was also compassionate to the sinful woman that washed His feet with her tears and Simon the Pharisee criticised Him within his heart saying, "This Man, if He were a prophet, would know who and what manner of woman this is who is touching Him for she is a sinner." (Luke 7:39). Christ then explained to Simon that whoever is forgiven much loves much.

With the same empathetic, loving and kind heart He had compassion on the woman that was caught in the act of adultery and saved her from those who wanted her to be stoned. They knew He was compassionate towards sinners, but they did this to, "Test Him, that they might have something of which to accuse Him. But Jesus stooped down and wrote on the ground with His finger, as though He did not hear." (John 8:6).

It is surprising that our Lord faced such acquisitions, rejections and insults from the leaders of His time. He endured a series of accusations and insults. They said to Him, "Do we not say rightly that You are a Samaritan and have a demon?"(John 8:48). What astonishing words that were said about the Lord of Glory, who cast out demons, that He should be accused of having a demon! They said to Him, "You have a demon!!? And those Blasphemers thought that they "spoke rightly"!

My brothers and sisters, do not dwell on what others say about you, for it was said about Christ that He was a Samaritan and had a demon. When the Lord heard these insults He answered calmly and peacefully.

What is this Lord? Just send fire from above to destroy them. Kindness does not work with this nation, be hard on them so they honour you! As if the Lord replied: this is not my way, I will leave them in their wrath and after sometime they will return and repent and look up to Me whom they have pierced and wounded and they will regret it.

There is no greater endurance than what our Lord endured of criticism and accusations. Even every miracle He preformed they tried to cover its glory by their insults, criticism and false accusations. He used to cast out demons from the demon possessed, so they said, "This fellow does not cast out demons except by Beelzebub, the ruler of the demons," (Matthew 12:24), as if the Lord was one of Satan's soldiers.

He opened the eyes of the man born blind; such a miracle had never been witnessed before and the Pharisees said about Him, "This Man is not from God", instead of believing Him. They put pressure on the blind man who had received his sight saying, "Give God the glory! We know that this Man is a sinner." (John 9:24).

When the blind man defended Christ they reviled him and said, "You are His disciple," as if the discipleship of Christ is shameful. What an astounding thing that the Lord should be described as a Samaritan and as having a demon, a ruler of demons, described as a sinner, and that He is not God, and His discipleship is an insult!!! What else?!

They said about Him that, "This Man is not from God, because He does not keep the Sabbath." (John 9:16), also they said, "Look, a glutton and a winebibber," (Luke 7:34), and "a friend of tax collectors and sinners!" (Matthew 11:19). What else did they say about Him? They said that He is "a blasphemer! And speaks blasphemies." (Matthew 9:3).

Then they took up stones to throw at Him (John 8:59), trying many times to stone Him (John 10:31). Their reason for attempting to stone Him was, "For a good work we do not stone you, but for blasphemy." (John 10:33). When the high priest charged Him with death, it was for the exact same reason, the charge of blasphemy! The high priest tore his clothes saying, "He has spoken blasphemy! What further need do we have of witnesses? Look, now you have heard His blasphemy." (Matthew 26:65).

It is amazing that the Author and finisher of faith, the Good Teacher, the One in whom are hidden all the treasures of wisdom and knowledge is called "blasphemer"!! While He is "the power of God and the wisdom of God." (1 Corinthians 2:10). They also accused Him of political offenses. They said that He was against Caesar and that, "He stirs up people", "perverting the nation" (Luke 23:5,2).

Those who wanted Jesus as their King to deliver them from the hands of Caesar wanted to take Him by force to make Him King (John 6:15). But Christ refused the earthly kingdom, because His Kingdom is not of this world (John 18: 36). They accused Him of being against Caesar and started to complain about Him saying, "We found this fellow perverting the nation, and forbidding to pay taxes to Caesar, saying that He himself is Christ, a king." (Luke 23:2). What an amazing thing, they accused Him without shame and His words were, "Render to Caesar the things that are Caesar's, and to God the things that are God's." (Mark 12:17).

Those who were angry with Caesar and wanted a king to save them were now putting Christ in Caesar's hand as a criminal. And Christ was silent and did not respond because He "carried our sins." They did not stop accusing Him of blasphemy and made many political accusations, but they also accused Him of deception, even after His death on the Cross for them, and for the entire world.

They went to Pilate and said to him; "Sir, we remember, while He was still alive, how that deceiver said, 'After three days I will rise.' Therefore command that the tomb be made secure until the third day, lest His disciples come by night and steal Him away, and say to the people, 'He has risen from the dead.' So the last deception will be worse than the first.'" (Matthew 27:63-64).

Indeed the Lord Jesus Christ was not treated with the same sort of love that He gave so that the words of the prophecy would be fulfilled, "they hated Me without a cause." (John 15:25, Psalm 69:4). This is Christ who was accused of being against the people because He wanted to change their customs and culture. They also accused Him of wanting to destroy the Temple and rebuild it in three days, as well as being angry with Caesar and refusing to pay taxes to him. This is the One who is meek and humble, Who does not quarrel nor cry out, nor will anyone hear His Voice in the streets. This is the Christ who was rejected by many. The scribes, Pharisees, Sadducees, the elders and the Jewish priests tried to entangle Him in His words (Matthew 22:15). They rose against the Lord and against His anointed saying; "Let us break Their bonds in pieces And cast away Their cords from us." (Psalm 2:3).

It was also said of Him that, "He Himself has suffered, being tempted." (Hebrews 2:18), so the depth of the spiritual life is to "suffer with Him" or to enter into the "fellowship of His sufferings" (Philippians 3:10). So all suffering for the sake of righteousness, is considered as fellowship with Christ's suffering. It was said that He was sorrowful and distressed (Mark 14:23). In the Garden of Gethsemane He said, "My soul is exceedingly sorrowful even to death." (Matthew 26:38). It is enough what was said of Him in Isaiah about His sorrow, "Surely He has borne our griefs And carried our sorrows." (Isaiah 53:4). This means that all the sorrows and suffering of mankind have been placed on His shoulders and was carried in His heart.

In the Scriptures it is recorded that He cried more than once. He wept at the tomb of Lazarus (John 11:35). He wept over the city of Jerusalem, "He saw the city and wept over it." (Luke 19:41) foretelling what would happen to it. The Bible reveals to us Christ's human nature. It shows us how delicate and emotional He was and sensitive towards individuals who suffered, as well as, cities and wept over them.

Why did He weep at the tomb of Lazarus? Was He affected by the sorrow of Mary and Martha? Perhaps! Or was it because He loved him? Maybe, however, there is a much deeper meaning. Perhaps He wept for all those who reached death by sin. Also, because man was created in the image of God and His likeness reached the stage that his sister said about her beloved brother that there would be a "stench". It was the first man's sin that lead to this: death, stench, decay of the body and weeping of family and friends. All this was before Christ's eyes when he wept at the tomb of Lazarus.

Lazarus' death represents human imperfection, that dies and decays. Mankind suffered from much pain, grief, sadness and tribulation, until our Lord had compassion on them, "But when He saw the multitudes, He was moved with compassion for them, because they were weary and scattered, like sheep having no shepherd." (Matthew 9:36) and He said to them, "Come to Me, all you who labor and are heavy laden, and I will give you rest." (Matthew 11:28).

He joined them heartily, bearing their pain, but how did He comfort them? He comforted them in a practical way. Just as He carried their sins He also carried their sorrows and pains. As Isaiah the Prophet said, "He was oppressed and He was afflicted, yet He opened not His mouth; He was led as a lamb to the slaughter, and as a sheep before its shearers is silent, so He opened not His mouth." (Isaiah 53:7).

So when we contemplate on Christ's suffering, we contemplate on our transgressions and our sins that He bore and carried for us, and because of it "He poured out His soul unto death, and He was numbered with the transgressors." (Isaiah 53:12). Christ's suffering is an evidence of His love for mankind. His love for us crucified Him, if it wasn't for His love for us, neither Pilate nor the Jews would have been able to crucify Him. "I lay down My Life that I may take it again. No one takes it from Me, but I lay it down of Myself. I have power to lay it down, and I have power to take it again." (John 10:17-18). And why did He lay down His Life? Because of His love for the world.

His great love for you and me, made Him to lay down Himself to save us. So we were saved by His death, "For God so loved the world that He gave His only begotten Son, that whoever believes in Him should not perish but have everlasting life." (John3:16). It is His great love that led Him to carrying the sins of the whole world and to wipe them by His blood and die for us.

He carried our sins and pain joyfully. St. Paul said of the Lord's suffering, "Looking unto Jesus, the author and finisher of our faith, who for the joy that was set before Him endured the cross, despising the shame, and has sat down at the right hand of the throne of God." (Hebrews 12:2). He endured the Cross with joy, because He found joy in salvation. He was joyful in this complete salvation that He offers on the Cross. He offered Himself as a sacrifice of love.

So do you offer yourself as a sacrifice of love? Do you look at the passion of Christ, forgetting yourself? Do you take it as your example and benefit from His suffering? We can learn from this and sacrifice for others. Do you offer yourself as sacrifice of love, accepting any pain and suffering for the love of others? If not, then start now; learn to give yourself up to death as the Lord did.

Christ's love reached its pinnacle when He was crucified on the Cross, giving Himself up with a loving and compassionate heart. He accepted death on our behalf so that by His death we may live.

Christ's pain was not only in His flesh. It was not only physical pain that Christ experienced when the crown of thorns was placed on His head or when He was slapped or whipped or when He fell beneath the heavy Cross...but more importantly it was that He carried the sins of the world since Adam until the end of the ages; the sins which went against His nature.

He stood before the Father and mankind as a sinner. Before the people, "He was numbered with the transgressors." And before the Father, on behalf of all of mankind's sins, carrying our sins before the divine justice to satisfy the Father and became a "burnt offering a sacrifice for a sweet aroma to the Lord." (Leviticus 1:9), "For He made Him who knew no sin to be sin for us, that we might become the righteousness of God in Him." (2 Corinthians 5: 21). It is hard for the Holy One to carry sins, it is a very painful matter, but He accepted it joyfully. He died as a sacrifice of sin, as a carrier of sin. Do you also do so?

Do you carry other people's sins as Christ did? Can you take the sins of others and attribute them to yourself saying, "It is my mistake not his or hers?" And if another's sin is attributed to you, can you accept it in silence? And if you cannot carry the sins of others, can you at least endure it? Meaning to endure the sins of those against you? If you cannot carry the sins of others and attribute them to yourself, at least do not condemn them. Look at what Christ has done for us on the Cross and compare it with what you do. Are you like Him, offering yourself as a sacrifice of love for others? Are you a sacrifice of sin that carries the sins of others? Are you a burnt sacrifice that is accepted before God the Father? What are you during Holy Week?

If you do not carry people's sins, then carry their suffering. Carry people's suffering as Christ carried it, who told them "Come to Me, all you who labor and are heavy laden, and I will give you rest." (Matthew 11:28). Join in with Christ in comforting others, be a big heart which suffers with those who suffer, visits the sick, comforts those the broken hearted, helps to solve people's problems, or at least prays for others and comforts them in their tribulations and helps them to follow God. As St. Paul said, "Rejoice with those who rejoice and weep with those who weep." (Roman 12:15).

But many of us do not follow half of this commandment. They rejoice with those who rejoice, but it is hard for them to weep with those who weep. Joy is what attracts them, sadly not pain, and if they join others in their distress, they quickly get bored and leave, because joining others in their pain causes us pain too, that is why they run away from it, while it is beneficial to them.

Always remember during Holy Week that the pain will benefit you and spending just an hour with those who are suffering or in pain is better than many months of joy and happiness. So set this rule before you.

People like joy, but they benefit from pain. King Solomon said, "Better to go to the house of mourning than to go to the house of feasting, for that is the end of all men; And the living will take it to heart. Sorrow is better than laughter, for by a sad countenance the heart is made better. The heart of the wise is in the house of mourning, but the heart of fools is in the house of mirth." (Ecclesiastes 7:2-4).

But because one cannot live in pain and suffering all the time, therefore Solomon said, "To everything there is a season, a time for every purpose under heaven …. a time to weep, and a time to laugh; a time to mourn, and a time to dance." (Ecclesiastes 3:1 & 4). So try to benefit from times of pain, in the pain of others, and benefit from meditating on the sufferings of Christ for you.

We look at Christ's suffering and we are comforted. During our times of pain we find comfort in Christ's pain. We think about His suffering and compare it to our own and we are comforted knowing that He also suffered. He suffered and carried our pain so that we may be comforted. But Christ's sufferings were due to His righteousness and ours due to our sins.

Before the first sin there was no pain. Pain came to the world as a result of sin. Pain and sadness entered into people's hearts. God did not want this to happen, and so what did the Lord do? He carried the pain instead of us ….. and what else? Our Lord Jesus sanctified pain by His pains. So pain becomes a gift and blessing. As St. Paul said, "For to you it has been granted on behalf of Christ, not only to believe in Him, but also to suffer for His sake." (Philippians 1:29). And pain became the way of glory, as St. Paul also said, "And if children, then heirs - heirs of God and joint heirs with Christ, if indeed we suffer with Him, that we may also be glorified together." (Romans 8:17), indeed the Lord has sanctified the pain. And He will continue to sanctify it, until we depart from the world of pain. Here we find pain is holy and there are crowns for it, as St. Paul said, "For as many as are led by the Spirit of God, these are sons of God." (Romans 8:14).

Indeed the Lord has blessed pain. So pain and suffering are rewarded by heavenly crowns for those who endure it, as St. Peter said, "But even if you should suffer for righteousness' sake, you are blessed. And do not be afraid of their threats, nor be troubled." (I Peter 3:14). There will always be pain and suffering in the world, and if we endure it we will obtain its blessing until His second appearance, "the place which has fled all sadness, distress and sighing" as we say in the litany of the departed. "And God will wipe away every tear from their eyes; there shall be no more death, nor sorrow, nor crying. There shall be no more pain, for the former things have passed away." (Revelation 21:4). And those who live in complete devotion to Christ will gain an everlasting joy, inexpressible happiness that is full of glory.

So if we suffer here, we will rejoice there. Do not be like the rich man to whom father Abraham said, "Son, remember that in your lifetime you received your good things, and likewise Lazarus evil things; but now he is comforted and you are tormented." (Luke 16:25). Therefore, we should take the position of Lazarus, and suffer here on earth so as to rejoice in heaven. We use the narrow gate and walk in the way of anguish because "narrow is the gate and difficult is the way which leads to life, and there are few who find it." (Matthew 7:14). For that reason let us suffer for Christ's sake, because this will open the way to eternal glory.

The Church places the martyrs in the highest ranking because of the suffering that they endured. In the Church's rituals we place the martyrs before our fathers the patriarchs and the heroes of the faith, and before the monks and hermits. And as much as those martyrs suffered, as much as the Church praises and gives tribute to them and God honours them. Those martyrs entered into fellowship with Christ's pain. They suffered with Him and so they also were glorified with Him. But how about those who did not have the chance to obtain the crown of martyrdom? To those we say, every type of pain for Christ's sake, has its blessings and its rewards and crowns.

The blessings and heavenly crowns are not only a reward for the suffering and pain of the martyrs, but any type of suffering and pain is acceptable before God and each one will receive their own reward according to their own labour (I Corinthians 3:8). An example of such suffering and pain is the suffering which is endured from the service and ministry and preaching. St. Paul explained this in 2 Corinthians 4, 6 & 11).

Likewise the pain that we suffer in our spiritual struggle. As St. Paul said, "For we do not wrestle against flesh and blood, but against principalities, against powers, against the rulers of the darkness of this age, against spiritual hosts of wickedness in the heavenly places." (Ephesians 6:12). This wrestle is against, "the fiery darts of the wicked one." (Ephesians 6:16). All these kinds of pain, suffering and spiritual struggles have their own crowns. This also applies to every insult we bear for the sake of Christ. As the Lord Himself said, "Blessed are you when they revile and persecute you, and say all kinds of evil against you falsely for My sake. Rejoice and be exceedingly glad, for great is your reward in heaven, for so they persecuted the prophets who were before you." (Matthew 5:11-12).

These insults are fellowship in Christ's pain who was also insulted and it was said about Him that He is a deceiver and blasphemous. In your pain be confident that Christ is a friend of all those who are in pain and suffering. A friend and a companion for you at times of pain and He will never leave you, as the Bible says, "In all their affliction He was afflicted, and the Angel of His Presence saved them; in His love and in His pity He redeemed them; and He bore them and carried them all the days of old." (Isaiah 63:9). Even your pain He considers as His pain, just as He reproached Saul (Acts 9:4).

You should be comforted that Christ shares your pain and

suffering. And let your heart be strengthened, "Wait on the Lord; Be of good courage, And He shall strengthen your heart" (Psalm 27:14) and place this before you that:

Christ was strong and powerful in all His suffering. During His crucifixion He was steady like a mountain that is not affected by storms and wind. He was steadfast during the time of His arrest, He was charged, insulted, slapped, mocked, crucified and put to death. He was the perfect example of a great, strong and courageous heart that bore the injustice of the wicked and said, "Father forgive them." This beautiful phrase has moved and moved the hearts of people throughout the generations. Thus, He transformed the Cross of shame to a Cross of glory and transformed pain and suffering to blessings and crowns.

When we see the sufferings of our Lord Jesus, we are comforted in our pain. And when we see His suffering, we feel guilty within ourselves because we caused His pain. Many people grieve over the Lord's suffering, but they increase His pain by their actions and everyday they add new pain to Christ. Many people see the image of the crucified Christ and they cry and feel pain in their hearts, but they crucify the Lord everyday.

If we truly want to ease His suffering, we must repent. This way we do not sadden His heart with new sin and not adding another drop to His cup of pain because of our sins. So let us leave sin and make God's heart happy. So let our repentance be mixed with the love of Jesus who was crucified for us.

Many people turn away from sin from the fear of hell and the eternal punishment. But let us leave sin because it hurts the Lord and injures His loving heart, and not because of our fear of losing the Kingdom, or caring for ourselves. Do not let our repentance revolve around ourselves, its purity and determination, but rather let it be centred on God who loved us. He considers sin to be betrayal from us, receiving His love with ingratitude and we add to this pain by our sins.

So let us ask the Lord to help us to live in righteousness, so we do not hurt His heart which does not hurt anyone, His heart which is full of love for us, and has compassion on us, even when we sin.

The Lord in His suffering for our sins has compassion on us and does not judge. Judgement has its time in His second coming. But during His suffering, he put before us a comforting fact, which is, "For I did not come to judge the world but to save it." (John 12:47). In fact the point which truly heralds admiration in Christ's suffering is, in all the sins of the people it never changed His love towards them. In spite of all the betrayal and rejection and all the false accusations and deception.

In spite of the charges and lies, and all the assaults and beating, slapping and mockery, all this did not shake His great love which had no limits. It remained the same big heart, who could bear all, it could bear the weakness of His loved ones, and bear the betrayal of people who He was good to. This is the big heart which He prayed for those who crucified Him saying, "Father, forgive them, for they do not know what they do." (Luke 23:34). Truly the love of Jesus was more powerful than His suffering.

Another amazing thing about His suffering is that it was the cause of His pleasure. St. Paul says, "Looking unto Jesus, the author and finisher of our faith, who for the joy that was set before Him endured the cross, despising the shame, and has sat down at the right hand of the throne of God." (Hebrews 12:2). The Lord Jesus found gladness in enduring the pain because of His joy for our salvation therefore He despised the shame. He did not complain when He suffered for us, but He was joyful, because of His great love for us, and His love of satisfying the Father. So His Crucifixion was, "An offering and a sacrifice to God for a sweet-smelling aroma." (Ephesians 5:2).

Thus, the Lord gave us salvation and God loves the cheerful giver. He gave His life as redemption for the world. And His giving was mixed with love, and was with joy for the great salvation and completion. And there was beauty in the suffering of Christ and He sanctified suffering. Suffering came as a result of sin; it entered the world and its impact was death. The Lord wanted to save us from both suffering and death. So by death He trampled death, and by suffering He sanctified suffering, and turned it into a sign of love, and a sign of obedience, obedience to the Father and love for mankind. And when we look at the suffering Christ we remember His love, and we remember how He sanctified suffering, and sanctified the suffering of those who bore suffering for His sake, such as the martyrs and the confessors, and all who carried the cross in their life. So when we love suffering and its sanctification, we enter the company of Christ's suffering.

HOW CAN WE BENEFIT
SPIRITUALLY FROM
HOLY WEEK?

Whoever does not benefit spiritually during Holy Week will find it hard to benefit during ordinary days, because suffering affects the soul in a deeper way. Feeling joy can be superficial. But feeling pain is deep, and goes inside the person and touches the heart, the feelings, the emotions and the senses. So did we benefit from the week? So what advice can we offer on this topic?

I   *Our behaviour outside and inside the Church* - What I noticed in many individuals during Holy Week is that they behave completely differently outside Church from how they behave inside. Why is this so?

a- Inside the Church there are black curtains, sad hymns and readings which concentrate on Jesus' suffering, in order to promote reverence, then outside the Church there is laughter, joking and playfulness. So what we built inside the Church, we destroy outside. We lose all the spiritual benefits we gained while we were inside the Church.

b- Inside the Church we think only of Jesus' suffering. Even the Psalms of Agpya we do not pray because they do not concentrate on His suffering, but other events in His life. We want only to concentrate on His pain. And what about us whilst we are outside the Church? Many, topics we think of and speak of, as if we are not in Holy Week. So we hope, according to our own ability that we focus on the pain and suffering of Christ and meditate on the events of this week.

If we were with Christ during that week we would have followed Him outside the city. So let us live with Him outside the city during this week away from the media of the world which surrounds us. This leads us to the next point:

2   *The Sacred Assembly* - If we were in the ordinary fasting days we would put before us the verse, "Blow the trumpet in

Zion, Consecrate a fast, Call a sacred assembly." (Joel 2:15). So let us do this during Holy Week. Let us stay away from useless interactions and discussions. The days of Holy Week are not days to meet with friends to talk and tell stories. And they are not days of arguing and debating many different topics. But the days of Holy Week are to be differentiated by having a sacred assembly with God, and also by staying away from all forms of entertainment. Do not waste your time in reading magazines and newspapers, and being preoccupied with what is in them, from latest news to jokes, or getting into discussions about what you have read with family and friends. Do not waste time during Holy Week with listening to the radio or watching television. But try to be alone, and enter into yourself, and sit with God, and shorten the time of your meetings and discussions with people to only the important things. And make your spiritual work suited for the Holy Week.

No doubt that maximum concentration on the Lord's suffering through complete devotion may only suit the monks who have been liberated from the tiring earthly work. What I am very impressed with are lay people who take holidays during Holy Week to spend in church.

Taking holidays during this week allows one to devote themselves to the Lord and experience the feelings of this holy week, and they do not just use their holidays for going to the beach and other important matters, but they use it for the Lord. The people of Nineveh were faithful to God in their fasting, and they were exemplary to us and from this we got some of our holiest fasting days.

If you can't take time off, then at least concentrate on God during your free time. Do not waste any of your free time during Holy Week, but take advantage of it as is befitting of the Holy Week. You can go to Church or have special meditations, or prayers and readings suited to the sufferings of the Lord Jesus. Women, do not be too preoccupied during Holy Week in the preparations for the Feast.

Do not let the demands of this period occupy you, from cleaning the house to preparing the food to buying what is necessary for the Feast day, but rather prepare yourself as much as possible before hand so that you can let the sufferings of Christ be the centre of what occupies your mind during this week. And what else is suitable to these days?

3   *Follow the steps of Jesus* - We follow Jesus' life, step by step during this week. The Lord refused the earthly kingdom on Palm Sunday, and the Jews lost their hope in Him, till they crucified and placed Him in the tomb. So have your contemplations each day of this week according to what is suitable for it.

If the Lord refused the earthly kingdom on Palm Sunday because He has aspiritual kingdom, you should find out if you have pleased God in His spiritual kingdom? Do you have anything that the Lord does not own? How can you subject all that you have to His kingdom?

And during the general funeral, tell yourself: If it happens that I died during this week and they will not have a funeral for me, then let's hope that I will benefit from this general funeral as I prepare for eternity and let me consider this general funeral especially for me. If you find that the Church prevents greetings and kisses from the evening of Tuesday of Holy Week, then let me remember Judas' kiss. Say in your prayers; How many times Lord did I give you the kiss of Judas? How many times do I bow before your altar and kiss it and I betray You with my sins? How many times do I wear a cross close to my heart, symbolising that I am a child of Yours and yet my heart is far from Your love?

How many times do I say words of love for You in my prayers; however, my heart is far from You? I hope that when I kiss you Lord it is with honesty and sincerity and with a heart full of love for You and that I don't betray You with my sins. All this as we follow the events of Holy Week. Also, take the Church readings during this week as a form of meditation.

4   *Look after the sanctity of this week* - This week has the holiest days of the year. The Lord exerted Himself for us, and gave all that we needed for our salvation. He said about this salvation, "It is finished." (John 19:30). It was a sacrifice of love, and for us He bore the injustice of evil, bore the mocking, the insults, the beatings, the spitting, the whipping, the thorns and the Cross and all manner of pain. So keep all this in your mind. If you do not feel the holiness of this week you may not be following it as should be.

Let your days be spiritual days and not ordinary days, by severe scrutiny in your behaviour, look after your spirituality and devote yourself to worship according to your ability, with your heart feeling compunction to who placed the sufferings of Christ before your eyes.

5   *Share in His suffering* - St. Paul said, "That I may know Him and the power of His resurrection, and the fellowship of His sufferings, being conformed to His death." (Philippians 3:10). Can you train yourself to enter into sharing the Lord's suffering being conformed to His death? St. Paul, who entered in sharing His suffering, said, "Always carrying about in the body the dying of the Lord Jesus, that the life of Jesus also may be manifested in our body. For we who live are always delivered to death for Jesus' sake, that the life of Jesus also may be manifested in our mortal flesh. So then death is working in us, but life in you." (2 Corinthians 4:10-12).

"For Your sake we are killed all day long. We are accounted as sheep for the slaughter." (Romans 8:36). So have we entered, with St Paul, in sharing with the Lord's pain? Did we follow the Lord's suffering, and resurrect to the Cross with Him?

Have we participated in pain with Him? Have we carried the shame for Him? Are we ready, deep in our hearts, for all this? Are we ready to go out of the city for the Lord? Are we ready to be crucified with Him? And can we say with St. Paul, "I have been crucified with

Christ; it is no longer I who live, but Christ lives in me; and the life which I now live in the flesh I live by faith in the Son of God, who loved me and gave Himself for me." (Galatians 2:20). The way to make Christ live in you, is to be crucified with Him. Do you bear all things for Him? Is it for Him that we are patient? Do we carry our Cross for Him every day and follow Him?

Do we get tired and complain whenever pain comes our way for Him? We whinge, are unhappy and judge others, then we say our Cross is too heavy for us! It is good to enter into the company of Christ's pain, but it has to be with joy, gratitude and thanks to Him, whether this pain involves yourself or the pains of others.

During Holy Week, when you remember you have a Cross to bear, carry it with calmness to the Golgotha. You will bear the pain there for the Lord, till the Lord says to you, "It is finished." This brings us to another exercise we can enter into during Holy Week.

6   *Feeling the pleasure of pain* - Every pain you bear for the Lord, feel its pleasure, blessing and its crown. Our fathers the martyrs found joy in pain. For example, Anba Fam, who wore the best clothes when he went to be martyred, said, "This is my wedding day." And the saint who accepted the ropes that tied him. Because of feeling joy while being in their suffering, they were able to bear the pain. Are you like that? Or are you very sensitive to everything that comes your way? Do you get annoyed, tired, sad and or perhaps even angry! Practice getting over all this and learn to feel joy and pleasure in the pain.

If you are overly sensitive about your dignity and your rights, try to over come this, remembering what was said about the Lord Jesus, "He was oppressed and He was afflicted, yet He opened not His mouth; He was led as a lamb to the slaughter, and as a sheep before its shearers is silent, so He opened not His mouth." (Isaiah 53:7). If you are reprimanded often and are easily insulted and simple things hurt you or upset you, you know that you still have a long way to go and still have much training to do.

Rejoice in pain because God gives blessings. When Saul was called to be an apostle, he honoured this pain and He said, "For I will show him how many things he must suffer for My name's sake." (Acts 9:16). And the apostle entered in that pain and did not lose his joy, so he said, "As sorrowful, yet always rejoicing; as poor, yet making many rich; as having nothing, and yet possessing all things." (2 Corinthians 6:10).

We will get our reward in heaven, according to our bearing of pain for Him. "Now he who plants and he who waters are one, and each one will receive his own reward according to his own labour." (I Corinthians 3:8). So it is the case, we hope to test the pain with love, acceptance, joy and trust, having faith in the kingdom. And the wicked people, their deeds follow them, and the righteous their pains follow them, as well as, their good works.

And every person has his own kind of pain for the Lord. It is not necessary to enter the pain of the Cross itself or be whipped as Christ was or endure the injustices and false accusations which our Lord was exposed to. However, your pain could be the weariness and sacrifice of the service, "For God is not unjust to forget your work and labour of love which you have shown toward His name, in that you have ministered to the saints, and do minister." (Hebrews 6:10). It is a labour of love to give love to others, just as Christ Himself did, which was the image of love. What else can we do to benefit from Holy Week? No doubt we need to follow the rituals which are befitting of this week.

7   *Asceticism* - Whoever puts the suffering of Christ before him, does not have the appetite to eat, so he fasts and is reluctant to eat. Suffering by nature tends to cause one to lose their appetite. Whoever hungers for food has not felt the depth of the suffering within himself. And whoever feels the depth of the suffering tends to lose their hunger during this time. Many people go through this week

without eating at all, without feeling fatigue. The reason is because they are drowned in Christ's pain and they forget food.

If hunger persists easily with you then know that you have not entered into the pain as you should. Do not rush then into eating but rather acquire those feelings necessary for sharing the pain of our Lord. Then the hunger will ease and you will forget it. So have a special plan for this week. Stay away from delicious foods which stimulate your appetite. Be an ascetic this week.

If your inner self is battling with food do not listen to it. Triumph in firmness and know that the biggest joy to yourself is for you to conquer the soul. And as one of the fathers said, "Be happy, not for the desires you get, but for the lusts you humiliate." And every time you desire to eat, rebuke yourself saying, "On this occasion which the Lord suffered for me, do I delight in eating and drinking?" If you want to succeed in managing your ascetism you need to feed your soul on spiritual food so you live and bear the hunger. And from this we go to:

8   *Suitable reading* - Reading is food for the spirit, and Holy Week has suitable readings. The readings suit the suffering of Christ, and are about the events of the holy week. This includes spiritual interpretations and sermons of the saints. Also any books which includes the love of God. The Church rituals put before us the four Gospel readings, distributed over the days of the week. Also there are the readings from the Book of Revelation, on the night of Apocalypse. Also there are the hymns and the prophecies from the Old Testament along side the readings. We also read from Lamentations of the Prophet Jeremiah in the last hour of Good Friday. The readings of Job the Prophet are also very suitable. And the importance of all this:

The readings have to be in depth and with understanding and spiritual benefit. Every day of Holy Week has its suitable readings. And by the will of God we will try to introduce you to the readings. The spiritual reading is a wonderful spiritual food, it focuses the thoughts and prevents them from being scattered, and leads them to special emotions evoked by the readings. Also the readings are material for meditation and prayer. There is another food, which is hymns.

9   *Church Hymns* - The week of suffering has its own exclusive hymns which are full of depth and impact. So we hope that you live these Coptic tunes, which you listened to in Church, in your homes during Holy Week, and that they help you. You can play the tapes and CDs of these hymns in your homes and anywhere else so that wherever you are becomes like the Church choir. And let it be with the spirit of prayer so that you can benefit from the emotions which are raised from the melody in the soul. In addition, the tunes, like the readings, will protect the thoughts from being scattered. Even those who are not talented in memorising the hymns can still be affected by the tunes when they listen to them. The readings and the hymns are spiritual food. We can also include here prayers.

10   *Prayer* - We do not pray from the Agpya during this week, but the spiritual work of the Holy Week prayers is to have a strong relationship with God. Use deep heartfelt private prayers. Tell the Lord everything that is in your heart, openly and frankly, as a child does with their father, in love and emotion. Pray for yourself and for the Church and for all those who are in distress.

We also use the Pascha prayer instead of the Agpya. Cry out to the Lord in your prayers and say, "To You is the Power, the Glory, the Blessing and the Honour, forever Amen, Emmanuel our God and our King." Repeat this many times with spiritual meditation in every word you say. Remember that we have written a book about the meditations of this special Pascha prayer.

Also pray the short frequent prayers, any prayer represents the internal condition of your heart, whether it be a request, thanks, praise to the Lord or meditation on His beautiful qualities, or perhaps confessing of sin or a contrite heart. Any of these we can put in a short sentence, and talk to God from the depth of our heart.

Add to all this, the ritual prayers of the church. So Holy Week is characterised by the collective general prayers, as we all gather in the Church, praying in one spirit. We notice that in the last 3 days (Thursday, Friday and the eve of Saturday), that the general prayers include the whole day, and all night on the eve of Saturday night (the Apocalypse). The day and night is spent in prayers, hymns, readings and raising of incense, concluding with the Holy Liturgy. The spiritual person follows with his heart all these prayers, concentrating with his thought and emotions, asking the Lord who carried the sins of the world and died for them, to forgive and have mercy. This leads us to another point in the spiritual Holy Week, which is...

I I   *Confession and Holy Communion* - It is good during this week, that one sits by himself and remembers his sins, and collects them and puts them at the foot of our Lord's Cross. We put them on the Lamb of God who carried the sins of the whole world. And says to Him, in shame and pain, "Lord carry my sins as I am part of the sins of the whole of mankind which You carried. Take them Lord and nail them on the Cross with You and wipe them with Your blood."

During Holy Week, examine yourself carefully and diligently. Examine yourself and know that these sins are the cause of His crucifixion. In Christ's pain we rebuke ourselves knowing that we are the cause of His pain.

Many are upset over Christ's pain, but they increase His pain by what they do every day. They look at the Crucified image of Christ and cry, while they crucify Christ every day by their sins, "If they fall away, to renew them again to repentance, since they crucify again for themselves the Son of God, and put Him to an open shame." (Hebrews 6:6).

We do not feel grieved during this week over His pains, but instead over the sins of mankind which caused Him this pain. We are grieved over ourselves, because we are the cause of this pain, "So Jesus said to Peter, 'Put your sword into the sheath. Shall I not drink the cup which My Father has given Me?'" (John 18:11).

Indeed, how human standard dropped to such an extent, which caused it to lose her loyalty and all righteousness, and transmitted sin without shyness. It is befitting to cry over ourselves the sinner, and not on Christ who conquered death and gave the perfect salvation. Therefore, it was good that the Lord said to the women who cried over Him, "Daughters of Jerusalem, do not weep for Me, but weep for yourselves and for your children." (Luke 23:28). So whenever the heart looks to the Lord in His crucifixion, it calls:

I am sorry Lord that I made you suffer to that extent. Your suffering is actually my suffering, and You carried them instead of me, truly. Lord I am so grateful with the salvation You have offered to me and to the world with Your blood. I remember what the Apostle said, "For indeed Christ, our Passover, was sacrificed for us." (I Corinthians 5:7).

Also I say that Passover was eaten on bitter herbs. Truly, the Jews were happy because the blood of the Passover saved them from the destructive sword. The word of God said to them, "When I see the blood, I will pass over you." (Exodus 12:13), but they shall eat the Passover "with bitter herbs" as the Lord told them (Exodus 12:8). These bitter herbs remind them of their sins which caused them to fall into slavery under Pharaoh and their need for the Passover to pass over from slavery and death.

We too eat our Passover with bitter herbs in remembrance of our sins which required this blood so that the Lord purges us with hyssop to be clean. We remember our sins and to judge ourselves and not others. We stand before the Cross of Christ as sinners and not as a judge. Think of our sins and not the sins of others; we are all under judgement, "There is none who does good, No, not one." (Psalm 14:3).

We confess our sins and prepare ourselves for communion. We have three Liturgies during Holy Week: Covenant Thursday, Joyous Saturday and Sunday of the Resurrection. Before that were two very important occasions; the liturgy of Friday the Seal of the Fast and Palm Sunday liturgy. Covenant Thursday is the main liturgy and it is the liturgy which all other liturgies originated from.

12

The period of spiritual storage - Holy Week is the period of harvest for the whole year. You harvest all the spirituality which you need for the whole year. This is what we need; we don't just need spirituality for Holy Week only. We also need to store and save for the fifty days which follow. We need to store up a spiritual stock for Holy Week which lasts the fifty days in which there is no fasting, no mettanias, no Pascha hymns or praises. So prepare from now during these Pascha days.

There is no doubt that whoever weakens spiritually during the fifty days which follow, witnesses to themself that there was not enough spiritual storage during Lent and Holy Week.

OUTSIDE THE CITY

During Holy Week we follow Jesus Christ step by step; we notice that He was taken outside the city. What is the spiritual meaning of the words "Outside the city"? The city is the place of the believers. It is the place of the Saints. It is the place in which the believers are, or the place that the Lord is with the believers, the Saints, that is "the place of the Lord with the people". Therefore, it is said "Your Camp shall be Holy." (Deuteronomy 23:14).

How can we keep the holiness of the city? Anything which is defiled or not clean should be outside the city. Therefore, any sacrifices of sins had to be burned outside the city, although it was from the holiness of the Lord. Because all the sins of the people are transferred onto the offerings, they should be burned outside the city so that the city is not defiled. St. Paul the Apostle said of the sacrifices which carry the sins of the people, "For the bodies of those animals, whose blood is brought into the sanctuary by the high priest for sin, are burned outside the camp." (Hebrews 13: 11).

Jesus Christ, the sacrifice of sin was crucified outside the city. Truly, He is holy without sin, but He carries the sins of the whole world (John 1: 29, 1John 2:2). "All we like sheep have gone astray; we have turned, every one, to his own way; and the Lord has laid on Him the iniquity of us all." (Isaiah 53: 6). So, because He carried our sins, He became a sacrifice of sin.

He has to suffer outside the door, outside the city (Hebrews 13:12). They crucified Him, and the Bible says, "Cursed is everyone who hangs on a tree." (Galatians 3:13). So He had to go outside the city to be crucified there. The sinner was generally expelled outside the city so as not to defile it inside, that the city remain holy and without sin. They did the same with Jesus, "He was numbered with the transgressors." (Deuteronomy 53:12). He became a sinner in their eyes, judged and convicted. If they crucified Him in Jerusalem He would defile Jerusalem!!

What a degree of cruelty that was reached towards this great, soft, kind heart, who carried their sufferings. He came to save them from their sins, but "He came to His own, and His own did not receive Him." (John 1: 11). But we, who received Him and believed Him, we are joined with Him in His sufferings and go outside with Him, outside the city. We are the sinners who put all our sins on the Holy One. He carried them on our behalf when we follow Him in His sufferings, "Therefore, let us go forth to Him, outside the camp, bearing His reproach." (Hebrews 13:13).

In order to fulfil this, according to tradition in Holy Week, we close the sanctuary and go down from the first Khorous (the Khorous of the Saints). We spend the whole week of Pascha in the lower Khorous, away from the Holy of Holies, away from the sanctuary. This reminds us of when they took Jesus far away and He is the Holy, so that He would not defile the city! And we remain with Him, wherever they take Him, our city is beside Him. Outside the city, we remember our sins which took us away and took Him away. We say to Him: "You are Lord who makes the city holy, and without You it could not be holy. They took You away, outside because of us, so at least, we will go out with You. Let us meditate on this principle, the principle of "Outside the city."

THE PRINCIPLE OF BEING OUTSIDE THE CITY

When did the Lord begin to implement this judgement of putting the sinner outside the city? It was a judgement which was enforced since the beginning of humanity; since Adam. Adam lived in paradise, inside the city, with God. The Lord appeared to him and he talked with God. So what happened when he fell? He went outside the city, He and his wife who sinned before him, were expelled from paradise. The holy city was closed off and the Lord sent an Angel to guard paradise with a sword of fire. So Adam and Eve could not enter and were separated from the tree of life. (Genesis 3:23,24).

When does the judgment end? When the consequences of sin are paid; the ransom was paid on the Cross. Then Jesus took Adam and his children and returned them to paradise. He opened the city door for them which had been closed since the first sin. He returned them back after the punishment.

The Lord took Cain outside the city too. Cain realises this and he said to the Lord, "My punishment is greater than I can bear! Surely You have driven me out this day from the face of the ground; I shall be hidden from Your face; I shall be a fugitive and a vagabond on the earth." (Genesis 4:13,14). Cain going outside the city has two major meanings:

The first and more minor one is the Lord expelled him from the face of the ground. He would see neither his father Adam' face, nor the saints who were born of him and were called sons of God (Genesis 6:2).

The second and more serious one is he was expelled from before the face of God, "I hide from Your face." This was the thing which David the Prophet was most terrified of and he said in his prayers, "Do not cast me away from Your presence, And do not take Your Holy Spirit from me." (Psalm 51).

This is the punishment of staying "outside the city" which is from the beginning of mankind, from the time of Adam, Eve and Cain: The first who was punished was Satan who was expelled from the chorus of Angels. He was no longer with the Angels of God in heaven, but wandering around the earth.

How difficult were the words said of Satan's fall and his punishment in the Book of Isaiah the Prophet? It was said to him, "How you are fallen from heaven, how you are cut down to the ground, for you have said in your heart: 'I will ascend into heaven, I will exalt my throne above the stars of God; I will ascend above the heights of the clouds, I will be like the Most High'. Yet you shall be brought down to Sheol, to the lowest depths of the Pit." (Isaiah14:12-15).

Satan was outside the city for the same two punishments. He was outside the city of saints, outside the pure group of Angels. He was also outside the communion with God Himself. He lost His love, His company and His affection. He lost His company and was outside, in the darkness, he and all the angels who followed him. The punishment of "outside the city" was to include humans and angels.

This punishment affected the whole of humanity during the flood. The sinners defiled the earth with their deeds. The Lord wanted to clean the whole earth for a second time. He destroyed all sins and sinners, He got rid of them outside the city, outside the whole earth, outside life itself, outside the general destruction which has never been repeated in the history of mankind (Genesis 6). Now the city of God, the holy, is Noah's ark, which only includes 8 people who were saved by the Lord (1Peter 3: 20). But the sinners and the wicked were outside the city, outside the Ark, meeting their fate.

The same thing happened to Korah, Dathan and Abiram. They stole the honour of the priesthood for themselves. They spread bad thoughts among the people and they allowed 250 men to carry the censer and offer incense (Numbers 16:17).

So what did happen? The Lord sent them outside the city, outside the group of saints, when He said to the people, "Depart now from the tents of these wicked men! Touch nothing of theirs, lest you be consumed in all their sins." (Numbers 16:26). The Lord took them out of life as, "The earth opened its mouth and swallowed them up, with their households and all the men with Korah, with all their goods, so they and all those with them went down alive into the pit; the earth closed over them, and they perished from among the assembly. And a fire came out from the Lord and consumed the two hundred and fifty men who were offering incense." (Numbers 16: 32-35). They went outside the city without repentance and they died. The city became pure and holy again, after it had been cleaned from evil and the evil doers.

This may remind us of the verdict to Ananias and Sapphira from St. Peter the Apostle. He did not just take them outside the city and separated them from the assembly of believers, but he took them completely from life. Anianias died instantly and St. Peter said to Sapphira after 3 hours, "Look, the feet of those who have buried your husband are at the door, and they will carry you out." (Acts 5: 9). Where outside? Is it just being outside the city which is followed by repentance and return? No, they were gone from the city into death; Sapphira died instantly beside her husband's feet.

But the covetous person, he was put out, but repents. This sinner had this principle applied to him by the order of St. Paul the Apostle, "Therefore put away from yourselves the evil person." (I Corinthians 5: 13). He ordered to, "Put away from yourselves" and deliver such a one to Satan for the destruction of the flesh that his spirit may be saved in the day of the Lord Jesus." (I Corinthians 5:5).

So this sinner repented, cried severely over his sins until St. Paul's heart was soften and he forgave him. He sent to the Corinthians that they should accept him back inside the city, saying to them, "This punishment which was inflicted by the majority is sufficient for such a man, so that, on the contrary, you ought rather to forgive and comfort him, lest perhaps such a one be swallowed up with too much sorrow. Therefore I urge you to reaffirm your love to him." (2 Corinthians 2:6,7). So he returned back to the city with repentance.

The Church followed this principle during the first few centuries.

The Church is an Assembly of Saints and not just a group of believers. So, whoever departs from this faith and this holiness, will be taken out of the city and be isolated. It is not fitting for the Church to mix the Saints with evildoers, believers with non-believers. The Apostle said, "What fellowship has righteousness with lawlessness? And what communion has light with darkness?" (I Corinthians 5:11).

There were sinners who were completely prevented from entering the Church. Other sinners were prevented from attending the Holy liturgy, the liturgy of the Saints. But they were permitted only to attend the first part of the liturgy which is called the Liturgy of the Catechism (or the Liturgy of the Word). They attended and listened to the readings and the sermon and then they left before reconciliation, since the liturgy was for the saints.

The Church becomes a group of saints who want to have a life of holiness. These may stay and those who don't want to? Let them go since the Bible says, "Holiness adorns Your house, O Lord" (Psalm 93). When the Church isolates sinners outside the city for some years leaving the fellowship of the saints then the Church remains holy and pure. The Church was very scrupulous in their actions, "perfecting holiness in the fear of God." (2 Corinthians 7:1). This is from the punishment of the Church but there was another type:

Sinners took themselves outside the city. An example of this was the Prodigal Son. He desired to live his own way and to enjoy money and pleasures with his friends. He left his father's home by himself and went to a far country (Luke 15:13). And so he lived outside the city, away from his father. He stayed this way until he came back to his senses (Luke 15:17). He returned back to the city, to his father's house. The father was very happy in the return of his prodigal son and the whole family was happy, except for the older son. With pride and jealousy, his will was not according to his father's will, he said, "He was angry and would not go in." (Luke 15: 28). The father had to go outside to persuade his son. The Prodigal Son went outside the city completely of his own will; no one took him there but his wrong emotions.

This is just like the divided sects; anyone who becomes angry with the Church for any reason decides "not to go to Church from now on". He will be on his own outside the city.

Some leave the Church and go outside because of tradition and teaching. Just like division they leave, go far and follow their own teaching which is not according to the Bible. Or they may be judged by the Church with a sentence of Anathema. This will completely destroy them and take them outside the city, especially if there is a heresy and they insist on it, teaching others wrong ways. The Apostles says, "If we, or an angel from heaven, preach any other gospel to you than what we have preached to you, let him be accursed." (Galatians 1: 8,9).

John, the beloved gave the same verdict. The disciple which the Lord loved, who speaks of love more than any other apostle, says, "If anyone comes to you and does not bring this doctrine, do not receive him into your house nor greet him; for he who greets him shares in his evil deeds." (2 John 1:10,11). He will be sent outside the city, by thinking outside the apostolic thoughts, even before a verdict comes against him.

Another strange type, in those who are outside the city is he who is outside the city with his heart, but he is inside of the city physically. A person may seem to be inside the city, but from deep within he is outside. His spirit is different to the assembly of saints, his thoughts are not like theirs, and his ways are not the same. There will come a time when he will go outside the city in practice. For example, the Apostle said these impressive, emotional words: "They went out from us, but they were not of us; for if they had been of us, they would have continued with us; but they went out that they might be made manifest, that none of them were of us." (1 John 2:19). Truly, children of God are distinct and manifest (1 John 3:10), "from their fruits, they are well known." All of this is going outside the city on earth, but the cruellest and hardest type is going outside the city in eternity.

OUTSIDE THE CITY IN THE ETERNITY

Anyone who goes outside the city on earth has a rope to return with, but once outside the city in eternity, there is no hope. An example of this is the foolish virgins. The Bible said about the wise virgins when the Lord came, "Those who were ready went in with him to the wedding; and the door was shut." (Matthew 25:10). But the foolish virgins came late, after the door was shut. They stand outside that door, outside the city saying, "Lord, Lord open to us". All they heard was, "I don't know you." What terrible despair to hear the voice of the Lord saying, "Assuredly, I say to you, I do not know you." And these souls will be kept outside the city forever.

Another example outside the city is Lazarus the beggar and the rich man. This lost, rich man was outside the holy city where our father Abraham was with Lazarus the beggar in his bosom. He requested Lazarus to dip the tip of his finger in water to cool his tongue. But he heard the frightening words, from the mouth of our father Abraham, "Between us and you there is a great gulf fixed, so that those who want to pass from here to you cannot, nor can those from there pass to us." (Luke 16:26).

The righteous will be in eternity together with the Lord and the angels, in the heavenly Jerusalem. But the wicked will be outside. The place for the wicked is called the outer darkness. It is darkness because it is separated from God who is the true light. It is an outer darkness because it is outside the heavenly Jerusalem, outside the assembly of the saints, outside the city in eternity. The Lord said about the wicked and lazy servant, "Cast the unprofitable servant into the outer darkness. There will be weeping and gnashing of teeth." (Matthew 25:26).

In Revelation, "Blessed are those who do His Commandments that they may have the right to the tree of life, and may enter through the gates into the city. But outside are dogs and sorcerers and sexually immoral and murderers and idolaters, and whoever loves and practices a lie." (Revelation 22:14,15).

Then they are outside the holy city, coming down from heaven, the heavenly Jerusalem, the tabernacle of God is with men (Revelation 21: 27). They are outside the holy city, because their works are defiled, "But there shall by no means enter it anything that defiles, or causes an abomination or a lie, but only those who are written in the Lamb's Book of Life." (Revelation 21:27).

Whoever is outside the saintly believers is outside the Book of Life, but with all of this there is still hope. There is a bridge that reaches inside it called repentance. Returning to God can enter us into the city. And so the Lord said in His comforting promise, "the one who comes to Me I will by no means cast out." (John 6: 37). There is then a chance to Passover. The door is not yet shut and there is still time and the promise is still there, waiting.

THE LORD SUFFERED IN ORDER TO

GET US INSIDE THE CITY

He took our place outside the city in order to give us His position inside. Our position is outside the city, so He, the Holy One , went outside the city instead of us, in order to get us inside the city. He came down from heaven to earth to let us go up into heaven. He became a Son of Man in order to make us children of God, He took our sins, for us to be righteous and holy like Him. He took what is ours and He gave us what is His. He took our punishments so that we may receive

His crowns and His glory. He had gone outside the city to pay the ransom in order for us to enter. He accepts death, to give us life. He took our weakness, to gave us strength, and took our shame to give us His glory.

It has been said to Him, "If You are the Son of God, come down off the cross". He didn't want to do that, because if He refuses the cross and death, then we will receive the death sentence. He said to us "you are sentenced to death; I will die on your behalf." Your punishment is outside the city, I will go out instead of you. With all acceptance and joy, with all love and sacrifice, Jesus went outside the city, carried our shame, carried our sins and died on the cross on Golgotha, erased it with His blood by paying the ransom which we owed to the divine judgement.

When He commits His pure spirit, He descended quickly down to Hades to release the righteous for hope, and open for them the Paradise. He said to the angel who carries the fiery sword guarding the Tree of Life, "Put your sword back". "I have come with these righteous to the paradise, and they will be able to eat from the tree of life. The time of captivity which they spent outside the city is finished and now they have come back to their original state and it is better."

Let us remember all these things while we sit in Church, outside the Sanctuary. Enough time has been wasted outside the city by our own will, the time we wasted outside God's heart, outside the bosom of the Church and the company of Saints.

To You is the Power,
the Glory, the Blessing
and the Honour,
forever Amen

With this song we praise our Lord Jesus Christ during Holy Week, following Him step by step. This praise replaces the Agpya prayers during the five day and the five night prayers. We repeat the hymn twelve times in each prayer instead of the twelve psalms which are included in each of the Agpya prayers.

Our Lord Jesus Christ left Jerusalem to Bethany, and we follow Him saying, "To You is the Power, the Glory, the Blessing and the Honour." The Chief priests were annoyed when the Lord cleansed the Temple, and they planned to kill Him. But we protest against their plots saying, "To You is the Power, the Glory, the Blessing and the Honour, forever Amen." Our Lord Jesus Christ, in humility, knelt down to wash the feet of the disciples and we praise Him saying, "To You is the Power, the Glory, the Blessing and the Honour, forever Amen."

The Lord was praying in the Garden of Gethsemane. He was in so much agony that His sweat were drops of blood and we cry to Him saying, "To You is the Power and the Glory." We follow Him hour by hour; whilst He is arrested, put under trial in the presence of His enemies, crowned with thorns, flogged, falling under the Cross, nailed, till He committed His Spirit into the hands of the Father and when He took the thief on the right with Him into Paradise, and during all these events we sing to Him, "To You is the Power, the Glory, the Blessing and the Honour, forever Amen."

THINE IS THE POWER

The first thing we praise our Lord Jesus Christ for during Holy Week is His Power. Yes, Lord, To You is the power, as St. Paul said, "Christ the Power of God." (I Corinthians I:24). Some people may think You were weak on the Cross, but we know who You are. The first thing we know about Your Power is that You are the Creator. "All things were made through Him, and without Him nothing was made that was made."(John. I:3). And You have the power as a Judge who will come in His glory to judge both the living and the dead.

Indeed, this crucified Lord who seemed to the people weak, had they considered what He had done throughout all the days that He spent among them; they would have known how powerful He had been in everything.

HE WAS POWERFUL IN HIS MIRACLES AND HIS HOLINESS:

O Lord, You alone of all the powers, defeated sin, the world and the devil, while all the others were too weak to resist sin, "For she has cast down many wounded, And all who were slain by her were strong men." (Proverbs 7:26). As the Holy Bible says, "They have all turned aside, they have together become corrupt; there is none who does good, no, not one." (Psalm 14:3). But You God, You are the Only One who challenged the whole world, saying, "Which of you convicts Me of sin". (John. 8:46).

You are the only One who overcame the Devil and said, "For the ruler of this world is coming, and he has nothing in Me." (John. 14:30). In the Book of Revelation, they sang for You saying, "For You alone are Holy." (Revelation 15:4). You alone are powerful in Your Holiness, "Holy, harmless, undefiled, separate from sinners, and has become higher than the heavens." (Hebrews 7:26).

Lord, Your miracles proved Your wonderful Power, as You, "had done among them the works which no one else did." (John 15:24). Your Power over nature was shown: when You rebuked the wind and the waves and when You walked on the water. David sang for You saying, "You rule the raging of the sea: when its waves rise, You still them." (Psalm 89:9). To You is the Power, Lord.

You showed Your Power over the sick and the dead: as you healed all diseases and weaknesses of the people, especially the incurable ones. You opened the eyes of the blind, cleansed those with leprosy, healed the woman suffering from haemorrhage, the man who was a paralytic for 38 years, the paralysed man who was lowered down through the roof and the man with the withered hand. Lord, You raised the dead, even he who had been in the tomb for four days and there was a stench.

You showed Your Power as a Creator: when You fed thousands with five loaves and two fish. You even created a new substance when you turned the water into wine and also when you created eyes for the man who was born blind.

Your Power over the devils was shown by casting out evil spirits, who left many saying, "You are the Son of God." You rebuked the demons and did not let them speak. Your miracles are countless, Lord, as John the Beloved said, "And there are also many other things that Jesus did which if they were written one by one, I suppose that even the world itself could not contain the books that would be written." (John21:25). Beside all these aspects of the Lord's Power, the puzzling one is shown in His suffering and crucifixion where He gives us a new concept of the meaning of Power. What is this new concept of power?

THE LORD'S NEW CONCEPT OF POWER:

The world's understanding of Power differs from that introduced by our Lord Jesus Christ. To the world, it means being violent, being able to strike, being able to defend oneself and having the power to force others to surrender.

Our Lord set the example of the Power which loves and sacrifices oneself to others, endures and gives without limits. When we think of Power, we have to look at it from the spiritual side not the physical. That is how we should look at our Lord Jesus Christ's suffering.

The materialistic world thought that the Lord Christ was weak when they struck Him on the face, mocked Him and crucified Him. That would have been true if the Lord Christ had those insults due to His inability, but in fact, He was far more powerful than all those who struck, mocked and crucified Him.

He had the power to destroy them all, but He did not because He loved them and His love was more powerful than death. He was able to put them to death, but He did not because He came to save them from death, by His own death to give them life. We glorify the Lord's endurance, which proved to us that true Power is in endurance, as the Apostle says, "We then who are strong ought to bear with the scruples of the weak, and not to please ourselves." (Romans 15:1).

Some people are too weak; they do not have the ability to endure even the least insult. The smallest insult provokes them and causes them to lose control and turn to revenge. This shows their weakness and lack of power to endure. The Lord Christ was powerful in His endurance, and His endurance is the evidence of His power of love. For a person who has love is able to endure, while failure to endure shows lack of love.

The Lord Christ came to carry our sins, "All we like sheep have gone astray; we have turned everyone to his own way, and the Lord has laid on Him the iniquity of us all." (Isaiah 53:6). The Lord sacrificed Himself for our sins and for our sake, He endured the insults of those who struck Him and spat upon Him. In His deep love, He was joyfully singing in the ear of each of us, "Because for Your sake I have borne reproach; Shame has covered my face." (Psalm 69:7). We listen to these words and answer Him in humility, "For my sake, You endured the injustice of the evil, the flogging and the slaps, and never turned Your face away from the shameful spitting.

The power of the Lord Christ during His passion and crucifixion appeared when He was able to destroy all those who attacked Him, but He never did so because of His great love for us. He was punished for our sake and gave us His peace, took upon Himself our shame and gave us His Glory.

To understand the real Power of the Lord Christ we have to ask ourselves: what could have happened if Christ had refused the humiliation and crucifixion? Or if He had commanded the earth to open and swallow all who were on it, or fire to come down from heaven and burn them? He could have done so, but the consequence would have been our destruction, the Redeemer refused to die for us. So the Lord said, "I will die so that you may not die, and be mocked so that you may be glorified. I came in flesh especially for your sake to sacrifice Myself and endure insults for you out of love for you and for those who insult Me". Therefore, He did not only endure injustices, but loved, forgave and prayed for the wicked, interceding for them saying, "Father, forgive them, for they do not know what they do." (Luke 23:34). This is the real Power of a heart full of love, who tolerates those who trespass against Him, loves them, prays for them and sacrifices Himself for their sake. Who of us can do that? And when insulted by another of an inferior rank to himself, would forgive, defend and also support him!

St. Peter the Apostle, drew his sword to defend his Master when they arrested Him and he cut off the servant's ear, not understanding power in its Christian spiritual concept. The Lord asked him to put his sword back. It is good to have holy zeal, but violence is not our way. Our way is love. With this love the Lord healed the servant's ear and surrendered to the sinners for whose redemption He came. St. John and St. James the Apostles also did not understand the real meaning of power and when the Lord Christ was rejected by a City, the two Apostles said, "Lord, do you want us to command fire to come down from Heaven and destroy them?" But He turned and rebuked them saying: "You do not know what manner of spirit you are of. For the Son of Man did not come to destroy men's lives but to save them."

(Luke. 9:54-56). In the same way, the Lord came submissively to the Cross, to give His life a ransom for many.

Therefore My brethren, when we stand near the Cross, we do not weep as Mary Magdalene did and the daughters of Jerusalem, nor do we sympathise with the Lord, nor do we stand there to support Him, we stand near the Cross to glorify both the Cross and the Crucified, singing the beautiful hymn "To You is the Power..."

The Cross is our boast, as we say with St. Paul: "But God forbid that I should boast except in the Cross of our Lord Jesus Christ, by whom the world has been crucified to me, and I to the world." (Galatians 6:14). "For the message of the Cross is foolishness to those who are perishing, but to us who are being saved, it is the power of God." (I Corinthians I:18).

If the Cross had been a sign of weakness, it would have never been our boast and we should have never taken it as our symbol. If the Cross had been a sign of weakness, we would have never raised it on our Churches and our Domes or hanged it around our necks, tattooed it on our hands and drawn it in our writings. The Cross to us is a sign of power, the power of love, sacrifice, self denial and endurance. This is the real meaning of power.

Many said to the Lord Jesus Christ, "If you are the Son of God, come down from the Cross and we will believe." Had He accepted the challenge, it would have meant the destruction of humanity and loss of salvation. But He, however, was too powerful to be moved and He remained on the Cross. The Lord Christ was not overcome by this vain glory: save Yourself to prove that You are the Son of God, to prove Your power and surprise the world by the miracle. He was not overcome by such flattery, nor by the wrong concept of power. He was able to come down from the cross, but He did not do so, that we might be saved.

The Lord Jesus Christ never thought of Himself, instead He was thinking of us. He did not care about saving Himself from death, but He was concerned about saving us. By redeeming us, He did not yield to crucifixion out of weakness but out of love. He was unselfish, for love "does not seek its own, is not provoked." (I Corinthians 13:5). Had He been thinking of Himself and of how to be glorified according to the world, He would not have emptied Himself and took the form of a slave. He did not think of Himself because He came to give Himself up for us and thus He proved to the world the power of His love and sacrifice, "Greater love has no one than this, than to lay down one's life for his friends." (John 15:13).

That is how the Lord Christ set the example of Power and overcoming oneself on the Cross. It was amazing how the Lord Christ accepted all their iniquities: "As a sheep before its shearers is silent, so He opened not His mouth." (Isaiah 53:7). He was aware of the plot against Him, but He did not resist evil. He calmly said to Judas Iscariot, "What you do, do quickly." (John 13:27). The only justification for what the Lord Christ did is His desire to die for us. He had the power to destroy the Cross and those who wanted to crucify Him, but His power was greater; the power of love and sacrificing.

This Power which accompanied Him all through the journey of the Cross will be the subject of our contemplation in the following pages.

HE WAS POWERFUL IN ACCEPTING DEATH:

The Lord Christ was powerful in approaching death. People did not attack Him secretly or take Him by force. He knew that they would arrest Him and He knew the time, as He told the disciples, "You know that after two days is the Passover, and the Son of Man will be delivered up to be crucified." (Matthew 26:2). It would not be wrong to say He knew the exact hour and moment and even the place, and still He went to the place where they would arrest Him, and at the fixed time.

And when the time came, He went to wake up His disciples, who had fallen asleep in the garden and said, "Are you still sleeping and resting? Behold, the hour is at hand, and the Son of Man is being betrayed into the hands of sinners. Rise, let us be going. See, My betrayer is at hand." (Matthew 26:45-46). When the enemy approached, He went with His disciples to meet him. He wanted to give Himself up for our sake, as He said, "I lay down My life that I may take it again. No one takes it from Me, but I lay it down of Myself. I have power to lay it down, and I have power to take it again." (John 10:17-18).

The Lord Jesus Christ walked towards the enemy in power and courage, and we walk by His side saying, "To You is the Power, the Glory, the Blessing and the Honour, forever Amen." The Lord had the power to put away death, but He was content in accepting it, "To give His life a ransom for many." (Mark.10:45).

HE WAS POWERFUL WHILE BEING ARRESTED:

Our Lord Jesus Christ was powerful when He was arrested. The soldiers who came with their sticks and swords were afraid of Him. St. John the Beloved, who followed the Lord till the Crucifixion, explained this by saying, "Jesus therefore, knowing all things that would come upon Him, went forward and said to them, 'Whom are you seeking?' They answered Him, 'Jesus of Nazareth.' Jesus said to them, 'I am He.' And Judas, who betrayed Him, also stood with them. Now when He said to them, 'I am He,' they drew back and fell to the ground." (John 18:4-6).

The Lord's enemies fell to the ground and they were unable to confront His unarmed power which was more effective than their armed attack. Jesus could have gone away at that time, but instead He remained calm, courageous and dignified. When they stood up, He asked them once more, "Whom do you seek?" And they said, "Jesus of Nazareth". Jesus answered, "I have told you that I am He. Therefore, if you seek Me, let these go their way." (John 18:7-9).

That is how our Lord Jesus Christ was powerful when He was arrested. Others who may face the same circumstances would have trembled with fear. But with the Lord, it was the opposite, He was not afraid, but it was those who came to arrest Him who were too scared to face Him, until He presented Himself to them saying, "I am He".

The Lord's Power was also demonstrated when He healed the ear of the Chief priest's servant while He was being arrested. "Then Simon Peter, having a sword, drew it and struck the high priest's servant, and cut off his right ear." (John 18:10). But our meek Lord, who does not behave violently, turned to Peter and asked him to sheathe his sword. He refused to defend Himself or let others defend Him. He rebuked Peter saying, "Put your sword in its place, or do you think that I cannot now pray to My Father, and He will provide Me with more than twelve legions of angels?" (Matthew 26:53). The Lord refused to do anything to save Himself, but faced death in courage for our salvation. As for the servant's ear, it was healed by the powerful Lord who was to be arrested, "And He touched his ear and healed him." (Luke 22:51). The Lord showed mercy to His enemies even during the most critical times. We stand beside the arrested Lord who healed the servant's ear, whispering in His holy ear, "To You is the Power..."

This act of mercy puts to shame the soldiers, Judas and the Chief priests. It was also a witness against them or an invitation to believe in Him later. After being arrested, He walked among them as a King in the midst of His slaves or the Creator with His creation. He could have destroyed them all, but He wanted their salvation.

The Lord could have done what Elijah did with the Captain of the fifty who asked him to meet the king. "So Elijah answered and said to the Captain of the fifty: 'If I am a man of God, let fire come down from heaven and consume you and your fifty men.' And fire came down from heaven and consumed him and his fifty." (2 Kings 1:10). The Messiah could have simply done what Elijah did, but He instead came to die for man. His power was in controlling Himself and not destroying them. It is the power that saved us and the courage that made Him face death without fear.

HE WAS POWERFUL DURING THE TRIAL:

The Chief priests were afraid of the Lord, so they held His trial at night. They were confused and, "Sought false testimony against Jesus to put Him to death, but found none. Even though many false witnesses came forward, they found none." (Matthew 26:59-60). They were amazed to see Him calm and silent, "And the high priest arose and said to Him, 'Do You answer nothing? What is it these men testify against You?' But Jesus kept silent." (Matthew 26:62-63). Accusations did not upset the Lord Christ, neither did false witnesses. His silence was more powerful than words; it made them feel that their accusations and false witnesses were trivial.

They searched for something else to charge Him with and implored Him to admit that He was Christ the Son of God. "I put You under oath by the living God: Tell us if You are the Christ, the Son of God!" He could have remained silent, but He answered powerfully, "It is as you said. Nevertheless, I say to you hereafter you will see the Son of Man sitting at the Right Hand of the Power and coming on the clouds of heaven." (Matthew 26:63-64).

He was powerful in facing Pilate, as well as, Caiaphas. His dignity overruled that governor who repeatedly confessed, "I find no fault in this Man. And indeed, having examined Him in your presence, I have found no fault in this Man concerning those things of which you accuse Him. I have found no reason for death in Him." (Luke 23:4, 14 &21). No words were spoken to convince Pilate, but instead it was the

Lord's silence and the power that radiated from Him. That governor tried different tricks to set Him free and when he failed he washed his hands, announcing his innocence of the blood of our Lord Christ. And we stand beside the Lord during His trial saying: "To You is the Power..."

HE WAS POWERFUL DURING HIS CRUCIFIXION AND DEATH:

When the Lord was on the Cross, the sun was darkened and, "the veil of the temple was torn in two from top to bottom; and the earth quaked, and the rocks were split, and the graves were opened; and many bodies of the saints who had fallen asleep were raised." (Matthew 27:51-52). When the centurion and his men, who were guarding the cross observed the earthquake they were dreadfully frightened and said, "Truly this was the Son of God!" (Matthew 27:54). The centurion became a great saint and was martyred for the name of Christ. His name is Saint Longinus and is commemorated by the Church twice a year in the Synaxarium.

The sun's darkening had its effect on Athens in Greece. Due to this phenomenon, the astrologist and the council member, Dionosius Ariobagi, believed in Christ because of the preaching of St. Paul, who explained to him how the sun was darkened at the time of the crucifixion of the Lord Christ. Dionosius became the first Bishop of Athens.

Our Lord Jesus Christ was also powerful on the Cross when He forgave those who crucified Him and when He promised the thief on the right hand to be with Him in paradise that same day.

The Lord was Powerful in His Death. When His hour came, "Jesus had cried out with a loud voice and said, 'Father, into Your hands I commit My spirit.'" (Luke 23:46). St. John Chrysostom chose the phrase "with a loud voice" and contemplated on the power of the Lord during His death. How did the Lord have such a "loud voice" while dying and after He had reached a state of extreme physical weakness?

He struggled at Gethsemane, "Then His sweat became like great drops of blood falling down to the ground." (Luke 22:45). He was then arrested and had to walk on foot for a long distance. He was sent for trial five times before Annas, Caiaphas, Pilate, Herod then Pilate for a second time. Add to this the exhaustion and the unbearable pain He had, when He was whipped thirty nine times in the most savage way, while many before Him had died from such whipping or had reached near death! Then the crown of thorns caused Him to lose blood. He was also struck several times. Then He had to carry the Cross until He collapsed beneath it. "Now as they led Him away, they laid hold of a certain man, Simon a Cyrenian, who was coming from the country, and on him they laid the cross that he might bear it after Jesus." (Luke 23:26).

He endured more pain when He was nailed to the Cross. He was physically drained and His skin stuck to His bones, as David the prophet prophesied saying, "I can count all My bones." (Psalm 22:17). When Jesus reached the moment of death, He had no power left in Him even to whisper. How then did He cry out with a loud voice?! We stand by His side amazed at this holy moment, saying: "To You is the Power..."

The Lord was powerful in His death. He defeated death by His death, trampled the serpent's head and fulfilled the promise given to humanity since the time of Eve, "He shall bruise your head." (Genesis 3:15). Therefore His death revealed Him as the Saviour of the world. The Lord's most powerful moment was that of His death. At that hour He reigned over humanity and restored His Kingdom from the ruler of this world. "The Lord reigns, He is clothed with majesty; The Lord is clothed, He has girded Himself with strength." (Psalm 93). He reigned on the Cross. For this reason, we find in the prayer of the ninth hour, by which we commemorate the Lord's death, Psalms of praise, glory and worship. So we stand before the Powerful Lord in His death singing: "To You is the Power..."

HE WAS POWERFUL AFTER HIS DEATH:

The first thing the Lord did when He yielded up His Spirit was lay hold of the devil and bind him for a thousand years. The Lord also, "Descended into the lower parts of the earth." (Ephesians 4:9). He announced the good news to the dead and led them, with the thief on the right hand, to Paradise. It was the Lord's death that opened the gates of Paradise after being locked for thousands of years, since the fall of Adam and Eve. The One which they thought was dead in the sealed tomb was able to open the gates to Paradise and lead all who died in hope of His procession of victory.

One of the beautiful stories that were told after the Lord's death is that, while Nicodemus was shrouding Him, he contemplated saying, "How can I shroud the Lord and the Creator?! So the Lord looked at him and smiled and Nicodemus said, "Holy God, Holy Mighty, Holy Immortal," which is where the well known Trisagion originates from. We stand by the side of the holy tomb, saying to the Lord in His death, "To You is the Power..." The Lord was powerful in His Resurrection, powerful when He left the sealed tomb and conquered death.

THE LORD HID HIS POWER FROM THE DEVIL:

One of the main reasons which makes people think that the Lord Christ was weak was that He used to hide His power. It was an act of humility that confused the devil and made him wonder, 'Is that really Jesus Christ! Is it Him or not?! It was for the best not to let the devil know the truth about the Lord Jesus Christ, as he could have done his utmost to cripple the plan of redemption, for the devil never wanted the world to be saved. The following are some examples which illustrate the devil's confusion because the Lord hid His power.

The devil knew that the Lord Christ would be born from a virgin, as Isaiah the Prophet foretold, "Behold the virgin shall conceive and bear a Son, and shall call His name Emmanuel." (Isaiah 7:14). He also described the characteristic of this Son, "For unto Us a Child is born, unto Us a Son is given and the government will be upon His shoulder: and His name will be called Wonderful, Counsellor, Mighty God, Everlasting Father, Prince of Peace." (Isaiah 9:6). The devil heard a confirmation of this prophecy when the angel appeared to Joseph and said, "Behold! The virgin shall be with child and bear a son, and they shall call His name Emmanuel." (Matthew 1:22-23).

It was also confirmed in the angel's annunciation to Virgin Mary that, "The Holy spirit will come upon you, and the power of the Highest will overshadow you; therefore, also, that Holy One who is to be born will be called the Son of God." (Luke 1:35). And it happened that the Virgin Mary did conceive, and the devil witnessed what happened when Mary visited Elizabeth, "When Elizabeth heard the greeting of Mary that the babe leaped in her womb; and Elizabeth was filled with the Holy Spirit. Then she spoke out with a loud voice and said, but why is this granted to me, that the mother of my Lord should come to me?" (Luke 1:43).

The devil then said within himself that this was certainly the Son of God. But when the Incarnated God was born in a manger, the devil was very confused. How could that happen! It is hard to believe that this poor, homeless baby, who is surrounded by animals, is the Son of God. It cannot be Him, without the whole world celebrating His coming with ceremonies, without angels and heavenly lights surrounding Him to announce His arrival and heaven and earth shaking before Him. The devil was confused as he had no idea of the meaning of humility or self mortification; otherwise he would not have become a devil.

The devil also heard what the angel announced to the shepherds, "Do not be afraid, for behold, I bring you good tidings of great joy which will be to all people. For there is born to you this day in the city of David a Saviour, who is Christ the Lord. And this will be the sign to you: You will find a Babe wrapped in swaddling cloths, lying in a manger." (Luke 2:10-12). The devil said within himself, "This is certainly He". This was confirmed by the multitude of heavenly host, praising God saying, "Glory to God in the highest and on earth peace, good will toward men." (Luke 2:14). If peace was to return to earth, then it should be through the Lord Christ, the Saviour. This was also ascertained by the testimony of the wise men, the fulfilment of the prophecy about the baby of Bethlehem, the disturbance of King Herod because of the Child's birth and worship of the wise men to the Child. (Matthew 2:1-11).

However, the devil later suspected the matter when he saw that great Saviour who was praised by the angels and worshipped by the wise men and who caused Herod to tremble, flee in fear to Egypt. He thought: "Is it possible that God escapes from the face of man? Where is His power, His Kingdom and awe? It cannot be Him." But the devil then saw that when that Child entered Egypt, many of its idols fell and were broken. He knew this fulfilled the prophecy by Isaiah which said, "Behold, the Lord is riding on a swift cloud and comes to Egypt; the idols of Egypt will totter at His presence and the heart of the Egyptians will melt in its midst." (Isaiah 19:1). And the devil said within himself, "No doubt, He is the Saviour, the Son of God."

Once more the devil started to doubt when he realised that the Child returned only after the death of those who were seeking His life. "But when he heard that Archelaus was reigning over Judea instead of his father Herod, he was afraid to go there. And being warned by God in a dream, he turned aside into the region of Galilee. And he came and dwelt in a city called Nazareth." (Matthew 2:22-23). What a confusing situation! "Can anything good come out of Nazareth?"

(John 1:46). "'No, it cannot be He!" said the devil.

The devil remained in his doubts till the Child was twelve years of age and he saw Him sitting among the elders, and all who listened to Him were amazed at His understanding. The devil heard Jesus answering Mary and Joseph, "Did you not know that I must be about My Father's business." (Luke. 2:49).

The devil then said within himself, "It must be He. Who else will have such wisdom and talk about His Father's business!" When the boy submitted himself to Mary and Joseph, the devil started to doubt again. How could He yield to them while heaven and earth surrender to Him? It cannot be He! What increased his doubts even more was seeing Jesus Christ living for another 18 years, until He was 30 years old, as a simple carpenter, with no fame at all. The Lord would not waste the prime of His life in such a way. It cannot be Him.

The devil then heard St. John the Baptist, who testified for Christ saying, "but there stands One among you whom you do not know. It is He who, coming after me, is preferred before me, whose sandal strap I am not worthy to loose." (John 1:27). He pointed to Christ and said, "Behold! The Lamb of God who takes away the sins of the world!" (John 1:29). "There comes One after me who is mightier than I. I indeed baptised you with water, but He will baptise you with the Holy Spirit." (Mark 1:7-8). And the devil said, "It must be He."

The devil was especially amazed when he saw that great Lord who John the Baptist said was not worthy to stoop down and untie his sandal straps and was supposed to take away the sins of the world, be Himself baptised with the Holy spirit. That great Lord came to St. John to be baptised just like everyone else.

The devil expected Christ to baptise St. John and start His mission; that is what dignity means. But he saw exactly the opposite happen. He heard Christ saying to John, "Permit it to be so now." And St. John did baptise Christ. It was too much for the devil to understand this humility and he said in his heart, "It is not He!" During the baptism, a remarkable sign was given to prove that it was He. The devil saw the heavens parted and the Spirit, like a dove, coming down upon Christ. And there came a voice from heaven, "You are My beloved Son, in whom I am well pleased." (Mark 1:10-11). There was no doubting that clear testimony of the Father. It is certainly He.

The devil then returned to his doubts when he saw that He, to whom the Father and the Holy Spirit gave testimony during the baptism, was lying exhausted on the mountain, hungry after fasting. How could He be hungry while having the power to turn the stones into bread to eat? Surely it was not He. The devil was able to take Him and set Him on the pinnacle of the temple, then to a high mountain. (Matthew 4:5-8). The devil was then certain that it could not be the Son of God, and dared to say to Him, "All these things I will give You if You will fall down and worship me." (Matthew 4:9). But his fear returned when the Lord rebuked him saying, "Away with you, Satan! Then the devil left Him, and behold, angels came and ministered to Him." (Matthew 4: 10-11).

The devil's fear was increased and he began to think that it was He when he saw Him performing miracles that nobody else had ever performed before. But he found that the Lord hid some of those miracles behind His prayers. Other miracles He worked on the Sabbath, which led to the anger of the Pharisees and Scribes. The devil, seeing the Lord living without a title, no position, and no residence, surrounded by weak people said to himself, "No, it is not He!" The devil then heard Christ say to Nicodemus, "No one has ascended to heaven, but He who came down from heaven, that is, the Son of Man who is in heaven." (John 3:13). And the devil said, "Could it be He?! But how could He be in heaven while being on earth with Nicodemus!"

If He is to be found everywhere, then He must be God. It is also confirmed by the phrase, "descended from heaven". Besides, he heard the Lord saying, "For God so loved the world that He gave His only begotten Son, that whoever believes in Him should not perish, but have everlasting life." (John 3:16). These words nearly convinced the devil, whose doubts returned to him because of the expression "Son of Man", which the Lord often used. But why does He say that "the Son of Man must be lifted up so that whoever believes in Him may not perish but have everlasting life." (John.3:14-17).

The numerous miracles of the Lord Christ proved His divinity, and His power over evil spirits forced them to admit it. "And demons also came out of many, crying out and saying, 'You are the Christ, the Son of God! He rebuked them.'" (Luke4:41). The devil's suspicions started again when he found that the Lord was tired of walking, sitting by a well asking a woman for a drink!! When the Lord rebuked the sea and waves, the devil said, "It is He", but when He was asleep in the boat, he wondered how it could be when it says in the Psalms, "He will neither slumber nor sleep"! (Psalm 121:4)

Some people were just as confused as the devil himself. "Some say John the Baptist, some Elijah, and others Jeremiah or one of the prophets." (Matthew 16:14). The Lord asked His disciples, "But you, who do you say I am?" Simon Peter answered, "You are Christ, the Son of the Living God", and the Lord answered him, "Blessed are you, Simon Bar-Jonah, for flesh and blood has not revealed this to you, but My Father who is in heaven." (Matthew 16:17). The devil heard this clear, unquestionable confession and said to himself, "No doubt it is He."

The devil's confusion started again when he heard the Lord tell His disciples that He must go to Jerusalem to suffer, die and on the third day rise. And the devil could not understand how would the Son of God suffer and die. It must be His way of saving Man. Then He should be stopped. So the devil put words in Peter's mouth to say to His Lord, "Far be it from You, Lord; this shall not happen to You!" But He turned and said to Peter, "Get behind Me, Satan! You are an offense to Me, for you are not mindful of the things of God, but the things of men." (Matthew 16:22-23).

The devil then thought it might be He when the Lord left to Jerusalem where He was received as a great King and the awaited Messiah. Even the children praised Him in fulfilment of the Psalm, "Out of the mouth of babes and nursing infants You have ordained strength." (Psalm 8:2), and out of respect He cleansed the temple. But his doubts returned when the Lord retired to Bethany.

The Lord started to destroy the devil's kingdom, revealing to the people the hypocrisy of the scribes and Pharisees saying, "Woe to you, scribes and Pharisees, hypocrites." (Matthew 23:1-3). He did away also with the Levitical priesthood by telling the parable of the vineyard and the wicked tenants. (Luke 20: 9-19). The Lord put to shame the Pharisees, Sadducces and the Herodians that "No one dared question Him." (Mark 12:34). Thereupon the devil began to get ready to arrest the Lord and so the plot developed on Wednesday.

The devil saw the Lord washing the disciples' feet on Thursday and he was encouraged, saying in his heart it was not the Lord; for how would the Lord wash the feet of men?! And so the devil entered Judas after the piece of bread was dipped and made him carry out the plot. (John 13:2). When the devil heard the Lord's last conversation with the disciples and that He would send them the Holy Spirit, he thought it must be He; for who else could send God's Holy Spirit except God Himself!

The devil then hearing the Lord's long prayer to the Father, asking for the disciples, "That they may be one as We are." (John 17:11), "As You, Father, are in Me, and I in You." (John 17:21), "Keep through Your name those, that they may be one as We are." The devil trembled and said "It must be He?" He remembered the Lord's words before, "I and My father are One" (John 10:30)and His words to Philip, "He who has seen Me has seen the Father, so how can you say, 'Show us the father? Do you not believe that I am in the Father and the Father in

Me?'" (John 14:8-10), and the devil was filled with fear and said, "It must be He?"

But soon the devil saw the Lord in His agony on the Mount of Olives, asking the Father if He would remove that cup from Him, and exclaimed how would the One who said, "I and My Father are One", be in such agony, till "His sweat fell to the ground like great drops of blood." (Luke 22:44)! So the devil was reassured and said, "No, it is not He." The soldiers then came to arrest Him. The devil saw the soldiers who came armed with swords, weapons and sticks to arrest the Lord Jesus Christ, and they fell to the ground and were not able to face His overwhelming reverence, though He was unarmed, and the devil became puzzled. He saw the Lord heal the ear of the slave when Peter severed it with his sword, and the devil said "Certainly, it is He". Who else would have such courage and reverence? Who else would have such love towards His enemies and have such miraculous power? But soon the devil saw the Lord walking with them as a lamb to the slaughter, not opening His mouth. And the devil was reassured again and said, "No, it is not He."

Then the Lord was put to trial by the chief priests, and the devil listened carefully. He was trying to find an answer to the question he had in his mind since the temptation on the mount. The question this time came from the chief priest who asked the Lord, "Are You Christ, the Son of God?" And the Lord said to him, "Nevertheless, I say to you, hereafter you will see the Son of Man sitting at the right hand of the Power, and coming on the clouds of heaven." (Matthew 26:64).

The devil heard this clear confession and wondered if it was He who had said many times before, would come upon the clouds of heaven! But the devil's doubts returned when he saw the Lord despised and forsaken by the people who mocked and spitefully treated Him, and He opened not His mouth. He offered His back to be flogged and His cheek to be slapped, and did not turn His face away from the shame of spitting. He saw the Lord fall with exhaustion under the

Cross, and Simon of Cyrene carrying it for Him. The devil then said, "No, it is impossible that it is He? Dignity and power according to the devil meant false glory.

So he said to himself, "It cannot be He". And the devil shouted on the mouth of the public, "Crucify Him, Crucify Him." But the echo of the Lord's words remained, "I lay down My life, I voluntarily lay it down and I have authority to take it up again." The Lord was lifted on the Cross and the devil continued to be tormented with doubt. The Lord hid His power and the devil continued asking the old question, "Save Yourself! If You are the Son of God, come down from the cross." (Matthew 27:40).

The Lord's first words while on the Cross started with, "Father, Father, forgive them." The word "Father" disturbed the devil, and he asked himself, "Could it be He?" And by putting words in the mouth of the thief on the left of Christ, who asked, "If You are the Christ, save Yourself and us." (Luke 23:39).

The Lord said to the thief on his right, "Truly I say to you, today you will be with Me in Paradise." (Luke 23:42). And the devil was shaken with fear. What is He saying? Doesn't He know that Paradise has been closed for five thousand years? And at the east of the Garden of Eden He placed the Cherubim, and a flaming sword which turned every way, to guard the way to the tree of life." (Genesis 3:24). How would Paradise be open then? And how would the Crucified enter it with the other thief?! Could it be the Christ, by whose Crucifixion the world will be saved?! If that happened, Satan's kingdom would fail and all that he achieved since Adam. On the sixth hour, there was darkness over the earth, the veil of the temple was torn in two, the earth shook, the rocks were split and tombs were opened, and the devil's fear increased and he said, "It is He, no doubt, Christ the Saviour."

But in spite of the shaking of the earth and darkness, the devil heard the Lord say, "My God, My God, why have You forsaken Me?"

then say, "I am Thirsty", and then the devil calmed down and said, "It is not He."

The devil waited for the death of the Lord Christ to get hold of His soul, as he did with other human beings, and bring Him down to Hades. He was surprised when the Lord cried with a loud voice, "Father, into Your hands I commit My spirit." The devil was astonished to hear the Crucified still saying, "Father". Could He be truly the Son of God? What was the meaning of that loud voice? How did He get that strength? And the devil said to himself, "How would He entrust His spirit into God's hands? It has to be in my hands." But when the devil progressed to take the soul of the Lord while still in fear and doubt, the Lord held him with the power of His divinity and bound him for a thousand years.

To You is the Glory

During Holy Week, we see that the Lord Christ, as described by the Prophet Isaiah, "He is despised and rejected by men, and we did not esteem Him." (Isaiah 53:3). We see Him despised for our sake and follow Him, singing this immortal hymn, "To You is the Power, the Glory, the Blessing and the Honour, forever Amen, Emmanuel our God and King."

Despised and Rejected by Men!!

In fact, the Lord did not only abandon His glory during the Holy Week, He sacrificed His dignity for our sake.

He became without Honour in His own country. They reproached Him saying, "Is this not the carpenter's son?" (Matthew 13:55). For us He endured shame, insults and reproach, for us! Being humble, the

Lord sat with tax-collectors and sinners, but they called Him a glutton and a winebibber. For His love and concern, which was evident when healed the sick, they accused Him of breaking the Sabbath, to teach us in depth, instead of abiding by the letter of the Law. They said He violated the Law. We see Him abused for our sake and we follow Him with the same hymn, "To You is the Power and Glory..."

We know, Lord, why they insulted You. They insulted You because You were not like them and Your humility exposed them. You did not behave like them for, "But all their works they do, to be seen by men. They make their phylacteries broad and enlarge the borders of their garments. They love the best places at feasts, the best seats in the synagogues, greetings in the marketplaces, and to be called by men, 'Rabbi, Rabbi.'" (Matthew 3:5-7). But You lived a modest and meek life by associating with the lowly and despised, eating with sinners and tax-collectors. You let the sinner woman touch You, the Samaritan woman converse with You, and the children come to You. You walked in poverty, with no title, no money and nowhere to lean Your head on.

They refused to glorify You Lord, for You reviled their glory and said, "I do not receive Glory from men." (John 5:41). So You refused the kingdom and majesty. But know Your great Majesty, and to You we say, "To You is the Power, and the Glory." Their scorn did not decrease Your glory at all. They sold You for the price of a slave, "Thirty pieces of silver" and mockingly, they put a purple robe on You and a crown of thorns upon Your Head. As for us, we follow You in Your passion saying, "To You is the Power, the Glory, the Blessing and the Honour, forever Amen."

YOU ARE OUR GLORIFIED GOD:

They despised You, because You took the form of a servant, but we glorify You, as we know who You are. You are equal to the Father as You said, "All Yours are Mine." (John 17:10). And You are the Only

Begotten Son, who is in the bosom of the Father, since the beginning (John. I:18), "Who being the brightness of His Glory and the express image of His person." (Hebrews I:3). Yes Lord, we glorify You for the glory which, "You had with Your Father before the world was." (John 17:5), and because all authority in heaven and earth has been given to You. (Matthew 28:18).

You were glorified before we existed, and for You "Every knee should bow, of those in heaven, and of those on earth, and of those under the earth." (Philippians 2:10). Before we began to glorify You, You were and still are glorified by the Angels and Archangels, "Before whom stand thousands of thousands and ten thousands of the heavenly hosts ministering to You and carrying out Your word, O our Master."

You had been also glorified before the Angels or anything else existed, when You alone existed. You do not need any creature to glorify You, for You are glorified in Your Nature, Your attributes, and Your Divinity. You need no one to glorify You and as You said, "I am the Alpha and the Omega, the Beginning and the End, the First and the Last." (Revelation 22:13).

When we glorify You, Lord, we do not add anything new to You, even when you emptied Yourself taking the form of a slave, many events showed Your glory. You were glorified on Your birth, by the angels who brought the good tidings to the shepherds, and by the three wise men who brought You gifts that suited Your glory and worshipped You. You were glorified when the idols of Egypt fell on Your visit while still a child, (Isaiah 19:1). John the Baptist glorified You saying, "There comes One after me who is mightier than I, whose sandal strap I am not worthy to stoop down and loose." (Mark I: 7-8).

Your glory was shown during the Baptism, when the Holy Spirit descended on You like a dove, and a voice from heaven said, "You are My beloved Son; in You I am well pleased." (Luke 3:22).

Your glory was also shown on the Mount of transfiguration, when

Your face shone like the sun and Your garments became white as light, and God's voice from a cloud said, "This is My beloved Son, in whom I am well pleased. Hear Him!" (Matthew 17:2-5).

You showed Your glory, Lord, in numerous miracles, even the devils could not help but bear witness. And when You were tempted by Satan on the mountain, You showed Your glory. You rebuked the devil and he was gone, then the angels came and ministered to You. (Mark 1:13).

Your glory was shown through the Revelation to St. John the beloved, who saw You in the midst of the golden lampstands. Your face shone as when the sun shines in its full strength, Your eyes were like a flame of fire, and Your voice like the sound of many waters. When St. John saw You, he fell at Your feet as though dead. (Revelation 1:13-17).

In Your second coming, You will also come in Your Glory, on clouds of heaven, as it is said, "When the Son of Man comes in His glory, and all the holy angels with Him, then He will sit on the throne of His glory." (Matthew 25:31). "Clouds and darkness surround Him; Righteousness and Justice are the foundation of His throne, His lightning illumines the world. The mountains melt like wax before the Lord." (Psalms 97:2-5).

WE ALSO GLORIFY YOU:

When we glorify You, our mouths are sanctified, but that does not add anything to You. When we glorify You, Lord, we do not give You glory, but rather admit Yours. You are like the sun; it shines with or without our acknowledgment. What we say does not add to its light; it illuminates by itself.

We do not glorify You only in Your second coming, when Your glory will be obvious, but we glorify You in the depth of Your pain.

We follow You, step by step proclaiming, "To You is the Power and Glory …. Emmanuel our God and our King." We Glorify You with the beautiful hymn "Pekethronous", the magnificent, immortal melody which is incomparable in the world of music, in which we say, "Your throne, O God, is forever and ever; A sceptre of righteousness is the sceptre of Your Kingdom." (Psalm 45:6).

By glorifying You, Christ, we protest against the deeds of those who plotted and crucified You. We protest against what the ungrateful human beings did to You, and see Your true glory on the Cross which You endured for our sake. By glorifying You in Your crucifixion, we have pride in the glory of the Cross, taking it as a life and support for us in our ministry. We even sing with St. Paul, "I have been crucified with Christ; it is no longer I who live, but Christ lives in me." (Galatians 2:20).

With this beautiful hymn we glorify the Lord at the end of the prayers of Good Friday, after He paid His blood a price for the world's salvation, and began to reign on a tree. We sing to Him, "Your Throne, O God, is for ever and ever." With the same hymn, we also glorify Him on Tuesday of the Holy Week, the day on which He announced to the disciples the time of His crucifixion, "You know that after two days is the Passover, and the Son of Man will be delivered up to be crucified." (Matthew 26:2). And with the same beautiful tune we glorify the Lord with another hymn (i.e. **Ⲁⲧϭⲛⲟⲛ**). We glorify You, Lord, in Your crucifixion not only in Your miracles.

TO YOU IS THE BLESSING

We follow our Lord Jesus Christ in the Crucifixion, whispering in His ear, "To You is the Blessing." As the Holy Bible says, "Cursed is everyone who hangs on a tree." (Galatians 3:13). Hence, a criminal who was put to death in that way had to be buried on the same day and not remain all night hanged on the tree lest he should defile the land, as the hanged is accursed by God (Deuteronomy 21:22-23). And so the Lord took away the curse of the Law on our behalf and became accursed for our sake. But we know that He is holy, without sin, and the curse He took away was ours; the wages of our sins according to the Law (Deuteronomy 28:27). He is not a sinner, certainly not, but He takes away the sins of others, of the whole world. We therefore, follow Him regretting our bad deeds that resulted in Him carrying it, saying to Him from the depths of our hearts, "To You is the Power, the Glory, the Blessing... Emmanuel our God and King."

For this curse, they crucified Him outside the camp, so that He would not defile it, and we follow Him in His Holy Week, as St. Paul said, "Therefore, let us go forth to Him outside the camp, bearing His reproach." (Hebrews 13:13). We bear His reproach, as said about the Prophet Moses, "Esteeming the reproach of Christ greater riches than the treasures in Egypt; for he looked to the reward." (Hebrews 11:26).

Therefore, the Church remains outside the camp, away from the altar, away from the sanctuary, away from the first Chancel, the Chancel of Saints, remembering our sins that took us outside the camp like Adam when he was sent forth from the Garden of Eden. We follow the Lord outside the Camp saying, "You are righteous, we are evil, we deserve the curse and banishment, but You, To You is the Blessing forever Amen, my Lord Jesus Christ, the Good Saviour.

While the Jews see in the Cross of the Lord Christ a symbol of shame and humiliation, we say to Him, "To You and to Your Cross is the blessing. With Your Cross we are blessed in everything. The priests, with the sign of the Cross, bless the Congregation, and with the sign of the Cross, consecration and sanctification are completed. With the sign of the Cross in the baptistery, we obtain the blessing of the new birth and each member of our body is blessed and sanctified with the sign of the Cross in the sacrament of the Holy Baptism. Besides, all the Holy sacraments of Eucharist, Priesthood and the other sacraments of the Church are completed with the sign of the Cross by which we obtain grace, blessing and gifts. So, we cry out from all our hearts, "To You is the Blessing..."

To You, O Lord, is the blessing that we lost since the fall of Adam, and of which we are still, to this day dreaming and waiting for You to grant to us. By You all the nations of the world are blessed. When Man was created, God blessed him, and when he fell, a curse came unto earth, as God said to Adam, "Cursed is the ground for your sake." (Genesis 3:17). Then the curse spread among human beings themselves, so God cursed Cain (Genesis 4:11), then Cain and his descendants too. The curse extended and reached every sinner, as it was said in the Law, "But it shall come to pass, if you do not obey the voice of the Lord your God, to observe carefully all His commandments and His statutes which I command you today, that all these curses will come upon you and overtake you. The Lord will send on you cursing, confusion, and rebuke in all that you set your hand to do, until you are destroyed and until you perish quickly." (Deuteronomy 28:15-20).

Amidst the curses of the Law, mankind dreamt of God fulfilling His promise to Abraham, "In your seed all the nations of the earth shall be blessed." (Genesis 22:18). Mankind waited for Your coming, Lord, then You came, our loving, kind Lord to take away the curse of the Law and in You all nations were blessed. We stand by Your side while on the Cross, trusting Your promise to Abraham. We look at You, Lord, while You dipped hyssop in Your Holy Blood and sprinkled us to become clean. We sing for Your Glory and Holiness, "To You is the Blessing, forever Amen."

To You is the Blessing, thine is the blessing that You gave to the world in whom are blessed, all nations and generations. But for this blessing of Yours, the whole world would perish in its sins.

To You is the blessing as we say to You in the Holy Liturgy, "You blessed my nature in You." To You is the unlimited blessing by which the whole world is blessed.

To You is the blessing You gave to us, the nation who was called uncircumcised, "That at that time you were without Christ, being aliens from the commonwealth of Israel and strangers from the covenants of promise, having no hope and without God in the world." (Ephesians 2:12). With Your blessings Lord we "are no longer strangers and foreigners, but fellow citizens with the saints and members of the household of God." (Ephesians 2:19).

To You is the blessing because You are Holy. So, on the day of Your crucifixion, we sing this hymn saying, "Holy God, Holy Mighty, Holy Immortal, who was crucified for us, have mercy upon us." As we sing the hymn of Your Holiness, we clear You from all accusations. When we sing the "AGIOS" hymn i.e. "The Trisagion" with a sorrowful tune, our sorrow is not for You, but for those who led You to the Cross as a sinner and charged You wrongly. But You, the Holy, born of the Holy Spirit, the only Holy One, To You is the blessing forever Amen.

You first gave blessing to the thief on the right hand, when You brought him with You to Paradise. With this blessing, You blessed the foolish of the world and disgraced the wise, You blessed the weak vessels that carried Your Holy Name.

Who ever thought that those weak fishermen would become in Your hands, like the five loaves and fill up the whole world, "Their line has gone out through all the earth, and their words to the end of the world." (Psalm 19:4). Who would ever have thought this scared group, hiding in the upper room would go and face emperors, philosophers and religious leaders, and fill the whole world? It is Your blessing that was given to our mother Rebecca, when You said to her, "Our sister, may you become the mother of thousands of ten thousands; And may your descendants possess the gates of those who hate them." (Genesis 24:60). Indeed Lord, To You is the Power.

The sin hid the blessing, so, when the sin was taken away from us, the blessing returned. You restored Man to his first rank, as You said to him in compassion, "I will make you a great nation; I will bless you And make your name great; And you shall be a blessing." (Genesis 12:2). We ask You to keep Your blessing on us, with all its grace and abundance. Let the blessing we heard on the sixth day return to us, when You said, "Be fruitful and multiply, and fill the earth and subdue it." (Genesis 1:28), by which You also blessed our father Noah (Genesis 8).

TO YOU IS THE HONOUR

"To You is the Honour," and if You refused the earthly kingdom, You reigned in the hearts, and Your kingdom is inside us. And those who did not let You reign inside them feared You.

"To You is the Honour", because You have the charisma, the respect, and the awe. You were able to overcome Your dignity and abandon Yourself in humility, but without diminishing Your greatness and Your worth.

How many times did You abandon Your true nature, allowed Your enemies to throw stones at You, but they could not do anything to You. But you passed in the midst of them and went Your way (Luke 4:30) and no one was able to touch You. And they could not seize You until the hour had come, the hour which You alone had set, which You would deliver Yourself. All were afraid of You. Even when they questioned You and argued with You, You were gentle with them. Even when You were young they listened to You, were surprised and admired You.

Even the devil felt deep within himself that You are strong and undefeatable. Your humility allowed him to approach You. But Your glory overwhelmed him when You rebuked him. Hence, he escaped and was unable to continue his conversation with You. Thus his temptations towards You ended here.

You were glorious all Your life, feared and respected, and the story of the crucifixion is nothing but a reflection of Your enemies' fear of You. They felt that You were stronger than them in everything, closer to the hearts than they and more convincing to the people. So they were fearful for their positions because of You.

We stand at Your cross O Lord, saying to You, despite the insults and suffering, "To You is the Glory forever, Emmanuel our God and our King."

LET US FOLLOW THE LORD BY PARTICIPATING IN

HIS SUFFERING

During this week we follow Christ step by step. We follow Him in His suffering, in all the events which He passed through and we sing praises to Him saying: "To You is the Power and the Glory." To this praise we add more words according to the events of the day. We live with Him day by day, with our emotions, our thoughts and our spirit, with all our being. We know the events of the day and its prophecies from the Holy readings and we live the events with Him, just as St. Peter said, "See, we have left all and followed You." (Matthew 19:27). During Holy Week we leave everything and follow Him.

We also remember what was said about the blessed women that followed Jesus from Galilee and ministered to Him (Matthew 27:55). And the many other women who came up with Him to Jerusalem (Mark15:41). We hope that we can live with Him during this week with the same purpose, feelings and passion, following Him and going up with Him. Just as the beautiful words which Ruth said to Naomi,

"Entreat me not to leave you." (Ruth 1:16-17). In the same way we follow Christ day by day through the week, wherever He went. Our thoughts and contemplations go with Him, all along singing the same praise "To You is the Power and the Glory."

Here we express our protest to our fathers whom he said "Indeed the hour is coming, yes, has now come, that you will be scattered, each to his own, and will leave Me alone." (John 16:32). Lord we are not leaving You alone, separated each one to his own, but we will gather around You. We will gather around You in Your suffering, with all our feelings and our hearts. We can not leave You, and You who did not leave anyone in their suffering, and You did not leave anyone during Your suffering.

We excuse the three apostles whom You asked to stay with You, "Stay here and watch with Me." (Matthew 26:38) and they could not stay. You admonished them saying, "What, could you not watch with Me one hour?" (Matthew 26:40). Unfortunately, they left You and could not stay awake. But here O Lord, we will stay awake the whole night in prayer, not just one hour, for we like to stay awake the whole of Pascha Week.

I admire what St. Paul said in Philippians 3:10, and this can be used as a slogan for this week, "That I may know Him and the power of His resurrection, and the fellowship of His sufferings, being conformed to His own death." Many have lived with our Lord Jesus and until now do not know Him yet! But even in during Holy Week we hear the Lord admonishing His disciple Phillip saying, "Have I been with you so long, and yet you have not known Me, Phillip?" (John 14:9). It seems to me that the Lord Jesus says the same thing to most of us. And many knew Him but did not enter into a relationship with His suffering. Thus during Holy Week we would like to say to Him, "Allow us Lord, even from far a distance, to share Your suffering with You or even to just be with You."

We will follow the events and the account of this great week. We offer our feelings on each day, the Scribes, the Pharisees and the priests did not know You, but we know You, and the mistakes of those who took advantage of You. So let us go back to the events of these days. Although Lazarus Saturday and Palm Sunday were not days of the Holy Week, we will talk about them as a brief introduction.

PALM SUNDAY AND CLEANSING THE TEMPLE

LAZARUS SATURDAY

It was the great miracle of our Lord raising Lazarus from the dead that caused many to believe. This miracle, however, did not spiritually affect the country's leaders, or the priests and Pharisees. Rather, Christ said of them, "If they do not hear Moses and the prophets, neither will they be persuaded, though one rise from the dead." (Luke 16:31). They did not have faith, but chose instead to turn the people against Christ, "Then the chief priests and the Pharisees gathered a council and said, 'What shall we do? For this Man works many signs,'" "Then from that day on they plotted to put Him to death." (John 11:47, 53).

Why did these people miss the message? Of course it was their ego and their hardness of heart. Their ego stood in the way of Christ and themselves. They were preoccupied by their own personal grandeur and their positions of power, so they saw Christ as a threat to their status and to their influence over the people. They sought to kill Him, and they did not say, as St. John the Baptist said, "He must increase, but I must decrease." (John3:30). We hope that on this day we can contemplate on how many times our ego gets in the way of loving God. The ego includes our pride, our desires and the love of praise.

Also, the hardness of the heart quenches any work of the Holy Spirit. It is strange that the previous two miracles of Holy Week had been performed on the Sabbath, that is, the restoration of the blind man's eyes and the raising of Lazarus. Did God want to rectify the thinking of the Jewish people about doing good on the Sabbath, or to prove that humans should not depend on their pride?

Let us take this idea of doing good on the Sabbath, and trust that God can raise us from our sins if we repent and repair our spiritual eyes if they have been lost. We know that sin is spiritual death and that Christ can raise the body and the spirit even after a long time. So let us prepare for Lazarus Saturday, and let us have Holy Communion on Palm Sunday. As we remember Lazarus' death and resurrection, we remember our sins and being raised from them and we prepare to have Holy Communion on Sunday as we receive Christ as our King.

PALM SUNDAY

Because this is a major feast, we celebrate it with the joyful tunes before entering into the sorrowful tunes of Pascha week. On this day the Jewish people welcomed Christ as their King to rule over Jerusalem and save them from the Romans. However, Christ refused this type of earthly kingship because His Kingdom was a spiritual one.

Although Jesus refused to reign in Jerusalem He is delighted to reign in your heart.

Your heart to God is greater than Jerusalem; it is the temple of the Holy Spirit and the dwelling place of God. Contemplate on whether the Lord rules in you completely: in your heart, your thoughts, your senses, your body and your time.

Say to Him, "Come Lord and reign. Here I am, I am Yours"

If Your kingdom is not of this world, then come, I have a kingdom befitting of You, rest Your head and relax. Perhaps You will find Your rest in my heart. We hope that You will not find disobedience or rebellion (Psalm 44). Do not be preoccupied with the palm leaves on this day, but rather prepare your heart to welcome Christ as your King, to rule over you and manage your household.

On this day Jesus entered Jerusalem as a King. He had no problems with the Romans because He was not competing with Caesar. The problem was from within His people and from the Jewish leaders.

They quarrelled amongst themselves over the meaning of King.

DISPUTE OVER THE MEANING OF KING

Our Lord accepted to enter Jerusalem as a King, as His kingdom draws near. Yes the day was approaching which would destroy Satan's kingdom, trample death, the death that brought sin into the world. So our Lord established a special Kingdom, but the Jews did not understand this type of Kingdom.

Christ wanted a spiritual kingdom, but they wanted an earthly one. Christ wanted to establish a Kingdom not of this world, but rather a spiritual one built on love with Christ ruling not man. But they wanted a worldly kingdom built on power and strength like their previous leaders Samson, Gideon and Joshua. To have God reigning on them was a concept they could not understand.

They shouted saying, "Hosanna to the Son of David!" The word 'Hosanna' means 'Save us'. But they asked for salvation as the Son of David, as an inheritance of David's crown and kingdom not as the Son of God. Thus they only wanted salvation from the oppression of the Romans. Christ, however, wanted to save His people from their sins, so His name Jesus means Saviour (Matthew 1:2). He wanted to save them from Satan's slavery, from sin and from the world. The slavery of Caesar is confined to this world, but Satan's slavery leads to complete loss of one's eternity.

Our Lord Jesus wants the heart, but the Jews wanted the throne. Christ wanted to release them from sin, but they wanted to be released from the slavery of their oppressors. The spiritual side of the salvation as the following words of Christ reveal, "Therefore if the Son makes you free, you shall be free indeed." (John 8:36). So the difference in thoughts eventually had to clash.

When Christ entered Jerusalem as a King the meek people were happy. But the priests, elders, scribes and Pharisees were annoyed. The people were happy with Him because He was modest and did not oppress them, "Behold, your King is coming to you; He is just and having salvation, lowly and riding on a donkey, a colt, the foal of a donkey." (Zechariah 9:9) so too; "And when He had come into Jerusalem, all the city was moved, saying, 'Who is this?'" (Matthew 21:10), also because of the many miracles which He had performed, "Then a great many of the Jews knew that He was there; and they came, not for Jesus' sake only, but that they might also see Lazarus, whom He had raised from the dead." (John 12:9). Also St. Luke said, "And were unable to do anything; for all the people were very attentive to hear Him." (Luke 19:48). They all shouted praises to Him and placed their clothes on the road welcoming Him.

Therefore the leaders were threatened by Him due to their ego. This ego tired their hearts and controlled their actions, produced malice, and led to conspiracy and corruption. It contradicted their positions as the spiritual leaders of Israel, it undermined their understanding and their principles.

They were troubled by the way the people greeted Him and were filled with jealousy and envy. They criticised the yelling of His disciples and the children's shouting and they said, "You see that you are accomplishing nothing. Look, the world has gone after Him!" (John12:19).

It is surprising to see them troubled, what damage would have happened if the world went after Him. John the Baptist said he who has the bride is the bridegroom and the friend of the bridegroom, stands afar off and looks on and rejoices greatly (John 3:29). But the leaders and the teachers were not like John the Baptist. And when Christ asked them where the baptism of John the Baptist was from, they claimed that they did not know, but in fact they did (Luke 20:3-7).

Their prejudice led them to love their leadership position over the crowd. Their love of self, of falsehood and lies and the love of external appearances led them to look upon Christ as a competitor and therefore hated Him.

When Jesus entered Jerusalem as a king, they did not welcome Him and refused to have Him reign over them. Later they shouted and said, "We have no King but Caesar!" (John 19:15). They were awaiting the coming of the Messiah who would save them from the oppression of Caesar, this was their understanding. Truly, it is clear that the love of self and flattery leads to hypocrisy. Their understanding is completely misguided.

By refusing to allow the people to worship Christ they have not harmed Jesus, but themselves. This offended them and not Him. The Lord was establishing the kingdom which they deprived themselves of. He was building the Church and He prepared the plan of salvation. These priests, elders and teachers were too busy with their negative thoughts, organising conspiracies, encouraging treason, seeking false witnesses, and plotting to have Christ put to death. Satan was there helping them to satisfy their sinful desires. Yet the objections of those priests and their plots, did not prevent the kingdom of Jesus.

This meek King who came to Jerusalem rode on a donkey. He refused to reign in Jerusalem, but preferred to rule on the cross and He established His spiritual Kingdom, and with the nails in His hands His kingdom spread to the ends of the earth in spite of all the plots.

And you, what is your contemplation on Palm Sunday? This day which the people wanted Jesus to be King over Jerusalem? Tell Him, "Come Lord and reign." Let your Kingdom come into my heart, and into the hearts of all the people. Let your Kingdom come on all the people and in all the countries, so the earth and all the Gentiles will know Your salvation (Psalm 66).

Lord take away anything which is preventing Your Kingdom from reigning in me. Take away my ego which prevents Your kingdom. Take away the letter of the Law which relegated the Pharisees from Your kingdom. Take away from me the envy and the jealousy which caused the scribes, elders and the leaders to be away. Ask The Lord to reign over your heart, but do not close it by yourself. Open your heart to all holy influences and accept the work of God in you. Do not quench the spirit. Do not ignore the voice of the Lord inside you.

JESUS IS KING

We all confess that Jesus is King. He did not refuse to reign in general, but He refused an earthly reign. Jesus' reign is eternal. It is written twice about Him in the Book of Revelation, "And He has on His robe and on His thigh a name written: KING OF KINGS AND LORD OF LORDS." (Rev 19:16) and "These will make war with the Lamb, and the Lamb will overcome them, for He is Lord of lords and King of kings; and those who are with Him are called, chosen, and faithful." (17:14).

Since His birth He was honoured as King. The Wisemen came asking, "Where is He who has been born King of the Jews?" (Matthew 2:2). The first gift which was presented to Him was gold which symbolises His Kingship. During the Annunciation of Archangel Gabriel to St. Mary it was said, "He will be great, and will be called the Son of the Highest; and the Lord God will give Him the throne of His father David." (Luke 1:32).

So what is the spiritual meaning of sitting on the throne of David His father? Because David was anointed at a young age he did not receive his kingdom straight away. It was only after King Saul died that David became King. Also our Lord Jesus was anointed as King and David said of Him, "Your throne, O God, is forever and ever; A scepter of righteousness is the scepter of Your kingdom." (Psalm 45:6), but He waited until He saw Satan cast out, "Now is the judgment of this world: now shall the prince of this world be cast out," (John 12:31). He waited till he saw the devil, head of this world (John 12:31), and He said unto them, "I saw Satan fall like lightning from heaven." (Luke 10:18), and then our Lord Jesus, in the end, reigned on a cross.

We also say of our Lord Jesus that He is King of Peace. In the hymn Eporo we say, "O King of Peace, give us Your peace." Also, facing the East in the Church, we find an Icon of the Lord, sitting on His throne, surrounded by the four living creatures which symbolise the four Gospels.

Jesus is the King of all mankind not just a specific group of people. The Jews wanted to make Him King over them alone, in a specified region of land and for a limited period, but His Kingdom has no end. On our Lord's Cross was placed a sign: "THIS IS JESUS THE KING OF THE JEWS" (Matthew 27:37).

Even the thief who was on His right side on the Cross confessed that He was God and King and asked the Lord, "Remember me when You come into Your Kingdom." (Luke 23:42). So Jesus has a spiritual reign which rules over the heart and a heavenly reign which is eternal.

We believe that His kingdom will come to judge the living and the dead and His Kingdom has no end. The Gospel of Matthew says He will be the Judge of His Kingdom, "And before Him shall be gathered all nations; and he shall separate them one from another, as a shepherd divides his sheep from the goats; and He shall set the sheep on the right hand, but the goats on the left. Then shall the King say unto them on His right hand, "Come, you blessed of My Father, inherit the kingdom prepared for you from the foundation of the world." (Matthew 25:34). So we wait for the time when He will come in His Father's glory, on the clouds, with the Angels and the Saints.

Our Lord Jesus refused the sort of reign which the people wanted. After the miracle of the five loaves and two fish, the people wanted to take Jesus by force and make Him King (John 6:15). On Palm Sunday, they shouted out wanting to make Him King. Christ refused this for two reasons: because it was an earthly kingdom and because it was not appropriate for Him to take the Kingdom from the hands of the people. As He said, "I do not receive honor from men." (John 5:41). He has His Kingdom with His Father through His divine nature, and He has His Kingdom by blood as He bought us by His blood. He paid His Holy blood to redeem us. He bought our life, for Him after we were sold to death because of sin. With that blood we become owned by Him. Thus, it is said, "He reigned on the cross." Hence, Satan tried many times and using many different methods to prevent His reign, which was His by the Cross, displaying different kinds of reign.

Satan tempted Jesus by offering Him a reign on earth, "Again, the devil took Him up on an exceedingly high mountain, and showed Him all the kingdoms of the world and their glory." (Matthew 4:8). The Lord refused this reign, rebuked the devil and he left Him. The Lord has His own Kingdom and does not take sovereignty from any one. On Palm Sunday, our Lord began His spiritual reign by cleansing the temple and confronting the Pharisees and their wrong behaviour.

CLEANSING THE TEMPLE

CLEANSING THE TEMPLE FROM THE MONEYCHANGERS

When Christ cleansed the temple He demonstrated His power and authority (Matthew 21:12-13), (Mark 11:16) and (John 2:14-16). This shows us that the meek Christ was also firm. No doubt Christ's personality was complete with all virtues. So, although He was meek and humble of heart (Matthew 11:29), when it was needed He was firm. He had never behaved in this way before and there were mixed feelings on the action, "It is written, 'My house shall be called a house of prayer.'" (Matthew 21:13). Therefore, Christ did what was necessary to correct the wrong.

The temple needed to be cleansed by any means. The temple is the house of the Lord and it is holy. This holiness needs to be preserved; holy zeal calls for that. Christ gave us an excellent example of this holy zeal and later Christ's disciples remembered this, "Then His disciples remembered that it was written, "Zeal for Your house has eaten Me up." (John 2:17). The Lord had compassion on those who sinned in the temple for a long period and treated them with calmness, and when they did not change by calmness and patience, He used a more severe approach.

In order to bring about change in a person the Lord uses calmness and gentleness. He, However; can also use firmness as was demonstrated in the temple. So, which method would you prefer to bring about reform in you? If you have a sensitive nature your heart will reproach itself quickly from within. It can respond to a spiritual word which you have read or heard, from a sermon, from a hymn or from a video. This is enough for the Lord. If you do not respond quickly to such things our Lord may use more severe methods to make your heart respond such as illness, temptation, an accident, an affliction and so on. And the Lord chooses what suits you, in the same way a doctor uses medicine. If the medicine doesn't work, the doctor may have to resort to surgery.

Our Lord Jesus did not only cleanse the temple, but also warned of the destruction of the temple, and the destruction of Jerusalem. He cried for Jerusalem and said, "For days will come upon you when your enemies will build an embankment around you, surround you and close you in on every side, and level you, and your children within you, to the ground; and they will not leave in you one stone upon another, because you did not know the time of your visitation." (Luke 19:43-44). And He also said, "See! Your house is left to you desolate." (Matthew 23:38). He also mentioned to His disciple, "Then Jesus went out and departed from the temple, and His disciples came up to show Him the buildings of the temple. And Jesus said to them, 'Do you not see all these things? Assuredly, I say to you, not one stone shall be left here upon another, that shall not be thrown down.'" (Matthew 24:1-2). And said, "Therefore when you see the 'abomination of desolation,' spoken of by Daniel the prophet, standing in the holy place" (whoever reads, let him understand), "then let those who are in Judea flee to the mountains." (Matthew 24:15-16).

You also my beloved children, when you hear during Holy Week that the Lord cleansed the Temple and warned of its destruction, you then shout saying, "Come Lord in power and clean my heart too." Aren't we an altar of the Lord and the Spirit of God dwells in us? "Do you not know that you are the temple of God and that the Spirit of God dwells in you? If anyone defiles the temple of God, God will destroy him. For the temple of God is holy, which temple you are." (I Corinthians 3:16). Then come Lord and clean my temple, turn the tables in me, before it turns on me and I lose my eternity. Do not leave my heart to desires and emotions, so that it becomes a marketplace for selling and buying. But purge me with hyssop and I shall be clean. Then I can say with You that my house is a house of prayer. Lord do it quickly before the temple is destroyed.

Our Lord Jesus did not only cleanse the Temple from sellers and buyers, but He also cleansed it from its corrupt religious leaders. This cleansing was a prelude to His spiritual leadership and His spiritual Kingdom.

CLEANSING THE TEMPLE FROM THE LEADERSHIP

In order to understand why our Lord did this we need to follow the events of what led to this action.

How did the Jews react to this cleansing? They could not confront Jesus or make Him stop and they were afraid of what the people would do, as the people were amazed by His teachings, "And the scribes and chief priests heard it and sought how they might destroy Him; for they feared Him, because all the people were astonished at His teaching." (Mark 11:18). So they waited for an opportunity to implement their plot, "And He was teaching daily in the temple. But the chief priests, the scribes, and the leaders of the people sought to destroy Him." (Luke 19:47).

What they did instead was try to trick Him through their questioning, "Now when He came into the temple, the chief priests and the elders of the people confronted Him as He was teaching, and said, 'By what authority are You doing these things? And who gave You this authority?'" (Matthew 21:23), "and spoke to Him, saying, "Tell us, by what authority are You doing these things? Or who is he who gave You this authority?" (Luke 20:2). Christ did not answer them, but rather asked them a question about John the Baptist. In this way He silenced them.

The Lord planned to appoint leaders for His Church. It was natural for Christ to change the spiritual leadership as these people did not understand His spiritual Kingdom. They were not spiritual, instead they mislead and controlled the people.

These leaders vowed that if any one who confessed that Jesus was Christ was to be taken out of the synagogue, "His parents said these things because they feared the Jews, for the Jews had agreed already that if anyone confessed that He was Christ, he would be put out of the synagogue." (John 9:22). So these leaders became a hindrance for the way of the Kingdom of God, therefore they needed to be changed. The Lord waited patiently with these people, the Scribes, the Pharisees, the Sadducees, the priests, and the elders. He bore with them in long suffering, in calmness and in meekness. But now the time has come and there were only a few days left till the Golgotha.

This Jewish type of leadership needed to be changed for two

reasons:

I Christianity would be based on another type of priesthood; that of Melchizedek. This differed from the priesthood of Aaron which presented animal sacrifices, symbolising Christ's sacrifice. But the era of animal sacrifices was over. Also, the priesthood of Aaron was by inheritance from his offspring, but the Christian priesthood would be according to individual merit and would not adhere to any particular tribe or family line.

"Therefore, if perfection were through the Levitical priesthood (for under it the people received the law), what further need was there that another priest should rise according to the order of Melchizedek, and not be called according to the order of Aaron? For the priesthood being changed, of necessity there is also a change of the law. For He of whom these things are spoken belongs to another tribe, from which no man has officiated at the altar." (Hebrews 7:11-13).

2 The Jewish leaders were corrupt and committed many sins. They were not worthy of the priesthood. Christ needed to rebuke them publically so that they would not be a stumbling block to others and in front of the new Christian priesthood that would follow.

Therefore our Lord made a public example of them. Christ told them, "Therefore I say to you, the kingdom of God will be taken from you and given to a nation bearing the fruits of it." (Matthew 21:43). Christ showed them that by rejecting Him they would be ruined. He also said, "The stone which the builders rejected has become the chief cornerstone." (Psalm 118:22). And He warned them, "And whoever falls on this stone will be broken; but on whomever it falls, it will grind him to powder. Now when the chief priests and Pharisees heard His parables, they perceived that He was speaking of them." (Matthew 21:44-45). They did not repent and they did not benefit from His warnings. But after they heard the warning the Bible says, "But when they sought to lay hands on Him, they feared the multitudes, because they took Him for a prophet." (Matthew 21:46). But after a day of these teachings they agreed with Judas that he would betray Christ, his Master, and deliver Him to them in exchange for money. Our Lord destroyed the idols which were present during His time, to ease His disciples before He delivered His Spirit into the Father's hand.

So the Lord rebuked the Scribes and the Pharisees. Our Lord met their criticism and insults calmly and taught them patiently. However, they were not affected and they did not benefit, even after cleansing the Temple. He confuses them during these discussions and they were embarrassed especially after they questioned Him about the relationship between Jesus and David, "If David then calls Him 'Lord,' how is He his Son? And no one was able to answer Him a word, nor from that day on did anyone dare question Him anymore." (Matthew 22:45-46).

Therefore the Lord rebuked them sternly saying, "Woe to you, scribes and Pharisees, hypocrites! For you travel land and sea to win one proselyte, and when he is won, you make him twice as much a son of hell as yourselves." (Matthew 23:15). Then He told them what would happen after two days, "You know that after two days is the Passover, and the Son of Man will be delivered up to be crucified." (Matthew 26:2).

Christ told them that their leadership was blind, "Woe to you, blind guides." (Matthew 23:16). He told them that they love the best seats and love the praise of people and they cause the people to carry heavy weights. He warned them saying, "Serpents, brood of vipers! How can you escape the condemnation of hell? Therefore, indeed, I send you prophets, wise men, and scribes: some of them you will kill and crucify, and some of them you will scourge in your synagogues and persecute from city to city, that on you may come all the righteous blood shed on the earth, from the blood of righteous Abel to the blood of Zechariah, son of Berechiah, whom you murdered between the temple and the altar. Assuredly, I say to you, all these things will come upon this generation." (Matthew 23:33-36).

He also silenced the Sadducees and those who followed the Law of Moses. The Sadducees did not believe in the spirit, in angels or in the resurrection, although they had a very good standing amongst the Jewish people and from them came many religious leaders.

During this week they tried to trick our Lord and embarrass Him by questioning Him regarding the resurrection of the woman who married one man after the death of another. They asked him whose wife will she be after the resurrection? Christ silenced the Sadducees when He answered them saying, "You are mistaken, not knowing the Scriptures nor the power of God. For in the resurrection they neither marry nor are given in marriage." (Matthew 22:29).

Thus the Lord led the movement of cleansing. He did not leave it to His disciples in case it was difficult for them, but He Himself led it. He stood up to the priests, religious leaders, scribes, Pharisees, Sadducees and the lawyers. Then they all conspired against Him saying crucify Him. But this was the reason why He came, to give Himself for the whole world, and to give the people the correct teachings.

Our Lord is not going to put a new piece on an old dress. Likewise in Christ's Church, all these old communities have disappeared. No more scribes, Pharisees, Sadducees nor the followers of the Law of Moses. The Lord Himself paid the price for this cleansing and He suffered on our behalf and bore the injustice of the wicked for us.

As you are standing before the cleansing of the altar ask yourself:

Am I one of the wicked? Or is my service accepted?

Am I one of those who are against Christ?

Am I causing others to carry a heavy load?

Am I working with Jesus to cleanse my altar?

Am I resisting Him like those who resisted Him and He took the

Kingdom from them?

By Jesus' cleansing of the temple, I ask Him to cleanse every holy place which has His name on it and say with Christ, "My house is called a house of prayer."

THE HOUSE OF BETHANY

IN THE HOUSE OF BETHANY

In contrast to those who plotted against Him, there were those who were loyal and loving and who welcomed Him in the House of Bethany and He lodged there. "Then He left them and went out of the city to Bethany, and He lodged there." (Matthew 21:17)

The House of Bethany represents the loyal heart which loves the Lord and He finds comfort in it, just as He found comfort in Bethany after facing the many problems in Jerusalem. Jerusalem was a great city full of conspiracies, full of noise and tired leaders. But in Bethany there was Lazarus whom the Lord cried for until the people said, "See how He loved him!" (John 11:36). And Bethany has those loving people who surrounded Him after He raised Lazarus from the dead. And there is also Mary who represents contemplation and Martha who represents service and there was simplicity which is not found in the city of Jerusalem.

This blessed village had loyal hearts to God. Therefore He preferred it in His last days before the crucifixion. Yes, He preferred it to Jerusalem. Jerusalem the big city, but her heart is not big like it. Jerusalem is the city of the great King. It conspired against the great King and did not deserve Him, "He came to His own, and His own did not receive Him." (John 1:11). Therefore, He left it and lodged at Bethany. This great city Jerusalem has no love and the Lord cried out saying, "O Jerusalem, Jerusalem, the one who kills the prophets and stones those who are sent to her! How often I wanted to gather your children together, as a hen gathers her chicks under her wings, but you were not willing!" (Matthew 23:37).

Jerusalem had a famous name, but Bethany did not. Perhaps many of you do not know the history of Bethany or where it is. It is not famous like Jerusalem. But it is full of loyalty, sincerity and love. So the Lord found His rest there. Therefore, our Lord looks at each persons love and not how great or famous they are. The Jews were famous in their faith but the Gentiles were not. Their hearts, however, were ready, so they reached God's heart and arms before the Jews and the Lord found His rest in them.

The Gentiles represented the House of Bethany. St. Paul experienced this; when the Jews rejected his preaching, he turned to the Gentiles, and found there open hearts filled with more readiness than those who followed the Law of Moses, "Therefore let it be known to you that the salvation of God has been sent to the Gentiles, and they will hear it!" (Acts 28:28).

There are many examples in the Bible of the spiritual symbolism of the House of Bethany.

I Many times we find ourselves in the midst of darkness, but with the memory of Bethany, the light restores us. These 'lights' are the beginning of a new start and covenant between God and people, when God finds, amongst sinners, loving hearts and finds rest in them. And here we give examples from the bible other than the example of the Gentiles.

2 In time, the whole world was full of evil and all became corrupt and moved away from God. So God decided to destroy all life on earth. But in the middle of all that widespread corruption He found loving and obedient hearts in Noah and his family. So God took and placed them in the ark and He began with them a new history to mankind, as He found His rest in them.

The ark was the House of Bethany, so He rested there. The ark was a dwelling place for God with the people, the only place which God could lay His head. He found love, fulfilment and purity of heart, in that dark era.

3 The same thing was repeated when the Lord wanted to destroy Sodom and Gomorrah. Her evil was great and her sin was greater. And the Lord could not find anyone in Sodom, other than Lot the righteous, and the two angels went to his house (Genesis 19:3-4).

So Lot's house was the House of Bethany for the two angels and for the Lord. It was the only house in the city which provided rest for the Lord away from the noise of the outside world. Therefore, God rescued Lot from the destruction which came upon Sodom and its people.

4 Our Father Abraham was Bethany to the Lord - The evil was great on earth, even in the offspring of Lot the righteous. People practised the worship of idols and it spread among them. So the Lord searched for a heart to rest in, so it can be a new start for people to know Him and have a covenant with them. He found Abraham, blessed him and had a new people. So by his offspring the tribes of the earth were blessed, "And in you all the families of the earth shall be blessed." (Genesis 12:3). Thus, Abraham became a friend of God and God opened His heart to him and did not hide anything from him, "And the Lord said, 'Shall I hide from Abraham what I am doing?'" (Genesis 18:17). This is a picture of the House of Bethany.

5 Also Joseph in Egypt was a House of Bethany - All of Egypt worshipped many idols according to her old religion under the gods Ra and Amon. The only one amongst them who worshipped the true God in Egypt was Joseph, and then his family joined him later. So the Lord found His Bethany in Egypt, so He rested there.

6 Moses the Prophet on the mountain - He went up the mountain to receive the tablets of the Law from God. He stayed with God for 40 days. When the people found that he delayed, they made an image of a molded calf and worshipped it. And there was no one left in all the earth who worshipped God other than Moses.

He was Bethany to God, the only heart which He found to rest in.

7 Elijah and the seven thousand knees - The worship of idols had spread far and wide during the reign of King Ahab and his wife Jezebel. And the people worshipped Baal and killed God's prophet and destroyed His temples, until Elijah said, "I have been very zealous for the Lord God of hosts; for the children of Israel have forsaken Your covenant, torn down Your altars, and killed Your prophets with the sword. I alone am left, and they seek to take my life." (I Kings 19:10). But the Lord kept for Himself 7000 knees which did not bow to Baal, "Yet I have reserved seven thousand in Israel, all whose knees have not bowed to Baal, and every mouth that has not kissed him." (IKing 19:18). Elijah, Obadiah and the 7000 were the Bethany for God during the days of Ahab. They were the only people loyal to God, so He rested there.

The Lord did not leave Himself without witness, "Nevertheless He did not leave Himself without witness, in that He did good, gave us rain from heaven and fruitful seasons, filling our hearts with food and gladness." (Acts 14:17). And the loyal souls are many, some are visible and others work in secret, without being seen. And everywhere in the world there is a House of Bethany for the Lord.

8 The twelve disciples were the first Bethany in Christianity. They were the sincere hearts towards the Lord whom He trusted over His Kingdom and His message. They were His own and the Bible said about them, "Nevertheless He did not leave Himself without witness, in that He did good, gave us rain from heaven and fruitful seasons, filling our hearts with food and gladness." (Acts 14:17). They defended Him with all their power and they witnessed to Him everywhere, "But you shall receive power when the Holy Spirit has come upon you; and you shall be witnesses to Me in Jerusalem, and in all Judea and Samaria, and to the end of the earth." (Acts 1:8). They were Bethany to the Lord. He rested there all the days of His life on earth. Perhaps John the Beloved was the most and he is the one who

followed Him to the cross.

9 He found Bethany on the Cross - The people denied and mocked Him, even one of the thieves who was with Him, but The Lord found other hearts which loved in sincerity and confessed Him to others and He was crucified in front of them. Before them was St Mary, John the Beloved, Mary Magdalene and Mary the wife of Cleopas. Those who were close to His Cross to the last moment, did not leave Him even after His death. Nicodemus and Joseph of Arimathea joined them and they were Bethany to the Lord who rested in them when all left Him. (Matthew 26:56-57; John 19:26-27).

10 The thief on the right of Christ was Bethany to the Lord - He shared the suffering, accompanied Him on the cross, he witnessed to the Lord, and Christ was in the depth of His suffering, and the Lord was comforted in his presence. Our Lord took him from the Cross to paradise. He was the first Bethany, entered from Golgotha to paradise. He took the Lord inside himself, or the Lord took him inside Himself, or both of them on the cross. Other than remembering the House of Bethany, the house of Lazarus, Mary and Martha, which the Lord took His rest in before His crucifixion, we also remember another house:

11 The House of Mary the mother of St. Mark - In that house, the Lord washed the feet of His disciples, He celebrated the Passover with them, and established the Sacrament of the Eucharist. And in this house He spoke to His disciples.

He had many long discussions with them which are recorded in 4 Chapters of the Gospel of St. John (John 13:17). He promised to send the Holy Spirit to them. The Holy Spirit came upon them in that house on the day of Pentecost. In that house, became the first Church in Christianity (Acts 12:12). It became the House of Bethany, not only for the Lord, but also for His disciples and the whole Church. All found their rest in this house. Finally, we salute the women who offered their homes to the Church.

Mary and Martha and Mary the Mother of St. Mark. We also give tribute to all the saintly women who opened their homes to God to become Churches, such as Lydia the Seller of Purple. Her home became a Church and a Bethany to St. Paul and Silas who went there after their stay in prison, "And when she and her household were baptised, she begged us, saying, 'If you have judged me to be faithful to the Lord, come to my house and stay.' So she persuaded us." (Acts 16:15). And also like Acquila and Priscilla who risked their life for St. Paul. St. Paul mentions their home, "Likewise greet the church that is in their house." (Romans 16:5).

There are many examples of Saints in the Old Testament. Like the widow who opened her house to Elijah the Prophet and he stayed in her upper room (1King 17:9-19). Her house was Bethany to him and he lived there during the famine. We remember also the Shunamite woman, who opened her house to Elisha the Prophet. He also stayed in the upper room which she had prepared for him (2 King 4:10). It was Bethany for him. He loved it, sanctified it and was happy in that house, and he rested there.

It is the love that these people give to God and His people. The Lord Jesus loved the love of this Bethany village, and their hearts, which were open in wondrous sincerity, away from the noise of Jerusalem and its conspiracies. The days before His crucifixion, He used to spend His days in the House of Bethany, then go to the temple, and come back again to Bethany and lodge there.

The holy house of Mary and Martha. This house was sanctified by the Lord during the days leading up to His crucifixion. And Mary, the sister of Lazarus, who took an expensive jar of Spikenard fragrant oil and poured it on the Lord's head when He was in their home. Also St John the Beloved said, on this occasion, that she wiped Jesus' feet with the perfume and anointed His feet and wiped them with her hair and the house was filled with the fragrance of the oil (John 12:2-3).

He visited the home of Simon the Leper in Bethany where a woman came to Him having an alabaster flask of very costly fragrant oil and she poured it on His head. His disciples were indignant saying, "To what purpose is this waste?" Christ replied, "Why do you trouble the woman? For she has done a good work for Me. For you have the poor with you always, but Me you do not have always. For in pouring this fragrant oil on My body, she did it for My burial." (Matthew 26:7-12). And Christ said of her, "Assuredly, I say to you, wherever this gospel is preached in the whole world, what this woman has done will also be told as a memorial to her." (Mark 14:9).

Blessed are these houses which received Jesus. Mary and Martha's house was not the only house which the Lord visited during these days. There were many others, who were sincere in their love and opened their homes to Him.

They did not leave Him when the others left. There were many houses which the Lord visited as a preacher or a teacher, such as the house which they opened from the ceiling (Mark 2:3), or hosted Him like Simon the Pharisee (Luke 7:36), or invited Him as a guest like at the Wedding of Cana of Galilee (John 2), or accepting the sinners like when He entered the house of Zacchaeus (Luke 19:7) and other tax collectors.

Here we want to just focus on the houses which the Lord visited and who opened their doors for Him during Holy Week only, while the Jews conspired to kill Him, especially the houses in which He lodged in Bethany.

So is your house also one of the houses which were opened to Jesus? Is your house ready to receive Jesus during these days? The Lord is ready to come into your house. But it is important that you should be ready to receive Him and not be too busy for Him. Your house needs to be holy so as to be fit for the Lord to come in. We hope that you welcome God into your heart and mind during these days.

The Lord was in the House of Bethany, and then, on Monday morning, on His way to the Temple, he passed the Fig Tree. So He approached it. Allow me here to contemplate together with you on the story of the Fig Tree.

THE FIG TREE

HUNGRY ON THE ROAD

On His way back from Bethany to Jerusalem, the Bible says, "Now in the morning, as He returned to the city, He was hungry." (Matthew 21:18). I was surprised when I read this verse as a man can be hungry at night if he has been fasting all day, but what does it mean that Jesus was hungry 'in the morning'? There is only one explanation; that He had spent the whole of the previous day in fasting and perhaps even many days before and He had not eaten in the evening. So He became hungry, and we understand from the following:

When He went to Mary and Martha, He did not eat there. Perhaps He was alone, and had spent the whole night in meditation. Perhaps He stayed on the mountain for some time (Luke 21:37), or perhaps He had spent some time guiding His disciples and followers how to live after His crucifixion. Could it be that Martha had prepared food for Christ, but He did not desire food? There were many issues occupying Him.

When a person is sad, he cannot eat. When one's mind is preoccupied it is difficult to put these things aside to eat. Food becomes more of a disruption. There is no doubt that, during these days, our Lord was preoccupied with what was to come; how He would save the world from the punishment of sin and save even those who conspired against Him, and those who would, in just a few days, shout

out 'crucify Him, crucify Him.' So, in the morning, when He was returning to the city, He was hungry.

Or perhaps, when He was in Bethany, He was nourished by the love of the faithful hearts around Him. And therefore, when He left Bethany and approached the treacherous Jerusalem which conspired against Him, He was hungry. We are surprised by the words 'was hungry' and we say: If He did not clear Himself and become like us, He would not become hungry! And would not be thirsty on the cross!

THE FIG TREE

When He was hungry He saw that the fig tree had leaves, so He came toward it hoping to find fruit. However, He did not find any, just leaves; beautiful from the outside but nothing on the inside. The fig tree reminds us of the sin of our father Adam who tried to cover his nakedness with the fig leaves.

Perhaps Jesus came to give him salvation before the time he committed his sin, that is, the time of the appearance of the fig leaves. He came to the fig tree, thinking perhaps it would change its old behaviour and would no longer remember sin, but He found it in the same state.

The fig leaves symbolise covering the sin without treating it. Adam covered his nakedness with fig leaves. On the outside this appeared to be covered. On the inside, however, he lost his purity and simplicity. So Adam took care of his external appearance, without curing the inside. From that, the fig leaves became a cover for the nakedness of Adam and Eve, symbolising hypocrisy, caring for the external appearance and the covering of sin without treatment.

The same hypocrisy was found in the fig tree – leaves without fruit. Beautiful appearance from the outside, but empty from within. Leaves do not cover fruit, but rather cover nakedness just as in the story of Adam and Eve. And when the Lord found in it leaves not fruits, He cursed it (Matthew 21:19). Immediately the fig tree withered away.

By cursing the fig tree, He cursed external appearance and hypocrisy. This is exactly what the Lord found during these days, external appearances and hypocrisy, white washed tombs from the outside. And immediately the fig tree withered away, the cup which they cleaned from the outside. They care only about frequent washing of the hands while their hands are stained with blood. The leaves give an illusion of fruit, but there is no fruit at all.

The Lord's rebuking of the fig tree symbolises the hypocrisy of the Scribes and Pharisees. The Scribes and the Pharisees were just like the fig tree - with leaves, but without fruit. So he rebuked them by cursing the fig tree. After that He said, "Woe to you, scribers and Pharisees, hypocrites!" (Matthew 23:13). Christ gave many examples showing their hypocrisy and love of external appearances.

The Lord saw in the fig tree the picture of hypocrisy during his time. He saw the fig tree in the priests, whom God placed among the people to lead them in the law and in goodness, but instead they led Judas into treason, and paid many to give false witness, and they persuaded the guard at the tombstone to take a bribe, and they misguided many and trapped them into their conspiracy. Christ likened them to the wicked vinedresser in the parable of the Wicked Vinedressers in Matthew 21:33-43. He also saw in the fig tree the picture of the Temple, which was supposed to be used for worship but instead they made it a den of thieves (Matthew 21:13).

During this week Christ placed all the sins of the world before Him. Wasn't it the plan that during this week He would carry it all? So He contemplated on all that was to come and His soul was filled with bitterness as He saw before Him the hypocrisy even between the teachers and the priests. Just as in Isaiah 5, He did not find good fruits in the vineyard, but rather bad fruits and not only in the vineyard, but also in the temple and in the blind leaders. Therefore in the end He was hungry as He did not find anything to eat. What can we say about all this hypocrisy and corruption which He had seen? So He cursed and condemned it, but:

He will carry it all on His cross to forgive the repentant. These whitewashed tombstones from the outside, for everyone who believes and repents the Lord Jesus carried all inside Him, from fetid bones, and He paid His Divine justice on the Cross. You too my brothers and sisters, look at yourself and examine it in that week. Are you also a tree that has leaves, but no fruit? Do you have an active service and a well known name in the Church and yet your heart is without the fruits of the Holy Spirit, free from the love of God and the knowledge of Him?

Are you covering your sins with the leaves of the fig tree so that they are not visible? These leaves of the fig tree could be your excuses and your justifications to cover yourself. Or they could be causes taking you away from the truth which you know inside yourself is lack of sincerity. Or you cover one sin with another sin, or place your sins upon someone else for them to carry the responsibility.

Ask yourself, is your life leaves or fruits? what are the fruits in my life? What are the fruits of the Spirit in me? As St. Paul said, "But the fruit of the Spirit is love, joy, peace, longsuffering, kindness, goodness, faithfulness, gentleness, self-control." (Galatians 5:22-23). And what are my fruits in the service and in building the Kingdom of God? And your work which is without fruits? What are the causes of being without fruits? Are the motives wrong? Are the means wrong? Are you doing it with laziness and complacency?

TREASON AND THE KISS OF JUDAS

From Tuesday night greeting one another with a kiss is not permitted, in protest of Judas' kiss of betrayal to the Lord. This continues for the remainder of Holy Week until the Easter eve. During the Covenant Thursday liturgy, the deacon does not say, "Kiss one another with a holy kiss," and likewise during the morning of the Joyous Saturday liturgy. All this is to instil in the believers how wrong were the actions of Judas the traitor towards his teacher. We also remember this act of treason every Wednesday throughout the whole year. We fast in order to remember this betrayal.

The Lord's disciple participated in this awful conspiracy. During this Holy Week, the believers sing a hymn which reproaches Judas and his actions. This painful hymn leaves deep and painful sentiments on the Church. Judas, however, was not the only person who betrayed Jesus during these days as there were many who betrayed Him. Many who treated Him well then later shouted, "Crucify Him, crucify Him. So why do we focus entirely on Judas? Because Judas' betrayal was of the worst degree.

The betrayal of Judas was a result of his deceptive heart. He came together with the soldiers, and when they had come closer to Him he gave Jesus a kiss. This kiss was a sign between him and them. St. Mark said, "Now His betrayer had given them a signal, saying, 'Whomever I kiss, He is the One; seize Him and lead Him away safely.'" (Mark 14:44) and "Immediately he went up to Jesus and said, 'Greetings, Rabbi!' and kissed Him." (Matthew 26:49). Truly we remember Judas with the fig tree which the Lord cursed.

Green leaves from the outside, but from within it is naked and without fruit. On the outside Judas kissed Jesus, but from within he betrayed Him and sold Him with money. On the outside he greeted Him, but in reality he betrayed Him to His enemies. He said to Him, "Peace my Master", but there was no peace in his heart and no respect or loyalty to his Master. His words 'peace' and 'Master' did not reproach Him, but his kiss reproached Him.

And the gentleness of Jesus did not stop him. Jesus knew what Judas intended to do and as the time drew nearer and He was in the garden, He said to His disciples, "Rise, let us be going. See, My betrayer is at hand." (Matthew 26:46). And even with that, he was not ashamed in front of the soldiers and the guards. He did not stop him from approaching and kissing Him and He did not use the word traitor to describe him, but rather said to him, "Friend, why have you come?" (Matthew 26:50). And He rebuked him gently and said, "Judas, are you betraying the Son of Man with a kiss?" (Luke 22:48).

It looked very bad when Judas betrayed Jesus because Jesus had been very good to him before. If the Lord offended him in any way in the past this would have been considered revenge and not betrayal. But his great Teacher was good to him, and He knew in advance his evil thoughts. It was enough that He chose him as one of His 12 disciples knowing his nature, "Jesus answered them, 'Did I not choose you, the twelve, and one of you is a devil?' He spoke of Judas Iscariot; the son of Simon, for it was he who would betray Him, being one of the twelve." (John 6:70-71).

Just as He did with the rest of the disciples, He sent him to preach, "And when He had called His twelve disciples to Him, He gave them power over unclean spirits, to cast them out, and to heal all kinds of sickness and all kinds of disease." (Matthew 10:1).

Did it suffice that He chose him to be a disciple and also leave the money box with him? So he was not just an ordinary disciple, but was given a greater responsibility than the rest of the 12. He was charged with giving to the poor from the box, and spent from it on the needs of the disciples, such as the needs for the Feast, "For some thought, because Judas had the money box, that Jesus had said to him, 'Buy those things we need for the feast,' or that he should give something to the poor." (John 13:29). Even though Judas did not care for the poor, because he was a thief, and he was taking money from the box, "This he said, not that he cared for the poor, but because he was a thief, and had the money box; and he used to take what was put in it." (John 12:6).

The Lord did not reveal his true character and He did not take the money box from him. The box, however, stayed with him until he died. And the Lord did not punish him according to his work, although the Lord knew of his betrayal, but He did not expel him as His disciple, and did not remove him from the twelve.

His position, nevertheless, remained as one of those closest to Him. As one of the twelve, he was with Jesus day and night, followed Him everywhere, and before everyone he was one of His own, lived with Him, ate and drank with Him. This was the general view, and on the private side he was close to Him. He sat very close to Him at the table, he could even dip into the same dish, "He answered and said, "He who dipped his hand with Me in the dish will betray Me." (Matthew 26:23).

It is a sign of love and intimacy to dip into the same dish. The Lord allowed him to do this. What special treatment? What a sign of love. Perhaps he should have been ashamed of this love and been deterred from following out his plan. He, however, did not benefit from this love, nor from eating with Jesus. This fulfils the prophecy, "Who ate my bread, has lifted up his heel against me." (Psalm 41:9).

It was enough that the Lord was His teacher. So Judas sold his teacher, and his spiritual father and guide and his friends who lived with him for three years, listening to the Lord's teachings and witnessing His miracles. Perhaps he even saw the miracle of raising Lazarus from the dead five days before he betrayed Him and the faith of many because of it (John 11). Perhaps he saw the miracle of opening the eyes of the man born blind (John 9). All that did not affect him, and did not stop him from carrying out his betrayal.

He sought to sell His Master and this made his betrayal even worse. The Jewish leaders did not approach him and tempt him or bribe him. It never entered their minds that one of the Lord's 12 would deliver Him! It was Judas who went to them, and the Bible says about Judas, "Then Satan entered Judas, surnamed Iscariot, who was numbered among the twelve. So he went his way and conferred with the chief priests and captains, how he might betray Him to them. And they were glad, and agreed to give him money. So he promised and sought opportunity to betray Him to them in the absence of the multitude." (Luke 22:3-6). And "Then one of the twelve, called Judas Iscariot, went to the chief priests and said, 'What are you willing to give me if I deliver Him to you?' And they counted out to him thirty pieces of silver. So from that time he sought opportunity to betray Him." (Matthew 26:14-16).

Therefore he sold his Master, in his betrayal, with a small sum. Thirty pieces of silver is the price of a slave! Perhaps the reason for the small amount is that he was the one who wanted to sell and he asked for the amount.

If millions were offered him, one could say that he was tempted by the money, but here there is no temptation, it was only thirty pieces of silver. This indicates how cheap Christ was in his heart and mind. Here we can mention the impressive action of Mary the sister of Lazarus when she poured the expensive perfume of spikenard oil on Christ. Its price was about 300 denari, but she did not care (John 12:3-5). She did not have money in her heart, but that disciple sold Him for thirty pieces of silver!

And he continued in his plan of betrayal for two days and his conscience did not rebuke him. If it had happened suddenly, perhaps we could say that he did not have a chance to review himself. But he continued through Wednesday to Friday, without thinking to go back on his plan, but rather he, "Sought opportunity to betray Him to them in the absence of the multitude," (Luke 22:6), in spite of many warnings from Jesus.

Out of love Jesus tried to warn Judas. The Lord did not leave him in this temptation alone, but he gave him many warnings to alert his heart:

1 After Christ washed the feet of the disciples He said to them, "'You are clean, but not all of you.' For He knew who would betray Him; therefore He said, 'You are not all clean.'" (John 13:10-11).

2 During the Passover He said to them, "The Son of Man indeed goes just as it is written of Him, but woe to that man by whom the Son of Man is betrayed! It would have been good for that man if he had not been born." (Matthew 26:24). And as they ate, Jesus took bread, blessed and broke it, and gave it to the disciples and said, "Take, eat; this is My body." This was a frightening warning from Christ who wanted Judas to turn back from his plan of betrayal. But he did not pay any attention and was not frightened

3 The Lord narrowed the circle by saying, "Now as they were eating, He said, 'Assuredly, I say to you, one of you will betray Me.' And they were exceedingly sorrowful, and each of them began to say to Him, 'Lord, is it I?' He answered and said, 'He who dipped his hand with Me in the dish will betray Me.'" And Judas' heart was still not moved.

4 The Lord said, "'It is he to whom I shall give a piece of bread when I have dipped it.' And having dipped the bread, He gave it to Judas Iscariot, the son of Simon." (John 13:26). Christ did this in love that he might return. The Lord fed him with His own hand, He put the bread in his mouth but Judas did not benefit.

5 At last Judas said, "Rabbi, is it I?" and the Lord said to him, "You have said it." (Matthew 26:25). The matter became

exposed and Judas had to work for his eternity and it would have been better for that man to never have been born. But Judas did not repent, instead the devil entered him.

Truly it is a tragedy that he allowed himself to reach this end, to deliver himself to the devil. The Bible says, "Now after the piece of bread, Satan entered him. Then Jesus said to him, 'What you do, do quickly.'" (John 13:27). He then made the decision to deliver the Lord, in spite of all the warnings.

6 So the Lord admonished him, "What you do, do quickly." (John 13:27). It was his chance to throw himself at Jesus' feet and say "Forgive me, I will not go ahead with my plan." But he did not repent and the Bible says, "Having received the piece of bread, he then went out immediately. And it was night." (John 13:30). He went at night, to carry out what was organised in the dark. And he knew that Jesus was aware of his plans and He told him.

By his exit he forever separated himself from the Lord and the disciples. The Lord did not remove him from His group of disciples, but Judas separated himself by his own hands. He chose a way different than the way the others went, and he joined the enemies of the Lord and became the traitor that all generations talked about.

So the devil did not only enter him after he took the bread, he entered him well before this when he approached the Jewish leaders and agreed with them to deliver the Lord. The Bible says, "Then Satan entered Judas, surnamed Iscariot, who was numbered among the twelve. So he went his way and conferred with the chief priests and captains, how he might betray Him to them." (Luke 22:3-4).

The devil entered one of the twelve twice! What a tragedy. This is a warning that all should be careful that the devil works in everyone, even the twelve. The Lord said to His disciples, "Simon, Simon! Indeed, Satan has asked for you, that he may sift you as wheat." (Luke 22:31). Yes, he sifted them and took from them mud, which is Judas and left the pure wheat for the whole world to feed on their faith and their preaching.

7 The Lord, however, presented to Judas a final loving touch. In reproach and compassion, He said to him when he was delivering Him "Friend, why have you come?" (Matthew 26:50). Is it with a kiss you deliver the Son of man?! Befitting from you as a friend to deliver Me? And deliver Me with a kiss?! This was the last sentence he heard from the mouth of Jesus and the last interaction he had with Him, forever. And the Good Teacher was arrested. He was tried, convicted and pushed to the Cross.

At last Judas' conscience was awakened, after Jesus was condemned! As if he was unconscious and woke up. And the words of Jesus echoed in his ears and he remembered the holy atmosphere in which he lived for so long, close to the Lord and he remembered the last words of Christ to him, "with a kiss you deliver the Son of Man?" and he could not bear it. The Bible says, "Then Judas, His betrayer, seeing that He had been condemned, was remorseful and brought back the thirty pieces of silver to the chief priests and elders, saying, 'I have sinned by betraying innocent blood.' And they said, 'What is that to us? You see to it!'" (Matthew 27:3-4).

He regretted and said I was wrong. But it was too late! The betrayal was complete and the matter ended, whether he has remorseful or not. His remorse did not prevent him from seeing before him the result of his actions; Jesus before him on the Cross, Jesus his teacher, his guide, his spiritual Father, his friend and his Master, disgraced in front of him, flogged and crucified, all because of his betrayal.

The remorse crushed him, perhaps it echoed in his ears the sentence of Cain, "And Cain said to the Lord, 'My punishment is greater than I can bear!'" (Genesis 4:13). The devil did not leave him for his remorse, but came to complete his work with him.

Perhaps the remorse would lead him to repent, and repentance leads to forgiveness, and perhaps inflicted by the words of Christ on the Cross, "Father forgive them for they know not what they do," (Luke 23:34), although he knew what he was doing, and the Lord warned him of this dangerous plan.

Therefore the devil filled him with despair and hopelessness and he perished. His tragedy ended with this sentence, "Then he threw down the pieces of silver in the temple and departed, and went and hanged himself." (Matthew 27:5). And the Lord's words were clear, "It was better for that man if he has not been born." And that was the end of the betrayal, Judas lost everything. He lost Jesus, the discipleship, thirty silver pieces and the Jewish leaders who said to him, "What is that to us? You see to it!" (Matthew 27:4). He lost earth and heaven, his eternity and his reputation and became a stain in the history of mankind.

What did he benefit from his betrayal? Nothing. The Lord did not escape from Judas' betrayal and He knew it. But He received him in the Garden of Gethsemane. He did not change it, but He was waiting for him, and bore his betrayal in silence, and changed it to be the salvation of the human race.

The Lord changed the evil into good. Not only the betrayal of Judas, but the betrayal of the people who said, "Crucify Him, crucify Him." Throughout history Judas was not just a person, but he became a symbol of whoever follows his example and his name represented shame on anyone who did what he did. The Lord did not punish him on earth, but He left him to himself. And Judas could not bear himself. He found himself despicable in his own eyes and felt he did not deserve to live.

What is harsher than a person who despises himself? Perhaps he can bear the scorn of others, but who can bear to despise himself? As it was for Judas; he could not bear himself, and went and hanged himself. And he died in his sin as a killer of himself. He lost hope and lost faith in life after death. But the Lord trampled death, and Judas' betrayal did not harm Him.

How was Christ so cheap in the eyes of the one who sold him? There are those who sold Jesus for less than thirty silver pieces. Those who shouted, "Crucify Him, crucify Him." They sold Him for no price. They did not take anything in return for their sale. And the Jewish nation who sold Him to the Romans, what did they take in return? Nothing! But they became dispersed.

They were dispersed for seventy years during the reign of Titus the Roman soldier after the Crucifixion of Jesus by less than 40 years. And the Temple and the city of Jerusalem were destroyed. If someone sells their enemy, perhaps they have an excuse, that this enemy abused them. But who sells his friend or his teacher, what is his excuse?

It is betrayal! At this point some may ask, what is the difference between Peter and Judas? Peter the disciple denied Jesus out of fear and weakness, but within his heart he loved Him, "He said to him the third time, 'Simon, son of Jonah, do you love Me?' Peter was grieved because He said to him the third time, 'Do you love Me?' And he said to Him, 'Lord, You know all things; You know that I love You.' Jesus said to him, 'Feed My sheep.'" (John 21:17). Judas, however, did not have that love inside him and externally there were no dangerous threats against him which would have caused him fear. But he is the one who led himself to deliver his Teacher by his betrayal, "and said, 'What are you willing to give me if I deliver Him to you?' And they counted out to him thirty pieces of silver." (Matthew 26:15). And also the Jews betrayed Jesus, and they asked for Barabbas to be freed instead of Him.

In spite of that He prayed for them on the Cross and said, "My Father forgive them." They had been led by their evil leaders and did not know what they were doing. So He forgave those who believed and repented.

How astonishing is the heart of Jesus! He loves without return, when we look at the Lord Jesus in His love and bearing with the suffering, and we sing to Him our renowned hymn, "To You is the Power and the Glory and the Blessing and the Honour, forever. Amen."

We are definitely not selling You, and if they put the treasures of the whole world at our feet, we will always remember that You bought us with Your precious blood. Whoever sells You for any worldly desire will lose their Godly image, and go down to the level of Judas, whom, when his eyes were opened, he could no longer see His image.

JOB'S WEDNESDAY

Our Church gave Holy Wednesday of Pascha Week the name 'Job Wednesday'. This may be due to two reasons:

1 On Holy Wednesday the Church reads the entire Book of Job. This book is a story of agony.

2 Throughout the Book of Job we see numerous parallels between the suffering of the Righteous Job and Christ. There are so many, but we can summarise them into the following:

- Job faced tremendous suffering just as Christ did.

- God said about Job, "That there is none like him on the earth, a blameless and upright man." (Job 1:8, 2:3). Here he resembles our Lord Jesus Christ.

- The trials which have happened in Job's life came from Satan's envy towards him (Job 1:9, 2:4). Likewise, Christ's sufferings came about when Satan entered the heart of Judas (Luke 22:3) and all of His enemies.

- Job's three friends hurt him as did Christ's friends hurt Him.

- Job's tribulations ended in a positive way when God restored all that he once had and more (Job 42:10). Our Lord Jesus' death was followed by His glorious resurrection, which granted salvation to the whole world.

We too, when we remember the sufferings of Christ and the sufferings of the Righteous Job, are consoled in all our pain and suffering and hence we are able to comfort others.

COVENANT THURSDAY

The Blessing of the Water Prayers (Lakan)

Our Lord Jesus Christ washed His disciples' feet on Covenant Thursday. He washed their feet before the Holy Communion, before He offered to them the Holy Sacrament. He said to them, after washing their feet, now you are purified. Perhaps here our Lord wants to give us a lesson on purity before Communion. We should be purified before going to the Holy Sacrament. Our Lord also wanted to teach us some spiritual teachings from this action.

He wants to teach us that purity is a gift from Him and that He is the only one who can give us this gift. By washing us we become pure. We notice here that He washes the disciples' feet without them asking. In the same way He offered us redemption without us asking.

Our Lord wants to teach us humility. How humble He is, our great leader who bows down to wash the feet of His disciples. And how humble the Lord is to wash His own creation. In order to explain this lesson to His disciples Christ said to them, after washing their feet: "Do you know what I have done to you? You call me Teacher and Lord, and you say well, for so I am. If I then, your Lord and Teacher, have washed your feet, you also ought to wash one another's feet. For I have given you an example, that you should do as I have done to you. (John 13:12-15).

By washing His disciples' feet, Christ wants to give us a lesson on love. Because of His great love to His disciples, Christ granted them purity, so He will grant them the same degree in love, His body and His blood. So it has been said of Him before washing His disciples feet, "Having loved His own who were in the world, He loved them to the end." (John 13:1).

We meditate on the water and take out of it so many lessons for our benefit. Let us contemplate on the water which we will use to wash the feet after the Lakan rites. What is water in the Holy Bible? And what does it represent for us?

Water in the Holy Bible has at least three meanings or three symbols. We will have some meditation on it as we continue our discussions.

WATER SYMBOLISES PURITY AND CLEANLINESS

The Bible readings of the Lakan prayers, tells of the washing of the feet of the disciples. Here we clearly see the work of cleanliness. There are many more examples in the Holy Bible.

In between the tabernacle of meeting and the altar in the Old Testament was a basin for washing which contained water. "For Aaron and his sons shall wash their hands and their feet in water from it. When they go into the tabernacle of meeting, or when they come near the altar to minister, to burn an offering made by fire to the Lord, they shall wash with water, lest they die. And it shall be a statute forever to them - to him and his descendants throughout their generations" (Exodus 30:19-21).

It was important to wash and be purified first before approaching the Altar and the sacrifice. This washing was of equal importance to the washing in the Jordan, the washing in the pool of Siloam and the washing in the pool of Bethesda.

Here we stop to meditate on the story of the purification of Naaman the Syrian. This man had leprosy. In the Old Testament leprosy symbolised sin and required purification. So how did he become clean and pure from his leprosy? Elisha ordered him to be washed in the Jordan River in order for his flesh to be restored and for him to be healed (2 Kings 5:10). The Jordan River reminds us of John the Baptist. It was here that he used to baptise the Jewish people who came to be washed, to receive forgiveness of their sins and be cleaned spiritually.

We can see from this story that the water of purification also symbolises baptism. Another story offered to us from the Bible is the one of the healing of the man from Bethesda. Once again this healing is linked to water. The most beautiful part of this story is the angel who went down at a certain time once a year into the pool and stirred up the water (John 5:4). The person healed was the one to step into the pool first after the water was stirred. The water was given power and healed effectively.

This reminds us of when the priest holds the cross in his hand and stirs the baptismal water. Or the water in the Lakan, when the priest does the sign of the cross on it and it becomes holy water for healing. Also there is the pool of Siloam which the Lord sent the man born blind to wash in and he returned with his sight restored. (John 9:7).

Tears can also be linked to water. Tears are water which cleans the soul and heals the spirit as we see in the pool of Siloam and the pool of Bethesda. In the story of the sinful woman who brought an expensive alabaster flask of fragrant oil to the house of the Pharisee, we see her tears as she washes the Lords feet, and wiped them with the hair of her head, and she kissed His feet and anointed them with the fragrant oil (Luke 7:38).

Which is greater, the perfume or the tears of this repentant woman? Believe me it was definitely the tears. The tears of this woman were the greatest and most precious and the Lord Himself blessed her. So water relates to purity; even the tears from the eyes. As in Psalm 51, "Purge me with hyssop, and I shall be clean; wash me, and I shall be whiter than snow."

In Christianity, washing can be one of two ways; either baptism or repentance. In Ezekiel 16 the Lord said, "When I passed by you and saw you struggling in your own blood. Then I washed you in water; yes, I thoroughly washed off your blood, and I anointed you with oil". The water here resembles the water of baptism which cleanses the person from all his old sins, the oil resembles the Holy Myron oil which gives us the Holy Spirit, but it comes after the water.

The water still represents cleanliness. Even when the priest starts the liturgy, he washes his hands three times and says, "I will wash my hands in innocence; so I will go about Your altar, O Lord." (Psalm 26:6). He doesn't say: "I wash my hands with water," but he says: "I wash my hands in innocence". The washing of the hands symbolises purity, and innocence as is also the white vestments the priest wears during the service. In the Old Testament, Aaron and his sons wash with water before offering the sacrifices on the altar.

The water symbolises purity. The gentiles also viewed water as a symbol of purity and innocence. When Pilate saw that he could not prevail at all and that a tumult was rising, he took water and washed his hands before the multitude, saying, "I am innocent of the blood of this just Person." (Matthew 27:24). We do not say here that Pilate was innocent, but rather we highlight that washing with water represented innocence.

We can meditate here on the water of the flood. We don't deny that the flood waters were due to God's punishment. But do we stop here? These flood waters were to clean the earth from sins and from the sinful people and to cleanse the earth from corruption and impurity. So the Lord washes the earth from its sins and renews it so that it becomes alive again in purity.

The washing of the disciples' feet by the Lord also symbolises purity. This was important in the feast of Passover and the Leaven Feast. We notice in the Church readings of Covenant Thursday that this blessed hour and the hour before it, that washing of the feet happened on the first day of the Passover Feast and the Leaven Feast.

The leaven represents the purity and the cleanliness which befits the Passover communion, and the leaven of the yeast represents evil. The Lord washes the feet of His disciples on this holy occasion in which He linked the Feast of the Passover and sacrificing Himself on our behalf.

St. Paul the Apostle highlighted all these things by saying, "For indeed Christ, our Passover, was sacrificed for us. Therefore let us keep the feast, not with old leaven, nor with the leaven of malice and wickedness, but with the unleavened bread of sincerity and truth." (I Corinthians 5:7-8). They used to eat the lamb of the Passover with the leaven bread (Exodus 12:8) which symbolises purity. Truly the lamb of the Passover saved them from death, and the angel of death passed over the homes which had blood on the doorposts. In order to enjoy this salvation, they were not permitted to have yeast in their homes for 7 days. "Seven days you shall eat unleavened bread. On the first day you shall remove leaven from your houses. For whoever eats leavened bread from the first day until the seventh day, that person shall be cut off from Israel." (Exodus 12:19). The Lord Jesus Christ washed the disciples' feet while the Passover symbolises the purity which has been indicated by the leaven bread.

Washing with water represents Baptism. The Holy Bible called it washing or the second Birth (John 3:6). In Baptism, there is a process of cleansing from all your old sins by the water and spirit. We will return to this topic later on. It will be enough now to talk in this occasion of Lakan on the water and its work in the cleaning process as we approach this great Sacrament which is the Holy Communion of the body and blood of our Lord.

WATER SYMBOLISES THE HOLY SPIRIT

This is seen in the Lord's words in the Holy Bible: "'He who believes in Me, as the Scripture has said, out of his heart will flow rivers of living water'. But this He spoke concerning the Spirit, whom those believing in Him would receive." (John 7:38). Because the Spirit of God symbolises water, so the disciples of the Lord full of the spirit were identified with the rivers and were moved by the Holy Spirit.

It is said about the Holy Church in Psalm 24, "For He has founded it upon the seas, and established it upon the waters". It was good what is written about the creation that it parted and became four riverheads that watered the Eden (Genesis 2:1-14). It could be that these 4 rivers symbolise the 4 Gospels which watered all the believers which was written by the Holy Spirit "who spoke in the prophets".

As water symbolises the Spirit, the Lord Himself is identified by the water. He said: "They have forsaken Me, the fountain of living waters, And hewn themselves cisterns, broken cisterns that can hold no water." (Jeremiah 2:13).

Then the person who lives a life filled with the Holy Spirit is like a tree planted by the rivers of water; living with this water, growing with it and dying without it. Water is linked to life and so the Bible is the fountain of the living water.

THE LINK BETWEEN WATER AND LIFE

Even physical life is linked with water whether it be the life of a person, a plant or an animal. It was said in the creation, "Let the waters abound with an abundance of living creatures." (Genesis 1:20-21).

The spiritual life is also linked with water. It starts with the birth from God, the birth which is from above, from water and the Holy Spirit (John 3: 3, 5), and why the water? Because the Holy Spirit works through the water, and with it. It will be purified and be alive, giving purity, cleanliness and life.

The person is washed with the baptismal water and becomes clean and pure. The old man has died and a new person is alive as the image of God. He has received life and has been saved from death. This is Baptism and it has so many symbols.

St. Paul the Apostle said: "Moreover, brethren, I do not want you to be unaware that all our fathers were under the cloud, all passed through the sea, all were baptised into Moses in the cloud and in the sea." (I Corinthians 10:1, 2). The cloud was water and both were to the Baptism.

It is the water that our fathers entered as slaves, under Pharaoh's bondage and exited as free people under the guidance of God and Moses. These people who flee from slavery, the water and the death followed them, but they went out with a new life conquering death. It was a great miracle that these people passed through the waters. The cloud was always covering them throughout their time in the wilderness as strangers just as we are strangers in the modern world.

The Lord Jesus Christ invites us to His water and says, "If anyone thirsts, let him come to Me and drink." (John 7:37). The Lord also invited the Samaritan woman to take from His living water and said, "But whoever drinks of the water that I shall give him will never thirst. But the water that I shall give him will become in him a fountain of water springing up into everlasting life." (John 4:14).

David the prophet called Him in the Psalm of the Shepherd "The restful water." The shepherd said on the Lord, "He leads me beside the still waters", which means "to the living water", the water of the Holy Spirit. What is the outcome? It says, "He restores my soul; He leads me in the paths of righteousness". This is truly the work of the Holy Spirit in humans which leads us to repentance and a spiritual life and gives joy, the Joy of salvation, or as David says, "Restore to me the joy of Your salvation" (Psalm 51).

Also, "There is a river whose streams shall make glad the city of

God." (Psalm 46). It is the spiritual joy, one of the fruits of the Holy Spirit (Galatians 5:22). This water, which makes glad the city of God, reminds us of another truth about water; we remember it when we approach the Holy Communion in the Holy Liturgy, after washing our feet with water. It reflects 2 words:

THE WATER AND THE BLOOD

When the soldier pierced the side of Jesus with a spear, and immediately blood and water came out (John 19: 34). St John the Beloved witnesses to this in his first Epistle (1 John 5:6), "This is He who came by water and blood, Jesus Christ; not only by water, but by water and blood." and he also said, "And there are three that bear witness on earth: the Spirit, the water, and the blood; and these three agree as one." (1 John 5:8).

How astonishing this verse is in our salvation? What is this mystery and what does it mean? This means that the salvation which the Lord offered with His blood on the Cross, you received with water and spirit in Baptism. These three: the Spirit, the water and the blood witness for your salvation. Without blood, there is no life, because "Without shedding of blood there is no remission and no forgiveness." (Hebrews 9:22). How can you receive this salvation offered to you with blood? The Lord Jesus Christ says, "He who believes and is baptized will be saved." (Mark 16:16). In Baptism you will be born of water and the Spirit (John 3:5) and receive the remission of sins (Acts 2:38).

The water and the Blood, are in the Eucharist. The Priest, in the Holy Liturgy, mixes the wine with the water and says in the prayers of the Holy Liturgy "Likewise after supper, He took the Chalice, mixed it of wine and water..." With this blood that we drink, mixed with water, we receive life. We can see from both the blood and the water the relationship with life.

Before I finish, I would like to say a word on the Lakan prayers and the washing of feet. Jesus Christ washed the feet of the disciples. Why did He specifically wash the feet? In addition to what we said earlier on the humility of washing feet, I want to meditate on St Augustine's words about the bride in the Book of Song of Songs 5:3. "I have taken off my robe; how can I put it on again? I have washed my feet; how can I defile them?"

St. Augustine said, the person is washed by Baptism, purified and exalted over worldly things. As he still lives on the earth, however, he is still bound to materialistic things and his feet become dirty from the soil.

Therefore, the bride in Song of Songs; when the Lord called her to serve Him, she was freed from the conflict which affects her purity, which she received from Baptism. So she took off her robe, the old person, not wanting to return to its problems after having washed her feet, which were defiled earlier in the soil. How can she return back to it?

The Lord Jesus calms the soul when it has been troubled due to problems. He solves our problems and attracts us to Him. So the Lord says to us, "Even if your feet defile you, I will come back and wash them just as I washed the feet of the disciples and told them, 'Now you are pure.'"

Something else about washing the feet - washing of the feet replaces washing of the whole body. When St Peter the disciple asked for his whole body to be washed, the Lord said to him, "He who is bathed needs only to wash his feet, but is completely clean." (John 13:10).

When the priest washes his hands before the Liturgy he says, "I wash my hands to be clean and I go around Your altar Lord." There is no need to wash the whole body, but only one part on behalf of the rest of the body. Just as when one part of our body sins, it is considered that the whole body received that sin.

The washing of the feet in the Lakan of Covenant Thursday, symbolises purity which is a precursor of the Holy Communion. So make the Lakan prayers of importance to all of you. I was once contemplating the verse said by the Prophet Samuel, when he went to Bethlehem and called on the sacrifice by saying: "Sanctify yourselves, and come with me to the sacrifice." (I Samuel 16:5). It is not proper for someone to come to the offertory without having repented. Therefore, sanctify yourselves first, be purified by repentance and then come and receive the Holy Communion.

The Church first washes the feet of the congregation and says, "Now you have all been purified and cleansed." And this is then followed by Holy Communion. This does not mean that you only come to Church on Covenant Thursday for the washing of feet, without repentance. If so you will hear the frightening words, "And now you are clean, but not all of you." (John 13: 10). "Not all of you"? No Lord, we need all to be clean and pure. Wash us with hyssop and we will be clean. Wash us so we will be white like snow. Yes, this is the aim of Lakan, to be clean and pure before Holy Communion.

The water which resembles cleanliness is found in the Church during every liturgy and not just in the Lakan liturgy. At the conclusion of the liturgy the priest sprinkles the holy water on the congregation before giving them the final blessing. It reminds us of when the Lord said in Ezekiel, "Then I will sprinkle clean water on you, and you shall be clean." (Ezekiel 36:25).

REPENTANCE AND HOLY COMMUNION

We thank God that when we were outside the city, carrying the shame of sin, the Lord opened the door of the holy of holies to us. He opens to us His holy altar and gives us His Holy Body and Holy Blood. It is a great blessing that the Lord remembered us during His week of suffering and cared for us after giving us the essential blessing of washing our feet.

Just as in the celebration of the old Passover, with all its symbols, He offered to us the Passover of the New Covenant. St. Paul said about the Passover, "For indeed Christ, our Passover, was sacrificed for us." (I Corinthians 5:7). And so the two Passovers united on one day, symbolically. And who is this symbol for? The Lord Jesus Christ gave this holy mystery to His disciples and said: "Do this in remembrance of Me." (Luke 22:15) and we do the same now according to His holy commandments.

The Lord celebrates the Feast with His disciples in His deep sufferings. He celebrates the Feast with them and says, "With fervent desire I have desired to eat this Passover with you before I suffer." (Luke 22:15). He sings praises with them that night, before they went to the Mount of Olives, "When they had sung a hymn, they went out to the Mount of Olives." (Mark 14:26, Matthew 26:30). Truly, He celebrated with them and rejoiced, "Knowing all things that would come upon Him." (John 18:4).

Truly how great is His heart, who rejoices with the joyful hearts. In the joy of the Passover, He talked to them about His Body which He sacrifices for them, and His blood which is shed for them (Luke 22:19,20). Consequently, He gave His Disciples a new feast and a new covenant. He gave them an idea that He would sacrifice His Body and shed His Blood for their sake and the sake of others, for the remission of sins (Matthew 26:28, Mark 14:24) and He said, "This is My body for the New Covenant."

He gave them warnings so that they would be prepared when they saw His blood shed in front of them. He told them before it happened so that, "You may believe that I am He." (John 13: 19). It is unusual that someone speaks of shedding their blood with a calm spirit. He talked objectively about shedding His blood in the midst of joy and praising, during the celebration of the Passover Feast. He is the loving and gentle Christ, who thinks of the salvation of all humanity and before thinking about Himself or His sufferings.

We observe here that He said My blood which is shed and not which will be shed. Likewise He said My body which is sacrificed and not which will be sacrificed. This is because His blood was shed on Friday and His body was sacrificed on Friday, the day which gave salvation.

On Thursday, He spoke of the salvation which would be on Friday. The Passover Feast which was celebrated on Thursday is the symbol of the true Passover of the New Covenant, which was sacrificed on Friday for our sake. The Lord wants to say, "This Passover which you eat today symbolises My body which will be sacrificed for your sake tomorrow and My blood which is shed for your sake tomorrow also.

These are the offerings that I give and eating the bread and drinking the wine you do this in remembrance of Me. The words, "Do this in remembrance of Me" indicate continuity of this Holy Sacrament until the end of age, "For as often as you eat this bread and drink this cup, you proclaim the Lord's death till He comes." (I Corinthians 11:26). And the words "till He comes" indicates that practising this great mystery will continue until the second coming to the end of age.

He said this is My blood which was shed for many for the remission of many sins. The meaning of many is, of who believes in Him, in His great redemption, in the effectiveness of His blood for the remission of many sins, and also their faith in His holy mysteries for practicing it. It requires from them to repent because the Lord Himself said, "Unless you repent you will all likewise perish." (Luke 13:5).

Repentance is then required for the believers to have the Holy Communion. This is an essential condition in order to deserve the Holy Communion. St. Paul explained it as, "Therefore whoever eats this bread or drinks this cup of the Lord in an unworthy manner will be guilty of the body and blood of the Lord. For he who eats and drinks in an unworthy manner eats and drinks judgment to himself, not discerning the Lord's body. For this reason many are weak and sick among you, and many sleep." (I Corinthians II: 27-30).

Then, this is very dangerous and very serious. Therefore, whoever receives the Holy Communion in an unworthy manner, will be guilty of the body and blood of the Lord, not discerning the Lord's body. This can even extend to a penalty in the body such as sickness or death as the Apostle said: "Let a man examine himself before the Communion. For if we would judge ourselves, we would not be judged." (I Corinthians II:28,31).

Then what does the word 'Worthy' mean? If we are to talk of being worthy no one would deserve it. The Great St. Roweiss, the Miracle Performer, was in awe when he approached the Holy Communion . He said, "Whoever approaches the Holy Communion must have purity and cleanliness inside them just as St. Mary who carried Jesus inside her womb!"

For this reason, the Priest says inaudibly in the Preparation Prayer of the Liturgy, "Lord who knows everyone's heart, the Holy One who rests in His saints, who alone is sinless and is able to forgive sin. You O Lord know that I am not worthy, nor prepared, nor deserving of this holy ministry which is Yours, and I dare not approach and open my mouth before Your Holy glory, but according to the multitude of Your compassion, forgive me, the sinner and grant unto me that I may find grace and mercy at this hour."

As a resultof this, each person should say before Holy Communion, "Lord, not because I am worthy, but because of my need, not because I am worthy, but for my healing." We all recognise that we are not worthy, as we say to the Lord, "It is not because of our purity that we approach His body and His blood. We have not been purified to have the Holy Communion but we approach the Holy Communion in order to be purified."

We have the Holy Communion, "For the purification of our souls, bodies and spirits." As we say in the beginning of the Litanies in the Holy Liturgy. The purity which which is due in order to approach the Communion, as the Prophet said, "Sanctify yourselves, and come with me to the sacrifice."(1 Samuel 16:5). This purity can be summarised in the following points:

Faith, repentance, reconciliation and physical

PURITY.

Faith: this means the true, right, Christian Orthodoxy which is free of heresies. Also, belief in this Sacrament and its effectiveness, following the Laws which the Lord established and has been kept by the Apostolic Succession.

Repentance: this means to leave sin with true determination not to go back coupled with the confession of sins and repentance from it. Some doubt that their repentance is genuine and avoid Holy Communion, giving the excuse that they still sin after Holy Communion. Then they are not truly repenting and are not worthy, so for some it is better not to have Holy Communion. We answer these people by saying:

The Holy Communion purifies and cleanses

There is no one without fault, even if we are saints or righteous, even if we confess and have Holy Communion. We are still weak until the end of our life. Weakness has many levels which will differ from one person to another.

"Now there is in store for me the crown of righteousness, which the

Lord, the righteous Judge, will award to me on that day—and not only to me, but also to all who have longed for his appearing." (2 Timothy 4:8). On that day there will be no more sin. Have Holy Communion and each time you do, it brings strength. Even if you have sinned, your heart will be troubled by this sin and you will repent quickly and you will rebuke yourself. But the life of negligence and carlessness prevents you from having Holy Communion. You will become a slave to sin and you will be obsessed with it and keep returning to it with no repentance.

The Lord commanded that we reconcile with one another. He said, "If you bring your gift to the altar, and there remember that your brother has something against you, leave your gift there before the altar, and go your way. First be reconciled to your brother." (Matthew 5:23.24).

Therefore, reconciliation with others must come before having Holy Communion. You cannot approach the "Sacrifice of love" when you are void of love. Here we remember that we pray the prayer of reconciliation before we begin the Commemoration of the Saints. We say in this prayer, "Make us all worthy our master, to greet one another with the holy kiss, to share Your immortal and heavenly gifts without falling into condemnation" Not reconciling causes us to fall into condemnation.

What does reconcile mean? And is it important to reconcile with others? The reconciliation means that the heart is free from hatred and is truly able to reconcile and return back to a amicable relationship. As the Apostle said, "If it is possible, as much as depends on you, live peaceably with all men." (Romans 12:18).

Many can not have peace with one another. The scribes, Sadducees, Pharisees and the Chief Priests who tried to arrest Christ did not have reconciliation with Him. What He needed is to have reconciliation first with them to have a pure relationship with the Father. St. Paul the

Apostolic was not required to leave his gifts before the altar and go and reconcile with Alexander the metalworker, who did evil against him and wanted to harm him and wanted to overcome the word of God (2 Timothy 4:14,15).

For this reason the Apostle said be reconciled with others "If it is possible" and said "According to your limit." This is because there are some cases which are impossible to reconcile. It is not held against you if others do not want to reconcile with you or if it is for a spiritual benefit.

Try to live in peace with others, and if it is not possible because of them not because of you, then you have done your best. Some examples include those who envy you because of your success, or gifts that the Lord has given you, or due to evil in their hearts, as what happened with Cain when he envied his brother Abel, and the case with the Jewish leaders when they envied Jesus.

In the Psalms David said: "Those who hate me without a cause are more than the hairs of my head." (Psalm 69: 4). Therefore, those who hate you without a cause, if you can't reconcile with them then you are excused and this should not prevent you from having Holy Communion. Likewise for those who persecute you (John 16:2).

Also there are those who you try to avoid for fear of them causing you to stumble and you want to protect your spirituality. As it is said in Psalm 1: "The path of sinners and the seat of the scornful" and also, "Evil company corrupts good habits." (1 Corinthians 15:33). In this case you don't have to leave your offerings and to go and reconcile with them.

Now when you leave your offerings before the altar and go to reconcile first, this is when: You have sinned against someone. The Lord said, "If you remembered something against your brother", and he has something towards you, that is, you sinned against him, then you have to go to him and reconcile with him before receiving Holy

Communion and obey the commandment of the Lord, even if he sinned against you. So you need to go and apologise to him (Matthew 18:15) to regain the love between both of you.

In all circumstances, you are one of two: either you are the offender or someone offended you. If you are the offender, leave your sacrifice, go and reconcile with your brother, and correct your mistakes. If you are not the offender and someone has offended you, reproach him or at least forgive him, because there are many kinds of people where reproach does not work and it may lead to the opposite consequence of what you intended. Or it may be that they are in a position where you can't reach them to reproach them. With these sorts of people it is better to forgive them and not make them your enemy. Remember the word of the Bible: "Forgive, and you will be forgiven." (Luke 6:37).

There is a request in the Prayer of Our Father, "forgive us as we forgive them" and the Lord explained this saying: "For if you forgive men their trespasses, your heavenly Father will also forgive you. But if you do not forgive men their trespasses, neither will your Father forgive your trespasses." (Matthew 6:14-15).

So far we have spoken about reconciliation, what about the preparation of the body. It is important first to prepare yourself with fasting, and the only one who can be excused is the sick or whoever has special circumstances to be exempt from fasting. The Church believes that a person requires at least nine hours of fasting before Holy Communion. This means not eating anything from midnight, the night before Holy Communion. If there are any exceptions it needs to be dealt with by the confession father.

The purity of the body also requires abstinence from sexual relationships so that the body may be pure and clean as it is cleansed by the spirit. There are many commandments written in the Bible on this topic.

We don't want anybody to abstain from communion if their excuse is they are not worthy or not deserving. If it is a matter of uncertainty always consult your confession father.

Let us then prepare for repentance as this is in our hand. Repentance is a work that happens inside the heart, so it is our choice then and it is not beyond us that we are unable to do anything about it. You are able to hear the voice of God inside you, so don't harden your heart, return back to God, benefit from the spiritual impact that you will receive during Holy Week. It is in your hands. The Bible says, "Today, if you will hear His voice, do not harden your hearts as in the rebellion."(Hebrews 3:15).

Let everyone give an account of himself and return to the Lord, and join in the joy of these holy days which the Church considers to be a Feast, having Holy Communion on the Great Covenant Thursday. All liturgies have Holy Communion originating from that day. Let us try and approach the Holy Communion with a pure heart.

You will not benefit anything from Holy Communion unless you have kept your heart pure. On Covenant Thursday, not all the disciples benefited from Communion to the same level. The disciple who loved the Lord the most, St. John the Beloved, after Holy Communion, followed Christ to the Cross. He heard one word from Him and the blessings. Peter the impetuous one, who was zealous in his love, followed Christ half way, but could not continue. He denied the Lord and repented although he received Holy Communion with the Lord just as John did.

The rest of the disciples also received Holy Communion at the same time, but they fled when the Lord was being arrested. They did not walk with Him even one step of His journey, they submitted to their weakness.

This reminds us of the seed which fell on the good soil. It produced fruit; the seeds were the same, the farmer who planted the seeds was the same, but some of his fruits produced thirty fold, some sixty and some one hundred. Let us prepare our hearts to also give one hundred.

Always remember the many blessings received from the Holy Communion. The Holy Bible spoke of this, the Lord said, "I am the living bread which came down from heaven. If anyone eats of this bread, he will live forever." (John 6:51). "Whoever eats My flesh and drinks My blood has eternal life, and I will raise him up at the last day. He who eats My flesh and drinks My blood abides in Me, and I in him." (John 6:56).

In the Liturgy we say, "Given for salvation and remission of sins, and eternal life for those who partake of them" and we also say, "Having Holy Communion from Your holies to purify our body, our soul and our spirits." Why then do we not approach for this purity, for this salvation and remission, and abide in the Lord and eternal life?

Christ grants us the grace of the Holy Communion and the results of this are so many blessings. At the same time, He made a Covenant between Him and us. Yes, we entered through the Communion in a Covenant with the Lord, for every time we eat and we drink from these holy mysteries, we preach His death, we confess His resurrection and remember Him till He comes.

We preach His death, which is His death on our behalf; we receive the salvation, the redemption and become holies with His blood. This Blood purified us from every sin (I John I:7). He said, "This is My blood of the new covenant, which is shed for many for the remission of sins." (Mark I4: 26). In this verse the Lord explains two things:

I- His blood is for the New Covenant

2- It is for the remission of sins, i.e for salvation.

Do we realise that every time we have Holy Communion it is a feast, "This is the day that the Lord has made, let us rejoice and be glad in it." Also, Covenant Thursday is a Feast. Do we truly understand how the Lord purified us with this blood which is shed for the remission of our sins, and we became saints, as is said in the Liturgy, "The holies are for the Holy people."

Perhaps this word "Holy" convicts us from within in a way we don't deserve and are not worthy. It encourages us to behave like people who have been sanctified by the Lord with His blood and purified from all sin.

How beautiful then to preach His death, who gave us all these blessings. Another verse which makes a Covenant between us and the Lord is, "To remember the Lord till He comes." What does the word "remember" mean? Does it mean that the Lord is constantly inside our minds as David said, "I have set the Lord always before me; because He is at my right hand I shall not be moved." (Psalm 16:8). How lovely is Your name Lord and to praise You all day.

We remember that everything the Lord did was for our sake. He put Himself, His incarnation, His teaching, His love, His suffering, His crucifixion, His resurrection and His ascension to heaven and sitting on the right hand of the Father, with all of these memories that carry great meaning and spiritual benefits. It means that we must remember all of this and continue to remember it till He comes.

In the words "Till He comes", believe and have faith in the Second Coming of the Lord. Prepare for this coming, watch always and prepare because, "Blessed are those servants whom the master, when he comes, will find watching." (Luke 12:37). Don't forget also that the Holy Communion is a gathering of believers, which are united together in one faith, one table and one priesthood. May the Lord give us the blessing of this day. Amen

THE FAREWELL GATHERING WITH HIS DISCIPLES

THE LORD CARED FOR HIS DISCIPLES

The most important thing in Christ's relationship with His disciples is this great love that He came down from heaven. But the love of the Lord appeared in its deepest form in the last week, the Holy Week. This following verse demonstrates this, "Having loved His own who were in the world, He loved them to the end." (John 13:1). The words "to the end" can be meditated on in depth and there will still be even deeper meanings.

The Lord knew that the crucifixion would affect His disciples deeply as they see their great teacher, who performed great miracles, scorned and nailed to the Cross and then die in the midst of mockery. Therefore, during this week we see the Lord giving all His attention to His disciples and preparing them spiritually and psychologically to face His death.

This matter affected Him greatly. He was not worried about Himself, nor His arrest, nor His trial or false witnesses, nor the insults that He would receive from hitting and slapping, nor the abusive and offensive words, nor from going from one place to another, facing Caiaphas, Pilate and Herod. He did not care about His sufferings, torture with thorns, whipping, nails and crucifixion.

His whole heart was deeply with others. He had two matters in mind: How to save the world and how to keep His disciples safe during the tribulation. He wanted to keep them safe during these dreadful hours so that the whole Church may believe and its faith to be not shaken. He wanted to strengthen the faith of His disciples, in the events before, during and after the crucifixion.

In order to strengthen their faith, He appeared to them after the crucifixion and the resurrection. He appeared to Mary Magdalene, to

Peter, to the disciples of Emmaus, to the blessed ladies, to the eleven disciples and to around five hundred others. He also appeared to Saul of Tarsus. He remained with His disciples for forty days after the resurrection to strengthen them and to talk to them about important matters relating to the Kingdom of God.

All of this was after the resurrection, but how did He strengthen them before the crucifixion?

1 Six days before the crucifixion He raised Lazarus from death (John 11). Four days after Lazarus' death, they said that there was a stench. Many believed after this great miracle and the Lord gave them an idea of the resurrection from death, giving them hope even after death. It was a miracle to strengthen their faith in His great power and His resurrection when they will see Him dead.

2 Before Lazarus was raised up from the dead, He gave the man who was born blind sight (John 9). This miracle was very obviously showing His divinity as it showed the power of His creation. He created eyes from the mud of the ground. This miracle had a huge impact and after his sight was restored this man said, "Since the world began it has been unheard of that anyone opened the eyes of one who was born blind."(John 9:32). In the end this blind man believed that the Lord Jesus Christ was the Son of God and worshipped Him." (John 9:38).

With these two miracles the Lord wanted to increase the faith of the Disciples. These two miracles had the results of some believing instantly and some stored these events until the crucifixion in order to strengthen the faith of the weak.

3 He showed them His power during the cleansing of the Temple. This happened on Palm Sunday, the day after raising Lazarus from the dead; He entered Jerusalem as a King and all the multitudes cheered Him and rejoiced. They laid down the olive branches and the Palm leaves.

On this occasion He cleansed the Temple with power and force, He rebuked the Chief Priests and scribes saying, "This is My Father's and you have made it a den of thieves." No one was able to overcome Him, He was the master. Each word He heard He answered in strength which no one could argue. All of these made His disciples strong and lifted their self-esteem.

4 With the same power He rebuked the Jewish leaders. He rebuked the Chief Priests with the Parable of the Vineyard. He said: "The Kingdom of God will be taken from you and given to a nation bearing the fruits of it." (Matthew 21:43).

He silenced the Sadducees concerning the resurrection of the dead (Matthew 22:34) and He did the same with the lawyers. He rebuked the Pharisees and the scribes with strength, saying, "Woe to you, scribes and Pharisees." (Matthew 23:13). He was stronger than all and St. Matthew said about Him, "And no one was able to answer Him a word, nor from that day on did anyone dare question Him anymore." (Matthew 22:46).

All of this increased the self-esteem of the disciples, strengthening them by seeing their teacher with such power and preparing them for the trial which was coming. And what else?

5 He cursed the fig tree which had no fruits and thus it withered away so quickly. This tree resembles hypocrisy in its appearance by having green leaves, but no fruits. By cursing the fig tree, He cursed hypocrisy and the Lord revealed His divinity and His power over nature. With one word the tree withered, "And when the disciples saw it, they marvelled, saying, 'How did the fig tree wither away so soon'"? (Matthew 21:20). The Lord gave them a lesson about faith and said to them, "Assuredly, I say to you, if you have faith and do not doubt, you will not only do what was done to the fig tree, but also if you say to this mountain, 'Be removed and be cast into the sea' it will be done.'"

"If you have faith and do not doubt", Christ wanted these words to stay with them during the time of the crucifixion of their master, His death and His burial. And what else?

6 The Lord washed their feet symbolising cleansing and purification. After He washed their feet, He said to them, "You are now clean." (John 13:10). Hoping by this cleansing they will be firm in their faith with the power that they receive after the Lord washed their feet. And what else?

7 He gave them the Sacrament of Eucharist. He granted them His Holy Body and His Holy Blood to give them spiritual power and strength. He told them, "He who eats My flesh and drinks My blood abides in Me, and I in him." (John 6:56). This sacrament was to hold on to the Lord and benefit the disciples during the time of tribulation. The Lord strengthened their weak nature by giving them a different, stronger and great nature.

At the same time He was preparing their minds to accept the news, "This is My body which is given for you; and this is My blood, which is shed for you." (Luke 22:19,20). "Which is shed for many" (Mark 14:24), "Which is shed for many for the remission of sins." (Matthew 26: 28). The words "shed His blood" was given to prepare the disciples for what would happen that night and on the following night.

8 He disclosed the truth so that they are not surprised. He told them many times, "He must go to Jerusalem, and suffer many things from the elders, chief priests and scribes, be killed, and be raised on the third day." (Matthew 16:21). He also said to them, "We are going up to Jerusalem, and the Son of Man will be betrayed to the chief priests and to the scribes; and they will condemn Him to death and deliver Him to the Gentiles to mock and to scourge and to crucify. And the third day He will rise again." (Matthew 20:18,19). So He linked the crucifixion and the resurrection and He talked to them providing them comfort.

Two days before the Passover, He repeated the same news to them and said, "You know that after two days is the Passover...one of you will betray Me."

9 After the Passover and Last Super He stayed with them for some time. This time was recorded in the Gospel of Saint John in Chapters 13,14,15,16.   He talked openly with them, comforting them with many words. He spoke of the resurrection, the Holy Spirit and His work with them and gave them guidance.

10 He continued to care for them even while they arrested Him. When the soldiers came to arrest Him, He said to them, "I am He. Therefore, if you seek Me, let these go their way, that the saying might be fulfilled which He spoke, Of those whom You gave Me I have lost none." (John 18: 8,9).

And so He pitied His disciples at the time of the arrest. He cared for them more than He cared for Himself. It was so important for Him that they were free, but He offered Himself to be arrested.

11 Even when He was on the cross. He cared for everything that is His, even in His deep sufferings. He didn't leave His mother, the Virgin St. Mary alone, but promised that she would be with His disciple, St. John the Beloved. "From that hour that disciple took her to his own home." (John 19:27). It was a great blessing for this disciple, as the Lord cared for him and granted him a spiritual mother. She is the most holy and gentle mother in the world.

12 Jesus' farewell to His disciples and His long prayer for their sake also indicated His care for them. Is it true He had a farewell with His Disciples? Farewell means leaving, Jesus never left them. Earlier He said to them, "For where two or three are gathered together in My name, I am there in the midst of them." (Matthew 18:20). Also, before the Ascension He said to them, "I am with you always, even to the end of the age." (Matthew 28:20). In all circumstances He only left them in the flesh and for a while. However,

it was very hard on them. The Lord knew it and that is why He sat with them to comfort and to ease them.

He knew it would be hard to take. This was revealed when He said to them, "But because I have said these things to you, sorrow has filled your heart." (John 16:6). So what did He say to them which made them sad? He said, "But now I go away to Him who sent Me". He said, "Little children, I shall be with you a little while longer". And as I said to the Jews, 'Where I am going, you cannot come.'" (John 13:33). He had to answer the question they asked Him, "Where are You going." (John 13:36). "We don't know where You are going." (John 14:5). He had to answer them in truth. So how did He answer? He said, "I go to the Father." (John 16:16). "A little while, you will not see Me." (John 16:17). And what else? "You will weep and lament, but the world will rejoice." (John 16: 20). There was another truth He had to tell them, "If they persecuted Me, they will also persecute you." (John 15:20).

The Lord gave them hope in every thing in order to comfort them. They will not see Him, but in a little while, they will see Him. The words "Not see Me", are the half truth, the agony part. So what is the other part which gives comfort? The Lord said to them, "A little while, and you will not see Me; and again a little while, and you will see Me." (John 16:17). "A little while longer and the world will see Me no more, but you will see Me." (John 14:19). It means that the world will not see You, You will die, so how can we see You then? Jesus will answer this by saying, "I am alive." "At that day you will know that I am in My Father, and you in Me." "He who loves Me... I will love him and manifest Myself to him." (John 14:19-21).

He gave them an idea of His resurrection, and they will see Him. He said to them that the Son of Man will be crucified and on the third day He will rise up." (Matthew 16: 21; Matthew 20:18,19). This day He emphasises the truth in a few words which are full of love, "I will not leave you orphans; I will come to you." (John 14:18).

Half the truth: "You will weep and lament, but the world will rejoice." What is the other half, the lighting one then? It is, "You will be sorrowful, but your sorrow will be turned into joy ... I will see you again, your heart will rejoice, and your joy no one will take from you." (John 16: 20,22).

It hurts Him very much that His disciples are sad because He is leaving them. He knows very well how much they love Him. About His love for them, it is enough to say what the Bible says, "Having loved His own who were in the world, He loved them to the end." (John 13:1). The Lord's heart is so sensitive that He got all those around Him, who love Him and He loves them to be comfortable. He then told them, "I will not leave you orphans." The word "orphans" tells them that they are His children. On this occasion, He used the words "My little children."

"Little children, I shall be with you a little while longer." (John 13: 33). You are My children, and I know that you will be orphans after I leave you, but I will not leave you and I will not let you be sad, I will come back. I will see you and your heart will be joyful, I will never leave you to grief because I can't see you sad.

I want, in this difficult farewell, to make your hearts happy, and to tell you that your sorrow is only for a while, a little while, and after a while you will see Me.

You are not only just My children, but my beloved too. "You are My friends if you do whatever I command you. No longer do I call you servants... but I have called you friends." (John 15:14,15). I will lay down My life for your sake, "Greater love has no one than this, than to lay down one's life for his friends." (John 15:13). "As the Father loved Me, I also have loved you; abide in My love." (John 15:9).

It is very nice to have a farewell with so much love. The Lord added, for their comfort, this beautiful parable, showing them that there is no separation between Him and them. It is the vine and the branches. He said to them, "I am the vine, you are the branches." (John 15:5). We are together, "You are in Me, and I am in you." My relationship to you is the relationship of the head with the body, you are not a stranger. "Abide in Me, and I in you", just like the branches are attached to the vine. Therefore, there is no farewell between you and Me because there is no separation at all. How beautiful is this comparison with all this love, passion and comfort at a time like this. Blessed are You Lord in all your great comfort.

Adding to that, His departure is for benefit and joy. He says to His disciples, " Let not your heart be troubled, neither let it be afraid. You have heard Me say to you, 'I am going away and coming back to you.' If you loved Me, you would rejoice because I said, 'I am going to the Father.'" (John 14: 27, 28). Yes, because at this stage the words "Made Himself of no reputation." (Philippians 2: 7) are ended. Now I return back to what is before these words: It is great, for if you love Me, you will rejoice because I am going.

My departure is beneficial for you in order to prepare a place for you "Let not your heart be troubled... In My Father's house are many mansions... I go to prepare a place for you, and if I go and prepare a place for you, I will come again and receive you to Myself; that where I am, there you may be also." (John 14:1-3). Yes, we will be all together.

Our presence will be over there not here. Let not your heart be troubled; this is the best, but here, Peace I leave with you, "My peace I leave with you, My peace I give to you." (John 14:27); this is a different type of peace, spiritual steady peace, not like the peace that the world gives. How can we have peace Lord and You are away from us?

This is the third benefit from My departure. I send to you the Holy Spirit. The Lord has elaborated here on this point specifically. He said to them that the Holy Spirit is the Comforter, the Helper, which will be their comfort. He repeated the words "The comforter and the Helper" several times. He said to them, "If I do not go away, the Helper will not come to you; but if I depart, I will send Him to you." (John 16:7). Also He says, "Nevertheless I tell you the truth. It is to your advantage that I go away." (John 16:7). "But the Helper, the Holy Spirit, whom the Father will send in My name, He will teach you all things, and bring to your remembrance all things that I said to you." (John 14:26).

When the Helper comes, whom I shall send to you from the Father, the Spirit of truth who proceeds from the Father, He will testify of Me. And you also will bear witness." (John 15:26). However, when He, the Spirit of truth, has come, He will guide you into all truth" (John 16:13). He comforted them by adding that the Comforter will abide with them forever, "And He dwells with you and will be in you." (John 14:16,17).

This reminds us of what Christ said before His Ascension, "But you shall receive power when the Holy Spirit has come upon you; and you shall be witnesses to Me." (Acts 1:8). Speaking of the Holy Spirit gave great comfort to the disciples. We note Jesus' farewell to His disciples was very honest. He wanted to comfort them according to the truth and reality, to strengthen their heart, but without hiding any of the truth. He was also honest with them in their mistakes and the problems they would face after His crucifixion.

This was beneficial for their faith and took away the element of surprise. He said to them, "Now I tell you before it comes, that when it does come to pass, you may believe that I am He." (John 13: 19, John 14:29). "But these things I have told you, that when the time comes, you may remember that I told you of them." (John 16:4).

He was very honest with them in telling them of their sins. He told them that the devil will fight you and will make you doubt this night. He said there will come a time when you will be scattered and will leave Me. He told Peter that he would deny Him and even that Judas would betray Him. He emphasised that by saying, "I shall give a piece of bread when I have dipped it." And Jesus convicting him, "What you do, do quickly." (John 13:21,26,27).

He was honest with them, telling them the troubles they would face. He said to them: "When they hate Me, they will hate you all," If the world hates you, you know that it hated Me before it hated you." "You are not of the world … therefore the world hates you." (John 15: 18-20).

He also told them more than that, "They will put you out of the synagogues; yes, the time is coming that whoever kills you will think that he offers God service." (John 16:2). Truly, honesty is a very important matter. Therefore , He said to them in these circumstances, "These things I have spoken to you, that you should not be made to stumble." (John 16:1).

The Lord Jesus Christ was very clear in this situation from the beginning, since starting with the narrow gate and carrying the cross. But He mixed speaking of the tribulations they would face with giving them comfort. He told them, "In the world you will have tribulation; but be of good cheer, I have overcome the world." (John 16:23) and as long as My strength is with you, you will overcome it.

We notice in this farewell that the Lord gave them many promises. Some are related to His appearances to them like, "I am coming to you." "After a little while, you will see Me." "I prepare a place for you... I come and take you to Me." There were more promises about sending the Holy Spirit to them, the work of the Holy Spirit inside them and staying with them till the end.

Also, there were more promises that were related to their needs. He said to them, "Whatever you ask the Father in My name He will give you." "Ask, and you will receive, that your joy may be full." (John 16:23, 24). "Whatever you ask in My name, that I will do... If you ask anything in My name, I will do it." (John 14:13,14).

Perhaps one of the promises which gave comfort to them was when the Lord told them, "Most assuredly, I say to you, he who believes in Me, the works that I do he will do also; and greater works than these he will do." (John 14:12).

In the farewell gathering, He gave them commandments. Regarding their relationship with one another, He gave them only one commandment: "This is My commandment, that you love one another." (John 15:12).

To what extent Lord was that love? He continues by saying, "To love each other as I have loved you." (John 15:12). Who can do this? That we love with the same measure as You have loved us, even to give Yourself for our sake. The love that He spoke of: "Having loved His own who were in the world, He loved them to the end." (John 13:1).

The Lord repeated the same commandment and in the same farewell gathering by saying: "A new commandment I give to you, that you love one another; as I have loved you, that you also love one another." (John 13:34). The Lord feels that this love, which is the same kind of love as His love, is a part of discipleship and He says: "By this all will know that you are My disciples, if you have love for one another." (John 13:35).

It is a great type of love that the Lord asks us to have. We love one another, as He loves us. How did He love us? The Lord deepens our understanding towards that love, He says: "As the Father loved Me, I also have loved you; abide in My love." (John 15:9). I speak out truthfully to You Lord, that this love is hard to understand and hard to fulfill. Here we reveal the commandment of love as it is given to us, in three points:

- The Father loves the Son (this love is unlimited without doubt).

- The Son loved us, with the same love (unlimited) in which the Father loved Him.

- It requires us to love one another in the same way.

This is a submission to You Lord. I repent but I still haven't reached and will definitely never reach that kind of love. Truly it is a new commandment. This is a new commandment in its understanding and in its level. No matter how much we have loved or given ourselves for others, we can never reach the level of the love of the Son to us or the love of the Father to the Son.

So we humble ourselves before You Lord and we ask You to pour the love from You, from the Holy Spirit, because it is impossible for human nature to love one another as You loved us! The Lord loved His disciples in their love towards Him and in their weakness. As He loved them they loved Him. He loved them in their fear, in their weakness, in their escape. He said to Peter, "You will deny Me three times." He didn't say that in anger or sorrow, but in love and kindness. He said to them: "I asked for you so your faith will not perish." He loves us in our weakness and our mistakes, to save us from our sins, "While we were still sinners, Christ died for us." (Romans 5: 8).

In the garden, when they left Him alone and slept, He accepted their weakness with sympathy. He referred the weakness in the body and said to them: "The spirit indeed is willing, but the flesh is weak." (Matthew 26:41). "Sleep now and have rest." The time will come for the body and the soul to be refreshed together. Now you are weak, this is true, " Behold, I send the Promise of My Father upon you; but tarry in the city of Jerusalem until you are endued with power from on high." (Luke 24:49). "This power you shall receive when the Holy Spirit has come upon you; and you shall be witnesses to Me." (Acts 1:8).

I don't despise weakness, but in My love I grant strength. This is My love to you. Then what is your love to Me? I will give you an example of this love: "I am the vine and you are the branches." (John 15:5). We love You Lord, as the branch loves the vine. There is no life in the branches without the vine and if it separates from it, it will dry up and whither away.

The Lord said to them in His farewell gathering: "Abide with Me in love. He who abides in Me, and I in him, bears much fruit; for without Me you can do nothing." (John 15:5). What about those who do not abide? The Lord said to them: "If anyone does not abide in Me, he is cast out as a branch and is withered; and they gather them and throw them into the fire, and they are burned." Therefore, "Abide in Me, and I in you. Abide in My love." (John 15:6,5,4). Perhaps the disciples were wondering:

How Lord can we love You, and abide in Your love? The Lord answered them in His farewell gathering: "If you keep My commandments, you will abide in My love, just as I have kept My Father's commandments and abide in His love." (John 15:10). Therefore, love is not just emotion, "Let us not love in word or in tongue, but in deed and in truth." (I John 3:18). Therefore our love for the Lord is evident in knowing and keeping His commandments.

Here the Lord reminds His disciples of His commandments and all that they heard from Him before, so they can do it. What happens if they forget what He taught them? He calmed them regarding this point too and said to them: "I am sending the Holy Spirit the Helper, He will teach you all things, and bring to your remembrance all things that I said to you." (John 14:26).

The Lord cares for His disciples and trusted them to preach the Gospel. He taught them with love so that they could endure and keep the faith which they would struggle in. The Lord spoke to His disciples about matters of faith. He included the doctrine of the Holy Trinity, He talked about the Father, the Holy Spirit and Himself. We remember what He said about the Holy Spirit, His work in them, His presence in them, His guidance.

He also talked in abundance about the Father: "I am going to My Father. I came forth from the Father and have come into the world.

Again, I leave the world and go to the Father." (John 16:28). "The Helper, the Holy Spirit, whom the Father will send in My name. The Helper comes, whom I shall send to you from the Father", "Proceeds from the Father, He will testify of Me." (John 15:26, John 14:26). These two verses very clearly speak of the Holy Spirit.

About the relationship between the Father and the Son, He said to them: "I am in the Father and the Father in Me." (John 14:10). He said to them: "I and My Father are one." (John 10:30). He repeated the same words in His prayers for their sake. He said to the Father: "Keep through Your name those whom You have given Me, that they may be one as We are." (John 17:11). He announced here that He and the Father are One. He repeated the same in His prayer saying: "That they may be one just as We are one. I in them, and You in Me; that they may be made perfect in one." (John 17:22-23), and He also said: "That they all may be one, as You, Father, are in Me, and I in You; that they also may be one in Us." (John 17:21). He presented this doctrine to them in His words and in His prayers.

He talked to them about the Father who loves them. He said: "He who loves Me, will be loved by My Father, and I will love him and manifest Myself to him." (John 14:21). "If anyone loves Me, he will keep My word; and My Father will love Him and We will come to him and make Our home with him." (John 14:23).

He wants them to be united with the Father, so He talks to them about the Father and His love for them. That is why He said: "The time is coming when I will no longer speak to you in figurative language, but I will tell you plainly about the Father." "Because the Father Himself loves you, because you have loved Me, and have believed that I came forth from God." (John 16:25,27).

In His prayers for their sake, He wanted them to know the Father. So He said: "Father... Glorify Your Son... this is eternal life, that they may know You, the only true God, and Jesus Christ whom You have sent." (John 17: 1-3). The disciples knew Jesus, but He wanted them to know the Father too, and all things are from the Father. He succeeded in this as He said in His prayers to the Father: "I have manifested Your name to the men whom You have given Me out of the world. Now they have known that all things which You have given Me are from You." (John 17:6,7).

When Jesus was going to the Father, He unites them with the Father. He said: "I am no longer in the world, but these are in the world... Holy Father, keep through Your name... I do not pray that You should take them out of the world, but that You should keep them from the evil one." "While I was with them in the world, I kept them in Your name... But now I come to You, keep them through Your name." (John 17:11-15).

Jesus prays to be with them always, He said: "Father, I desire that they also whom You gave Me may be with Me where I am." (John 17:24). These are extraordinary words which indicate that the love of Jesus Christ towards His disciples is very deep. The love of Jesus and His protection towards His disciples was very important. Because the devil's work will be to destroy them therefore, Jesus is working to keep them, guard them, care for them, strengthen and comfort them and prepare them for the tribulations which will follow. He did this through His love, His protection, His words and His prayers for their sake.

This love in His heart towards them encourages us. He reminds us that we are not alone, but He is with us all our days until the end of the age. He reminds us of His divine Helper, preparing His children before the tribulation, and also reminds us of the love of the Father and His protection. He reminds us that the prayer of Jesus includes us too: "I do not pray for these alone, but also for those who will believe in Me through their word." (John 17:20).

Blessed are You Lord in all Your love, protection and care. We ask

You to be with us, as You were with Your disciples and the apostolic Saints, with the same degree of love, protection and care. Truly Your prayers kept the disciples, even though they had some weakness, but their faith was still strong and firm, never hesitating.

The faith inside us reaches us, through their preaching. In the end Lord they brought many fruits just as You commanded them to. All of this is through the Holy blessings of Your sufferings Oh Lord, Your love to Your disciples, strengthening them on Covenant Thursday when You washed their feet, cleansed them, purified them, granted them Your Body and your Blood, sat with them to comfort and strengthen their faith.

To You is the Power, the Glory,

the Blessings and Honour.

Forever Amen.

GOOD FRIDAY

On Good Friday we see Jesus Christ in His great love and His great sacrifice. Love reaches its depth and its peak when You are raised on the Cross. Love is tested by pain, experienced in tribulation. If one loves, he offers and sacrifices himself for others. When he increases his love towards others, he increases in sacrifice until he offers everything. When He reaches the pinnacle of this love and sacrifice, He offers Himself up on the Cross and offers Himself for others. This is the lesson which we take from Good Friday, "For God so loved the world that He gave His only begotten Son, that whoever believes in Him should not perish but have everlasting life." (John 3:16).

The Lord demonstrates His love to the world in many different ways. He gave the world the grace of existence, gave knowledge and blessings. Also, He gave the world spiritual gifts. He offers the world His care and His love. But His love towards us reaches its peak when He offered and sacrificed Himself when He gave His life a ransom for many for the redemption of sins. He said to His disciples: "For even the Son of Man did not come to be served, but to serve, and to give His life a ransom for many." (Mark 10:45).

The first thing the Lord did was to offer Himself and He took the form of a slave (Philippians 2:7). He offered His glory and His greatness when He was incarnated for our sake, taking the form of a bondservant, and coming in the likeness of men. He offered His comfort too, and went around to do good and He had nowhere to lay His head (Matthew 8:20).

And in the end He laid Himself on the Cross for our sake. He showed His never ending love for our sake. And so the image of the crucified Jesus Christ is the greatest image in all of humanity as it shows the enormous sacrifice and deepest love.

The image of the Transfiguration on Mount Tabor and the image of Christ entering Jerusalem are rare pictures which are not found frequently, but the image of Christ crucified on the Cross is found everywhere. It is the most treasured image and leaves the deepest feelings inside every heart.

Mahatma Gandhi stood before this picture and cried saying: "It is a complete and great love, the full giver." "Greater love has no one than this, than to lay down one's life for his friends." (John 15:13).

So the Apostle St. Paul said: "But God forbid that I should boast except in the cross of our Lord Jesus Christ, by whom the world has been crucified to me, and I to the world." (Galatians 6:14). Every time we look at the image of Jesus on the Cross, we remember the great and amazing love. We remember our strong God, unlimited in His greatness and capacity. He laid Himself down, taking the form of a bondservant and sacrificing His life. He shed His blood because of His love to those who deserve death.

The finest expression written about this image of the crucified Jesus is, "He loved till He offered Himself." A sign was written about the Cross of Jesus, "Jesus of Nazareth, King of the Jews (INRI)", but a much more appropriate sign is one which reads, "The love and the sacrifice." "For God so loved the world that He gave His only begotten Son."

The lesson which we should take away from the crucifixion of our Lord is His love, His giving and His sacrifice. We don't love ourselves, but we love others, we love the Lord. We don't love our comfort, but we love to comfort others no matter how it affects us or our comfort. If you don't love and you don't sacrifice, then you didn't benefit from the lesson of the Cross of Jesus and you didn't use Him as a role model in your life.

The Cross of our Lord Jesus Christ teaches us to love until death. In our love to God we can do this, and in our love to people we can do that. "We don't love with words or by tongue, but by works and truth".

What is this true expression of love? It is the giving and the sacrifice until death. We like the love that leads us to the Cross, the love that reaches us to death for the sake of the one we love, or at least you are ready in your heart to go until death or offer yourself.

Consider repentance as an example of Love, how the Apostle reproaches us saying: "You have not yet resisted to bloodshed, striving against sin." (Hebrews 12:4). Do you want to love the Lord? Then you have to love Him till bloodshed. Resist the sins till bloodshed, rise to the Cross, and crucify your ego. "And those who are Christ's have crucified the flesh with its passions and desires." (Galatians 6 :4). Crucify the world inside your heart, so you crucify your ego so it disappears, and then the love reaches its peak, and now you can become proud of the Cross of Jesus Christ saying: "Whom the world has been crucified to me, and I to the world." (Galatians 6:14).

We learn that the Cross of Jesus Christ is to love and to sacrifice, and we can't do that unless we crucify ourselves. Before our Lord Jesus sacrificed Himself, He was incarnated for our sake, taking the form of a bondservant. So, if you want to love and you want to give, then you have to put away all the love you have towards yourself and feelings for yourself, that means to humble yourself, taking the form of a slave and then you can sacrifice.

Sacrifice is a true expression for love. Abraham, father of all fathers, showed his love towards God by first leaving his family, his tribe and his country for the sake of God and he became a stranger living in tents. Of all the things which Abraham has done, the greatest love was when he sacrificed his only son on the altar. He carried the wood of the burnt offering and he took the fire in his hand and the knife to offer the burnt offering to God.

There are some obstacles which prevent one from sacrificing. For example, the love of rest, the love of dignity and the love of the self. The true love is one that does not care about his own rest, but rather the person who loves.

Jacob the father of all fathers, when he loved Rachel, he offered himself. He worked twenty years for her; working in the sun during the day and in the cold during the nights. All these years were only like a few days in his eyes, because of his love towards her." (Genesis 31:40, 29:20).

Love can do miracles. Love bears all things, endures all things. If you can't sacrifice, then you love yourself and you don't love others. If the obstacle is your dignity, then you love dignity more. Also the obstacle can be the love of life or the love of freedom.

When Daniel loved the Lord, he didn't mind to be thrown in the den of the hungry lions. He wasn't afraid and he didn't see that his life was more important than the love. The love in Daniel's heart was stronger than the fear and worth much more than life itself. Just like the three youth (Daniel's friend) in their love, they didn't mind to be thrown in the fire, they didn't fear the fire nor death nor life for God's sake.

St. Paul the Apostle said when he was expressing his love to Jesus: "I also count all things loss for the excellence of the knowledge of Christ Jesus my Lord." (Philippians 3:8). "But what things were gains to me, these I have counted loss for Christ and count them as rubbish that I may gain Christ." (Philippians 3:7).Therefore, we find a life of sacrifice is agreeable and there are no regrets but with all enthusiasm is counted as rubbish and loss.

The Cross of Jesus Christ teaches us to offer ourselves in love. These offerings, however, may require some training. The spiritual person may be trained to sacrifice first by giving from his money, his obsession, before he can sacrifice himself. Truly, if one can not sacrifice his belongings, how can he sacrifice himself?

If you can't give your money to your Lord, your tithe and your first of every thing, how will you give him your life? How can you shed your blood for His sake? How? If you are not able to give one day of the week, how can you give Him your entire life?

During the era of the Martyrs, the Church trained her children to be able to die and not fear death. The Church trained her children to leave material belongings, leave home and family. "The time is short, so that from now on even those who have wives should be as though they had none, those who weep as though they did not weep, those who rejoice as though they did not rejoice, those who buy as though they did not possess, and those who use this world as not misusing it. For the form of this world is passing away" (I Corinthians 7:29-31)

For all to believe that "the world is passing away". The Church teaches her children in every Liturgy: "Do not love the world or the things in the world... the world is passing away, and the lust of it" (I John 2:15,17). Whoever loses interest in life and all that is in the world can easily offer himself and sacrifice his life for the sake of the Lord. You can say then "my kingdom is not from this world", wanting eagerly to be a child of Jesus in eternal life. Under those circumstances one can offer himself for the sake of his brothers and sisters and for the sake of Christ.

If one does not even want to offer just a bit, how can he offer much? And how can he sacrifice his life? How can he resemble Jesus in sacrifice. He refuses glory, refuses rest, no proper home, no money or wages, but offers His blood for the life of the whole world, in order for us to live by His death, and to live with His love to us.

The Lord Jesus Christ always offered before He died on the Cross. His love was everywhere, surrounding the people, giving them kindness, love and mercy. He gave healing, comfort and food. He called for the captives and the prisoners to be freed, worked continuously in order to give rest to all, but all of that was not enough. He was waiting for this love to give sacrifice, to rise on the Cross and shed blood on all humanity. The Lord Jesus Christ walked to Golgotha to offer Himself as a burnt love offering. He showed His love by His incarnation and His great sacrifice of love.

Satan was surprised with all this love. He tried to resist all this with his strength. He summoned all his powers and trickery to prevent the love of Christ reaching the Cross. It requires a great water to surround this huge, fiery love. This great water was in the form of mockery, challenging and aggravating insults using the horrible words, "If You are the Son of God, come down from the cross" and "He saved many but Himself He is unable to save."

The love of the Lord towards us was even more powerful than these challenging words.

The Lord defeated the war, He overcame all the insults and mockery to give us victory over death. He put in front of Him, His purpose for coming, which was to die in order to give us life. And so His love was raised to its peak on the Cross. In suffering and agony, He overcame every obstacle until, He reached the top where redemption was, which is crowned by great glory.

The Cross became a symbol of love for redemption and giving. On the Cross the Lord gave to the whole world full redemption and the remission of sins. Also on the Cross, He gave a promise to the thief on the right to be in Paradise with Him. He gave forgiveness to those who put Him on the Cross, if they repented. On the Cross, He gave John the Beloved a spiritual mother, St. Mary the Virgin and He gave the Virgin Mary a son who is John the Beloved.

Although Jesus was suffering on the Cross, He did not focus on His pain and sufferings or on Himself, but on the salvation of the whole of humanity and offering the price of the divine judge, the Father. Our eyes are focused on the Cross and His gift of giving to us. The Cross, which gives remission, salvation, life and hope until the joyful eternity. The Cross gives a great picture of the great sacrifice and great giving, with unlimited offering of yourself for others.

The Cross gives us the picture of giving in the midst of great suffering and the last drop of bloodshed to show His great love. And in return the world did not offer. The best offering can be the profound tears which flow from a loving heart. This has a great meaning of love.

Let us ask the Lord to bless us, to train us for that love and sacrifice, to give more than to take. Let us grow and give our souls for His sake for, "To You is the Power, the Glory, the Blessings and the Honour, forever. Amen."

THE FATHER PREPARED THE BURNT OFFERINGS

On this day the Holy Church celebrates the presentation of Jesus Christ, a sacrifice for our sake. Here we want to explain the meaning of the burnt offerings with some detail.

Since the Lord announced salvation to Adam by saying that the woman's seed will bruise the serpent's head (Genesis 3:15), He taught him how to offer sacrifices and to pass it on to his descendants. Adam learnt his first lesson, which is redemption. When Adam sinned he knew he was naked. The fig leaves were not enough to cover him so the Lord made a tunic of skin and clothed him. This skin was an offering to cover him. He knew that nakedness came with sin and the sacrifice was to be covered from sin. This was the first lesson, furthermore the offerings were from a clean animal. A clean soul doesn't sin, to die on behalf of human soul who sinned.

We read that the offerings of the Righteous Abel (Genesis 4) were offered "from his first born of his flock and of their fat". Where did Abel know that he should offer a burnt offering to the Lord? Perhaps he knew this from tradition which was handed down from his father Adam who received it from the Lord.

This tradition of offerings was passed down through the generations as happened with our father Noah (Genesis 8) from clean animal. The same lesson is learnt here, "A clean soul died for the sake of a sinful soul." This is the second lesson.

Also we read about the offerings made by the Righteous Job and his children: "It may be that my sons have sinned and cursed God in their hearts." (Job 1:5). Thus, Job did sacrifice regularly for the sake of the forgiveness of his children's sins. From the blood which is shed from these offerings and burnt offerings we get the third lesson, which is: "The wages of sin is death." (Romans 6:23) for the sinner or a soul on its behalf.

Moses the prophet explained in detail the offerings and the sacrifices for sin. Each one of them resembles Jesus Christ from a different point of view. Let us take a look and get an idea of each so that we know what our Lord offered for us on this day, the great day of redemption.

We understand that man has sinned and his sin was against God Himself. It is enough that it is disobedience and rebellion to God and it is separation from God and not loving Him. The sin of mankind had two results: First, it hurt God and second it was destructive. Jesus Christ came to correct these two things.

- Reconcile God the Father, bear his anger and pay the ransom of sin.

- To free mankind by dying on their behalf, whose punishment was death.

Pleasing God's heart symbolises the burnt offerings. That is why it is at the beginning of all sacrifices. Chapter 1 of Leviticus repeats this three times, "Offering is a burnt sacrifice, an offering made by fire, a sweet aroma to the Lord." (Leviticus 1:9,13,17).

Because it was especially for the Lord Himself, no one else could eat from it, no priest, no Levi, not the person who offered it, not even their friends, but it could only be eaten by the fire that was on the altar. This indicates the divine judge, the fire of the altar shall be kept burning on it until it turns into ashes. Then the priest takes up the ashes of the burnt offering, which the fire has consumed on the altar, and he carries the ashes outside the camp to a clean place (Leviticus 6:8-12). This indicates that God's right is met through reconciliation and was the ransom of sin. He was pleased from the fire consumed on the burnt offering until the end.

This pleases the heart of God, but what about man's salvation? The sin burnt offering is the offering that carries mans sin and has died so that man could be saved. Just like the trespass offering. Therefore there are two burnt offerings: one is for intentional sin and the other for unintentional sin which is later discovered (Leviticus 4,5). The two burnt offerings: the sin and the trespass burnt offerings must be pure and clean without fault.

The burnt offerings did not sin, but they carried sin. The person who carries the offering is the one who sinned, but when he lays his hands on the head of the offering, then the sin passes to the offering which dies on his behalf (Leviticus 4:4,15,24,29,33).

The Bible says this offering is most holy. "In the place where the burnt offering is killed, the sin offering shall be killed before the Lord. It is most holy. In a holy place it shall be eaten, in the court of the tabernacle of meeting. Everyone who touches its flesh must be holy. It is most holy." (Leviticus 6:24-29). Likewise this is the law of the trespass offering (Leviticus 7:1,2, 6) "it is most holy".

All these are symbols in the Old Testament. So what happened to Jesus Christ, who is the symbol of these sacrifices and offerings? On Good Friday, God the Father prepared the burnt offering on the Mount of Golgotha. Jesus Christ approaches by carrying the wood of the burnt offering. He raises Himself on the altar. No one compelled

Him to, but He Himself said: "I lay down My life for the sheep. No one takes it from Me. But I lay it down of Myself. I have power to lay it down, and I have power to take it again." (John 10:15-18).

The Lord Jesus Christ raises Himself on the altar of burnt offerings and the fire burnt the offering. The fire surrounded the burnt offering. Fire from everywhere. Fire from the different generations. It is all related to the sin of the people, from everywhere, it is the fire of the divine judgment on all the sins. The fire was alive for a full three hours, from the sixth hour through to the ninth hour.

The fire was consuming the burnt offering. The smoke went up and it pleased the Father to smell the sweet aroma. His hand remained on the burnt offering as it had on Isaac. Then the burnt offering cried out with a loud voice, "My God, My God, why have You forsaken Me?"

The Father did not leave the burnt offering for a single moment or a twinkle of an eye, but He left the fire of the divine judgment to burn until the end to please the Father and to remit every sin, every trespass and every unintentional sin. For everyone, in every place and for all generations.

Before the burnt offering was completely converted to ashes, the Lord said: "It is finished." "O Father, I have finished the work which You have given Me to do." (John 17:4). When the soul of Jesus Christ was laid in the hands of the Father, the Father took the ashes of the offering, according to the Law, and put it in a holy place in Paradise first, then on the right hand of the Father.

At the same time, on the same mountain, the mount of Golgotha, Jesus Christ offered Himself as a burnt offering for sin. To carry the sins of the whole world, as John the Baptist said, "Behold! The Lamb of God who takes away the sin of the world!" (John 1:29). And as St. John the Beloved said, "And He Himself is the propitiation for our sins, and not for ours only, but also for the whole world." (1 John 2:2).

Whether it be the new sins at the time of the crucifixion, or the old sins since Adam or the sins that will take place in the future till the end of age. Therefore, all have hope, by putting their hands on the head of the burnt offering and accept the offering on their behalf for the remission of sins.

The blood of the burnt offering is sprinkled across the whole earth. "He placed cherubim at the east of the garden of Eden, and a flaming sword which turned every way, to guard the way to the tree of life." (Genesis 3:24). This angel saw the blood, flowing from the burnt offering to atone for all sins and thus the angel said, "When I see the blood, I will pass over you." (Exodus 12:13).

The road to the Tree of Life is open to whoever is able to overcome. So, as the Lord said to the Church of Ephesus, "He who has an ear, let him hear what the Spirit says to the churches. To him who overcomes, I will give to eat from the tree of life, which is in the midst of the Paradise of God." (Revelation 2:7).

But the Holy Church stands in front of the burnt offering and the sin offering, to sing praises everyday during the Holy Pascha saying: Christ our Saviour came and suffered for us, that He may save us through His suffering. Let us glorify and exalt His Name according to His great mercy."

As the people mock the Crucified, thinking of Him as weak, the Church continues chanting the well known Holy Week praise, "To You is the Power, the Glory, the Blessing and the Honour, Emmanuel our God and our King."

When the people mocked the Crucified saying to Him: "If You are the Son of God, come down from the cross and save Yourself", the whole Church chants the hymn "Omnogenees": "You the only Son and the word of God the immortal and the everlasting." When "He was numbered with the transgressors" on the Cross, the Church continues, during the sixth and the ninth hour, singing the long hymn

"Agios" which means, "Holy... Holy... Holy..." He carried the sins of the whole world. The Church praises our Lord in the Trisagion hymn. The Church knows that His holiness is unlimited. He died on the Cross for us because He loves us.

It must be an offering without blemish, to carry the sins of all people. It must be a Man without sin, and if He dies, He will die on behalf of the sins of others, so He can redeem them. So the person who dies must be unlimited, to offer an unlimited redemption, enough for all the sins, for all people, throughout all generations.

PETER'S DENIAL, THE WEAKNESS OF HUMAN NATURE

The readings of Friday Eve of the Holy Pascha clarify an important truth: The Lord created us knowing the weakness of human nature. Although this human nature doesn't know itself and most of the time can be very arrogant and overly confident.

The Lord knows everyone's weaknesses. He knows that His courageous, zealous disciple, Peter, could deny Him three times in just a short time, in front of the high priest's servant girl and not the high priest himself, who has a higher status. And so the human nature is before the Lord. Our Lord warned Peter saying: "Indeed, Satan has asked for you, that he may sift you as wheat, but I have prayed for you, that your faith should not fail." (Luke 22: 31,32). But Peter, who was very confident in himself, not thinking of his weakness said: "Lord, I am ready to go with You, both to prison and to death." (Luke 22:33).

I thought that perhaps our teacher St. Peter would have a different answer! Forgive me my brethren, I am not criticising the Saint's actions and I am not deserving even of the dust that St. Peter walked on, it is just my opinion. When the Lord said: "Indeed, Satan has asked for you, that he may sift you as wheat" and in the result of that: "All of you will be made to stumble because of Me this night, for it is written: 'I will strike the Shepherd, And the sheep will be scattered.'" (Mark 14:27; Matthew 26:31). When the Lord said: "All of you will be made to stumble" and He didn't exclude Peter. Then St. Peter should be humble and ask for help.

He should have knelt at the feet of Jesus, pleading: "Lord help my weakness, give me grace to overcome my weakness, so that I don't deny You." He could say it in humility, "I am sure that if Your grace leaves me, perhaps I will deny You seven times and not just three in spite of my love towards You." "For without Me you can do nothing." (John 15:5). I am weak if I conduct myself with my own strength. But with You I can do everything, "I can do all things through Christ who strengthens me." (Philippians 4:13).

Peter didn't do this! He was so confident in himself, He was sure of his love towards the Lord and his capacity to withstand. Also, he was confident that he could endure more than the rest of the disciples!! He said, debating with the Lord: "Even if all are made to stumble, yet I will not be." (Mark 14:29; Matthew 26:33).

It is even more puzzling when the Lord looked at him intensely and said: "Assuredly, I say to you that today, even this night, before the rooster crows twice, you will deny Me three times." And Peter said all the more vehemently, "If I have to die with You, I will not deny You!" "And they all said likewise." (Mark 14:30,31; Matthew 26:34,35).

How easy it is for the soul which is ignorant of her true nature, to say to the Lord: "I will lay down my life for Your sake." (John 13:37). To say it so confidently and the actions that follows are in complete contrast to what was said! This soul, which is overly confident in themself needs to appreciate St. Paul's words: "For what I am doing, I do not understand. For what I will to do, that I do not practice; but what I hate, that I do. But now, it is no longer I who do it, but sin that dwells in me." (Romans 7:15,17).

We can offer some advice here: This person needs to understand the weakness of human nature and the power and tricks of the devil. We need always place our spiritual struggle before us, and know that Satan, our enemy: "walks about like a roaring lion, seeking whom he may devour." (I Peter 5:8). It is said that when Satan becomes free from his shackles, he will decieve the nations "And unless those days were shortened, no flesh would be saved; but for the elect's sake those days will be shortened." (Matthew 24:22). Because Satan has power, trickery and deception, he can even change his appearance: "And no wonder! For Satan himself transforms himself into an angel of light." (I Corinthians 11: 14).

Then our first advice, is to be humble, and to be broken from inside. We are meek and humble on the inside by the power and the strength of God's hands. Don't think that you have power over sin, and over the wars of the devil: "For she has cast down many wounded, and all who were slain by her were strong men." (Proverbs 7: 26). With meekness then, we realise that we can at any time fall into sin.

In addition to humility, we need to pray continuously. So that the heart always says: "Lord, give me grace, Lord, give me strength, protect me, I am weaker than sin, hold me to be saved." With humility and prayer we are vigilant. There are some sins we don't notice, we think they are only for the inexperienced! We have trained ourselves in a more spiritual life, lived always in Church, always practicing God's gift of grace. We do not fall into these sins easily and so we don't watch! And because we don't watch, we fall into the sins of the inexperienced!

Perhaps St. Peter thought the same, that he would never deny! Peter in whom the Lord said: "Blessed are you, Simon Bar-Jonah, for flesh and blood has not revealed this to you, but My Father who is in heaven." (Matthew 16:17,19). Peter in whom the Lord gave the keys to heaven and the power to bind or to loose: "Assuredly, I say to you, whatever you bind on earth will be bound in heaven, and whatever you loose on earth will be loosed in heaven." (Matthew 18:18). Peter who is one of the pillars of the Church and St. Paul said of him: "Who seemed to be pillars." (Galatians 2:9).

Peter, the most courageous of all the disciples who followed the Lord, who was zealous, who within seconds stretched out his hand and drew his sword striking the servant of the high priest and cutting off his ear, was the same person who denied Jesus. Don't you think this is impossible and unheard of for him? If Peter himself denied Jesus shouldn't we be humble? Shouldn't we say: "We are not any stronger than others who fell and we should be watchful.

If the Lord holds us tight and helps us in some instances and we don't fall, it is not due to our own strength, our steadfastness and our resistance to falling. Then we say with David in the Psalms: "If it had not been the Lord who was on our side... Then they would have swallowed us alive, Blessed be the Lord, Who has not given us as prey to their teeth." (Psalm 124).

Then let us maintain humility, prayer and vigilance. We shouldn't divide sin into big sins, which require lots of prayer and attention and other sins which don't require much strength, but we fall by them. The Lord, who knows our weak nature, when we say: "If I have to I will die with You", it is just superficial courage and a soft heart. But the truth of the matter is the will is not on the same level as courage.

Yes, you have the courage and the way, but the determination doesn't support it. The heart may be affected if the tribulation was difficult, where your weakness might show. Notice that the Lord said to Peter: "But I have prayed for you, that your faith should not fail." (Luke 22:32). Is it to that degree Lord that our faith would "fail"? Instead, the Lord could have said: "So your faith does not weaken , or your faith will not waiver. But "fail" is a very harsh and tough word, especially since He said it to a strong, Great Apostle like Peter. Yes, it was a harsh word, but it was the truth. Peter, your denial was the easiest of all and it was because He prayed for you! Without prayer, especially for you, it is possible that your faith will fail.

Lord, I am under Your feet. I don't say that I am strong. I am the weakest of the weak. I am too weak to fight even the smallest of all and I am not able to fight anyone. Hold me tight to be saved. If one day I manage to defeat sin then I will definitely say, "The right hand of the Lord does valiantly. The right hand of the Lord is exalted." (Psalm 118: 15). Without the Lord with us, they could have swallowed us and yet we are still alive.

The humble soul is the one who passes through tribulations in peace. But the arrogant soul, will hear the words of the Bible: "Pride goes before destruction and a haughty spirit before a fall." (Proverbs 16:18). The power of God protects us and not our strength. It protects the humble. Therefore the Lord said to the Father: "While I was with them in the world, I kept them in Your name. Those whom You gave Me I have kept; and none of them is lost." (John 17:12).

Yes, You kept them, not because of their strength, their caution, their wisdom, their will, their determination or their love for You (Peter loved You too), but because You kept them. Keep us Lord as You kept them. Gives us the power as You gave them: "Now thanks be to God who always leads us in triumph in Christ." (2 Corinthians 2:14). When You held Peter's hand, he was able to walk on water with You, but with his own power he fell. He tried, but he fell in the water.

If you walked on water my brethren and you didn't fall, know very well that the Lord was holding your hands very tightly. So keep these Hands with you, and watch and do not depend on yourself so you don't fall. Those who depend on their strength and their power (like Peter) need to transform these feelings into prayer.

Peter depended on his strength from two sides; his personality and his comparison. Peter depended on himself by his pride: "I put myself for your sake." He compared himself to others saying: "Even if all are made to stumble, yet I will not be." (Mark 14:29). He believes himself to be more senior than the others, more loving than them and stronger than them. But humility teaches us to seek others first before ourselves.

The Holy Spirit allowed only the recording of Peter's denial in the Gospels. The Lord said: "All of you will stumble" and: "The sheep will be scattered." He said that Satan will: "Sift you as wheat." Therefore, it is not only Peter's trial, but it is for all. The Bible only recorded Peter's fall because he boasted over the rest. Also, he believed that he loved the Lord more than the rest. Perhaps because of this our Lord reproached him after the Resurrection saying: "Simon, son of Jonah, do you love Me more than these? (John 21: 15). Pay particular attention here, our Lord called Peter by his old name, Simon son of Jonah, and not Peter (the name he received by Christ's blessing, Matthew 16:18). Here, he returned to the old man, a fisherman and not Simon Peter (John 21:3). He is not Peter the rock because he stumbled before the servant.

But the Lord returned him back to the apostolic position by saying: "Tend My sheep... feed My lambs." He didn't give account to what he had done: "But whoever denies Me before men, him I will also deny before My Father who is in heaven." (Matthew 10: 33).

The Lord allowed Peter's denial to be recorded in the Bible, so that later he does not boast over the rest of the disciples, because he said: "If the others stumble, I will never." When the Lord reproached Peter saying: "Do you love Me more than these," he replied: "You know Lord that I love You" and he didn't say "more than these". This was a lesson. Because of this lesson, when St. Peter's time of Martyrdom came he asked to be crucified upside down, because his heart came first before thinking.

As if he is saying to the Lord: "I am very embarrassed from You and my brothers, ashamed of my past confidence and strength. I thought that I was better than my friends and this caused me to say: "If all doubt, I will never." Now my head is inverted before You and the others and I say I am not worthy.

Likewise, when the Lord healed the paralysed man in front of the Beautiful Gate, by the hand of St. Peter, and the crowds surrounded him; he said to them together with St. John the beloved: "Men of Israel, why do you marvel at this? Or why look so intently at us, as though by our own power or godliness we had made this man walk?" So he diverted their eyes towards the Lord Jesus and said: "And His name, through faith in His name, has made this man strong." (Acts 3: 12-16).

Yes, not with our power nor with our strength, I tried that before! When Peter healed the paralysed man, he wasn't just trying to be humble, but he was convinced with all his heart that this power came from our Lord Jesus and not from himself. I tried my own strength and power before and I didn't benefit at all. There is no strength other than the Lords: "The Lord is my strength and song, and He has become my salvation." (Psalm 118:14). Peter used his strength and his power when the Lord Jesus Christ was struggling for our sake in the Garden of Gethsemane.

On that night there were two other pillars of the Church with Peter; James and John. The three of them couldn't stay awake with the Lord even one hour, although He asked them three times. "He found them asleep again, for their eyes were heavy." (Mark 14:40).

St Peter, one of the pillars of the Church, couldn't stay awake with the Lord for one hour in such a difficult time, when He was struggling for our sake and His sweat became like great drops of blood falling down to the ground. He reproached Peter saying: "Simon, are you sleeping? Could you not watch one hour?" (Mark 14:37).

Where is "our strength and our power" then? And where is the talk of "The rock?" If the eyes of these pillars were heavy sleeping, shouldn't we then be humbled? Shouldn't we then cry out to the Lord and say: "You know our weak nature." He definitely knows, without a doubt, as David said in the Psalms: "For He knows our frame; He remembers that we are dust." (Psalm 103:14).

As He knows our weakness, He doesn't reproach us too much, or blame us too much. Who should be reproached or blamed? Dust or ashes? David said: "Do not enter into judgment with Your servant, for in Your sight no one living is righteous." (Psalm 143:2). He also said: "If You, Lord, should mark iniquities, O Lord, who could stand?" (Psalm 130: 3). "Yes, no one can stand, all we like sheep have gone astray; we have turned, every one, to his own way; and the Lord has laid on Him the iniquity of us all." (Isaiah 53: 6).

Pity that person who tries to justify himself saying: "I... I..." We all are sinners so there is no point in saying "I". Believe me; no one can be saved if the Lord were to judge us all. It is the grace of God which helps us so that "your faith should not fail."

The Lord Jesus Christ was strengthening, encouraging, protecting His disciples, giving them grace and keeping them from stumbling. Therefore, in His preaching, He told them, because He knows their weakness: Don't pass through to the gentiles, and do not enter the country of the Samarians. Why? Because they will reject you and you may not be able to handle the rejection. You can't accept rejection; you are not at this level yet in the difficulty and hardship of the service. Instead, go now to the stray sheep of Israel, perhaps their service is easier.

The Lord tested them and they couldn't stand. He went to a village of the Samaritans, they didn't receive Him, they closed their door in His face. His disciples were angry and said: "Do You want us to command fire to come down from heaven and consume them?" (Luke 9:54).

Is your personal dignity at this level, that you can't even tolerate doors being closed in your faces! Don't you know that the Son of Man came to save the world and to protect everyone from destruction?

The unusual thing here is that one of these disciples was John the

Beloved, who was filled with love or he became filled with love after he accompanied the Lord. He and his brother were called Sons of Thunder. The Lord knows that their nature is weak and made of dust (Psalm 103).

During Holy Week the Lord dealt with dust, the dust in which when water was mixed with it became mud. He was patient with His enemies and all the bad friends.

He bore the evil, injustice and the weakness of the righteous. He bore the plots of the enemies and with the fear and denial of friends. He bore all of us. He came not to punish us for our mistakes, but to save us, and His name shall be called Jesus. (Matthew 1:21).

When He found His disciples weak and full of fear, He did not reproach them, but said to them: "But you shall receive power when the Holy Spirit has come upon you; and you shall be witnesses to Me." (Acts 1:8). Then, but not now, what I say now is, sleep and rest (Mark 14:41).

Now, you are leaving in fear, I don't blame you for your fear. But you will receive power from the Holy Spirit, and you will be changed. At that time you will no longer be afraid of the Jewish leaders, but you will say: "We ought to obey God rather than men." (Acts 5: 29). When you receive the Holy Spirit, you won't be afraid and hide in the Upper Room and you won't deny Me, but you will be witnesses to Me in Jerusalem, in Judea and Samaria and to the ends of the earth. It will not be you speaking, but your Father and you will stand before kings and leaders for My name's sake.

With the power that you will receive from the Holy Spirit, you will be able to preach and teach the entire world. I will reward you on the work of this power which is not from you, but you will be a good vessel to carry it.

See and understand well what I teach you. I will forgive your weakness and I will reward you in all the power that you will have upon receiving the Holy Spirit. I will forgive you of your present shortcomings and I will not remember them. But the righteousness that you will receive from the Holy Spirit, it will remain until the end. I will record it in the Book of Life. I will never forget your labour of love, even a cool cup of water that you give to the poor in My name.

That is how the Lord Jesus Christ spent the week, struggling by Himself. He carried the evil injustice, and the weakness of the righteous. Stood firm with friends, family and His disciples, bore their denial, fear and fleeing, bore all of this and did not leave them. Here Lord we ask You, after You saw all their weakness. Although they were, You will serve them in Your Kingdom. You tried them and found the denial, the doubtful, the fearful and the weak. Do they deserve to serve You after all of this? Yes, they are My children, their sins I have forgotten and forgiven. And their weakness I will strengthen. I will clean them, make them holy and write their names in the Book of Life. O Lord, You are so gentle, there is no God like You .

LIGHT IN THE DARKNESS

-

PLACE OF DARKNESS

On this Day, Good Friday, we stand and meditate quietly to see a picture which combines two things, The love of God and His great salvation on one side, and the ungratefulness of mankind and their betrayal of the Lord on the other side.

In His great love, meekness and giving, we see the Lord on this day, offering an unusual redemption to all of mankind; a complete forgiveness of sins, even to those who crucified Him and He made promises to the thief on the right.

In contrast to that love is the ultimate unimaginable cruelty and ugly betrayal. Although there was such joy in heaven, because of the great salvation which the Lord offered to humanity, at the same time there was darkness on the whole earth!

Everything was truly dark, idols dominated the whole world. What about the Jews who were committed to the prophesies of God, His promises and His covenants? (Romans 3:2). What about the Holy city which worshiped God? What about the Holy temple in which the sacrifices were offered and the prayers of praise, psalms and hymns? What about the people in which its members boast that they are sons of Abraham "to whom pertain the adoption, the glory, the covenants, the giving of the law, the service of God, and the promises; of whom are the fathers and from whom, according to the flesh, Christ came." (Romans 9:4,5).

Unfortunately, Jerusalem, during this entire week, was the centre of betrayal and intrigue. The Jewish Leaders and the priests planned the most dreadful crime in the whole of history. They planned to kill the great Redeemer who came to save them! They searched for charges to place on the Holy One, who is without sin and the whole world had never seen anyone like Him before.

They screamed against the great, soft heart, who loved everyone. He was good to all and they offered all their power to get rid of the Good Shepherd who gathered all people around Him. Even the plots, the false witnesses, the envy and the cruelty; all of this was found in the Jewish priesthood during this week. "Now the chief priests, the elders, and all the council sought false testimony against Jesus to put Him to death, but found none. Even though many false witnesses came forward, they found none." (Matthew 26:60).

At this particular time, He did not find joy in Jerusalem, the holy city, the city of the great King. He cried and said: "O Jerusalem, Jerusalem, the one who kills the prophets and stones those who are sent to her! How often I wanted to gather your children together, as a hen gathers her chicks under her wings, but you were not willing! See!

Your house is left to you desolate." (Matthew 23:37,38). Yes, the holy temple at that time was a centre of planning, plotting and crime and it had lost its holiness. The Lord wanted for the Holy temple to be seen on Palm Sunday, but the Jewish leaders didn't.

The plotting started on Sunday and humanity showed its ugliness. The envy started in their harden hearts and they said: "You see that you are accomplishing nothing. Look, the world has gone after Him!" (John 12:19).

One of the twelve disciples was tempted, the Lord Jesus' disciple! He was a well known one who had the money box with him. He was one of those who the Lord chose to be His followers! He was a traitor who sold his Master and Teacher for thirty pieces of silver. This is the price of a slave. He couldn't sit with Him at the table and eat from the same plate. The Bible said: "Who ate my bread, Has lifted up his heel against me." (Psalm 41: 9). If the enemies of the Lord stand against Him this is normal and not a surprise; but dishonesty from one of the group, that was outrageous.

Worst of all is to betray Him with a kiss. So, in remembrance of the kiss of Judas, the Church prevents any form of greeting starting from the eve of Wednesday (Tuesday night) until the end of Holy Week. It is for this reason (the plot of Judas), the Church fasts every Wednesday.

It is absurd what humanity brings to us this week, all related to the One who loved and gave Himself for her sake! An example of this is what the Jews did after claiming Christ as their King on Palm Sunday. They said He was the one who would save them from Caesar and they were focused on the destruction of the Roman Empire, but they went back on their claim and sided with Caesar against Jesus, saying He was against Caesar (Luke 23:2). They ran to Pilate the Roman to save them from Jesus and to have Him killed!

Surprisingly, Pilate said to them: "Shall I crucify your King?" They answered him saying: "We have no king, but Caesar!" (John 19:15). How much they lied and were disgraced in order to get rid of Jesus their Saviour, whom they called only a few days earlier their King!! How strange was their rejection and to be written on His cross, "King of the Jews" (John 19:21). Now they defend Caesar, who used to humiliate them and held on to him, who mixed their blood with their sacrifices." (Luke 13:1).

Judas was not the only one who betrayed Jesus in the crucifixion story. Didn't these also betray Him, who cried out saying: "Crucify Him, Crucify Him, His blood be on us and on our children." (Matthew 27:25). These are those who were healed by Jesus, who had demons cast out by Jesus, who were fed by Jesus when they were hungry. He performed so many miracles as had never been seen before. And in the end, they forgot all that He did and freed a thief and murderer, Barabbas, in His place! (Matthew 27:20).

They didn't just stop at accusations and complaints, but they threw on Him many other cruel things: they mocked Him, they treated Him with contempt, they exposed Him, they spat on Him, they beat Him and struck Him and said: "Prophecy to us, Christ! Who is the one who struck You?" (Matthew 26:68).

All of these things against Jesus the meek, the gentle, who the Bible said about Him: "He will not quarrel nor cry out, nor will anyone hear His voice in the streets. A bruised reed He will not break, And smoking flax He will not quench." (Matthew 12: 19, 20; Isaiah 42:3).

Truly, how cruel was humanity on Good Friday. These horrible actions were done by His enemies, but what about His disciples? It is true when He said: "Indeed the hour is coming yes, has now come, that you will be scattered, each to his own, and will leave Me alone."(John 16:32). Who would have thought that all eleven disciples would leave Him! But this is what happened in the Garden of Gethsemane, during His hardest and most difficult time, for our sake. The great pillars of

His disciples, the great three, Peter, James and John, these were the ones who Jesus told: "My soul is exceedingly sorrowful, even to death. Stay here and watch with Me." (Matthew 26: 38). They slept and left Him alone, although earlier He reproached them several times saying: "Could you not watch with Me one hour", even during this difficult hour, "Their eyes were heavy." (Matthew 26:43).

We read a very sad verse in the Bible when He was arrested: "Then all the disciples forsook Him and fled." (Matthew 26: 56). Although this was humanities position, He did not get upset because His disciples left Him and fled, but He wanted them to leave for their safety so that they were not harmed because of Him. Let the enemies do as they like as long as His disciples were safe. So He said to the soldiers who came to arrest Him: "I am He. Therefore, if you seek Me, let these go their way. That the saying might be fulfilled which He spoke, 'Of those whom You gave Me I have lost none'". (John 18: 8,9).

When Jesus stood for His trial, no one stood beside Him. No one defended Him, He was the one who protected the evil sinners. No one was courageous to say a word of truth. No one brave enough to stand up against these false witnesses. Jesus Christ accepted all these injustices. He didn't defend Himself. Isaiah prophesised about Him: "I have trodden the winepress alone, and from the peoples no one was with Me." (Isaiah 63:3).

It was painful that His disciples not only just left Him alone, but He said about them: "All of you will be made to stumble because of Me this night." (Mark 14: 27). How hard this must have been on a soft, gentle heart, to doubt the loving one, all of them, to injure Him in their house: "Those with which I was wounded in the house of my friends." (Zechariah 13: 6). How hard and cruel it is to be denied by your friends! Who can tolerate such a thing? But Jesus endured Peter's denial 3 times on one night in front of a servant. He swore and cursed and said: "I do not know the Man." (Matthew 26:70-74).

Did humanity reach this level on Good Friday? The enemies plotted against Him and delivered Him up to death. The friends who were afraid left Him and fled. Jesus stood alone, endured the evil betrayal, bore the weakness of His loving friends, and took pity on these, and said to God the father: "Father, forgive them, for they know not what they do."

The Lord Jesus Christ is the only light in the middle of this darkened humanity. He said to those who conspired against Him: "But this is your hour, and the power of darkness." (Luke 22:53). The darkness was in full power and then the grace started.

THE WORK OF GRACE:

Truly the whole thing was dark, powered by the prince of darkness (Satan). In the midst of all this, the work of grace began to work in people. As the apostle said: "But where sin abounded, grace abounded much more." (Romans 5:20). So we find the lights appearing on that day. Truly the light was shining and it kept on shining in spite of the prince of darkness. Some had light, but then the darkness covered it and the light came back again to continue glowing.

This last type resembles St. Peter the Apostle. This saint was very excited, grace worked very powerfully on this day. He followed Jesus Christ even after He was arrested. His courage appeared when he drew his sword, struck the servant of the high priest, and cut off his ear. Truly it was the wrong way to behave and the Lord scolded him saying: "Put your sword in its place, for all who take the sword will perish by the sword." (Matthew 26:52). But in spite of all this, he had a holy zeal, was full of courage and a willingness to fulfil all that was needed.

All these good qualities, however, quickly disappeared. He became weak, fearful and denied the Lord Jesus three times. He cursed and swore! But the grace of God was working in him and he repented and cried bitter tears. He became enlightened by repentance and this radiated after receiving the Holy Spirit.

Amongst those who had grace working in them, but it was swept away like the wind, was Pilate. No doubt grace was working in Pilate and without a doubt he responded initially. There was a very strong voice inside, warning him so that he doesn't fall.

Grace also worked in Pilate's wife through a dream. She sent for her husband and said to him: "Have nothing to do with that just Man, for I have suffered many things today in a dream because of Him." (Matthew 27: 19).

We notice that grace worked in Pilate when he said three times about Jesus Christ: "I have found no fault in this Man." (Luke 23). The Bible says: "Pilate invited the chief priests, the leaders and the people, and said to them: 'You have brought this Man to me, as one who misleads the people. And indeed, having examined Him in your presence, I have found no fault in this Man concerning those things of which you accuse Him; no, neither did Herod, for I sent you back to him; and indeed nothing deserving of death has been done by Him. I will therefore chastise Him and release Him.'" (Luke 23:13-16; Luke 23:4).

Then he said to them a third time, "Why, what evil has He done? I have found no reason for death in Him. Pilate, therefore, wishing to release Jesus instead of Barabbas." (Luke 23: 20; John 18:39). Pilate believed that the Lord Jesus was righteous. Pilate, however, was afraid to lose his position and desired to please the Jews, so he didn't respond to the grace hidden as a light inside him and instead surrendered to the devil (the power of darkness). So he betrayed the Lord Jesus to be crucified. In an unsuccessful attempt to please his conscious, he washed his hands with water and said: "I am innocent of the blood of this just Person. You see to it." (Matthew 27:24).

St. Peter reminds the Jews that Pilate wished to free Jesus; after he healed the lame man, "Jesus whom you delivered up and denied in the presence of Pilate, when he was determined to let Him go. But you denied the Holy One and the Just, and asked for a murderer to be granted to you." (Acts 3: 13,14). The work of grace in Pilate gave him the awareness of Christ's righteousness and innocence and he wanted to free Him, but he didn't respond to this grace for long.

The work of grace in the person doesn't force him to do good, it is the person's responsibility to accept it and act on it. Pilate is a perfect example to demonstrate this. He responded to the work of grace for a while, but due to his own desires, the grace left him to his own will. The grace of guidance can not override free will.

Another example of the work of grace is Judas Iscariot. Even Judas betrayed Christ, the grace didn't leave him, it continued to work in him and produce the great outcome of making him aware of what he had done wrong. His conscience reproached him and he tried to correct the damage which he did by going to the leaders and the elders and returning the 30 pieces of silver. He confessed in front of them that he sinned and said: "I have sinned by betraying innocent blood; he threw down the pieces of silver in the temple and departed." (Matthew 27:3-5).

Until this point the work of grace was beneficial and Judas was responding well. Now we can see that Judas' conscious was awake. After that, the people plotted against Jesus to have Him put to death. They had Him bound; they led Him away and delivered Him to Pontius Pilate the governor, then "Judas, His betrayer, seeing that He had been condemned, was remorseful." (Matthew 27:1-3). Seeing that He had been condemned and the whole matter finished he became remorseful!

His betrayal and conscious worked to deliver Jesus, but the results of the betrayal were too much and he reproached himself and was remorseful. Then the devil took the chance of this remorse and reproach and converted it into despair. He went and hanged himself. So the light in which grace worked was destroyed by the power of darkness.

THE SOULS WHICH WERE ENLIGHTENED DURING THIS TIME

Although the events of Good Friday were saturated in betrayal, plotting, weakness, fear and denial, and although humanity appeared very cruel and was dominated by the power of darkness; there were souls which were enlightened and we remember these souls with pride on this day and we honour them.

We greet those who stood at the Cross with our Lord Jesus Christ. They were firm till the last minute at the time of the crucifixion.

- The Virgin Saint Mary

- Her sister Mary the wife of Clopas

- St. John the Beloved

- St. Mary Magdalene

Those who accompanied Jesus till the Cross did not leave Him during this difficult time. They were not afraid of Pilate, or Herod, or Ananias and Caiaphas, or of the soldiers, or of all the powers of revolt and the noisy crowds saying, "Crucify Him, crucify Him!" The Bible says: "Now there stood by the cross of Jesus, His mother, and His mother's sister, Mary the wife of Clopas, and Mary Magdalene." (John 19:25).

These women stood beside the Cross in Christ's suffering. It was not a time for miracles, but rather a time when the Romans and Jews believed He was defeated, weak and was unable to save Himself. The Jewish people believed that they were rid of Him at last! These women, along with John the Beloved, stood with Him with all their hearts and their love, while the people mocked Him and nailed Him. They were with Him during all His suffering. It was the love that united

Him to them not the glory. We should also honour, the other women who followed the Lord, the people who followed Him earlier. Those who the Bible said of them: "And a great multitude of the people followed Him, and women who also mourned and lamented Him." (Luke 23:27).

"But all His acquaintances, and the women who followed Him from Galilee, stood at a distance, watching these things." (Luke 23:49). St. Matthew said about these women: "And many women who followed Jesus from Galilee, ministering to Him, were there looking on from afar, among whom were Mary Magdalene, Mary the mother of James and Joses, and the mother of Zebedee's sons." (Matthew 27: 55,56), also mentioned in the gospel of St. Mark. (Mark 15: 40,41).

We greet all these women who showed their sincere love in every step they took following Jesus. We greet also the women who went to the tomb carrying the spices which they had prepared; although they were aware of the Jewish leaders and the elders, the scribes and the Pharisees who hated Him; in contrast to Peter who was afraid and had denied Him in front of a servant girl. They were not afraid of all of these, but instead their deep and sincere love for Him was demonstrated at a time when everyone else left Him.

On this day we greet Joseph of Arimathea. During this difficult time "coming and taking courage, went in to Pilate and asked for the body of Jesus." (Mark 15: 43). He took Him: "Joseph had taken the body, he wrapped it in a clean linen cloth, and laid it in his new tomb which he had hewn out of the rock; and he rolled a large stone against the door of the tomb." (Matthew 27: 57-60; Luke 23: 52,53).

Joseph of Arimathea was courageous, brave and bold. How many followed Jesus in His glory, but in His sufferings we saw fear? It seems the crowds followed the glory and not the person Himself. Joseph of Arimathea, however, went to Pilate the Roman to take the body of a person who was sentenced by Pilate who had delivered Him to death, crucified by the Jews outside the city in order not to defile it! The leaders followed Him to destroy Him and even the disciples fled and hid. Joseph didn't flee. He wasn't afraid, but instead: "Approached Pilate and took Jesus' body." It is very emotional.

On this occasion we remember the beautiful words said in the Bible about Saint Joseph. St. Luke said: "Now behold, there was a man named Joseph, a council member, a good and just man. He had not consented to their decision and deed. He was from Arimathea, a city of the Jews, who himself was also waiting for the kingdom of God." (Luke 23: 50-51). St. Mark also said about him: "A prominent council member, who was himself waiting for the Kingdom of God." (Mark 15: 43). And St. Matthew said: "When evening had come, there came a rich man from Arimathea, named Joseph, who himself had also become a disciple of Jesus." (Matthew 27: 57).

The true disciples of Jesus appear here, who had genuine love in their hearts, courage and were not afraid. The unusual thing here is that the Bible never mentioned the name of Joseph of Arimathea before this moment, but it appeared at the right time in order to finish a job which no one else could do.

On this day we also greet Nicodemus. Nicodemus the Pharisee and a member of the Sanhedrin; he also came and shared with Joseph of Arimathea in wrapping the body of Jesus. St. John said: "Nicodemus, who at first came to Jesus by night, also came, bringing a mixture of myrrh and aloes, about a hundred pounds. Then they took the body of Jesus, and bound it in strips of linen with the spices, as the custom of the Jews is to bury." (John 19: 39-42).

His position was critical because he was one of the members of the Sanhedrin who had judged the Lord Jesus with injustice; but Nicodemus did not side with them. Instead Nicodemus said: "I shall announce my fellowship to Jesus, even if He is dead, crucified and counted among the sinners. I will not leave Him during this time; I will carry all the consequence on me. Truly, what a great soul which enlightens us until today.

If the Lord Jesus came today raising people from the dead and performing miracles, people would shout saying, "We are His followers." But to see the Lord crucified as a sinner and died, and then one of the leaders comes and says: "I am His follower," and then takes the Body and wraps it; what a great, noble, loving, caring and compassionate person this is? This is exactly what Joseph of Arimathea, Nicodemus and the women did and we greet their shining, glowing souls on this day and we also greet with them Simon of Cyrene, the man who fell under the heavy Cross on Good Friday. Simon of Cyrene came to carry the Cross on Jesus' behalf. He joined with Jesus in carrying the Cross (Luke 23: 26). Jesus before said: "Come to Me, all you who labor and are heavy laden, and I will give you rest." (Matthew 11:28). When He was in physical pain He allowed this saint to come and comfort Him, therefore He enters in "joining His pain."

We greet also on this day, a gentile, Saint Longenos the Centurion. This man who was a member of the army and the rulers, whose name was well known in the country and was appointed by the Roman Governor to guard the convicted man who was executed; proclaimed Jesus, in front of all, and glorified God saying: "Certainly this was a righteous Man!" (Luke 23: 47). "Truly this was the Son of God!" (Matthew 27: 54). "Truly this Man was the Son of God!" (Mark 15: 39). Later this commander believed and became a martyr. The Church celebrates this occasion in the Synaxarium on two days:

a- 23rd Abib: the day of his martyrdom (he was beheaded)

b- 5th Hatour: the appearance of his holy head

We greet the Commander Saint, as a soul shining its light, by grace on this day, for he gave the glory to Jesus Christ.

We also greet him who was on the cross, the thief on the Right hand of Jesus. He is another saint among all the saints; it is enough that the Lord said to him: "Assuredly, I say to you, today you will be with Me in Paradise" (Luke 23:43). The thief was attacking and reviling Jesus Christ along with his friend, as is mentioned in the Gospels (Matthew 27:44, Mark 15:32).

Then the grace worked in him and changed his heart when he was on the cross. When he heard his friend blaspheme Jesus, he rebuked him saying: "Do you not even fear God, seeing you are under the same condemnation? And we indeed justly, for we receive the due reward of our deeds; but this Man has done nothing wrong." (Luke 23: 39-41).

It wasn't enough for him to confess his sins which were deserving of death, reprimand his friend, defend Jesus Christ, but he confessed that Jesus Christ is the Lord, the King and that He was able to save him and he said to Him: "Lord, Remember me when You come into Your Kingdom." (Luke 23:42). And so he believed and deserved the salvation. He died with Jesus Christ and because of this his death is considered his baptism.

Let us praise him who confessed his sins and his acceptance of the work of grace and believed although he saw Jesus suffering, crucified with him, blasphemed by the crowd. The Church calls this saint the blessed thief, and praises him on Good Friday with a long tune hymn, which is called, "The Creed of the Thief on the Right." He is one of the luminous souls on this day which were enlightened in paradise; although he is given the name 'thief' and this name will follow him even in the commemoration of the saints; but he is a thief who was able to steal paradise in his last moments of life.

Praise also on this day, a group which are not human. We praise nature: the sun which darkened, the earth which shook, the tombs which cracked and the veil of the temple which was torn in two. Nature was unsatisfied with the evil injustice and praised Jesus in its own way. It was a brilliant thing that happened on that day. Maybe it was because of what happened that the centurion, the thief on the right and later

Dionysius the Areopagite (Acts 17: 34) all believed. Nature responded on this day to what Christ had said: "If these should keep silent, the stones would immediately cry out." (Luke 19:40).

All these are lights on Good Friday, but the true great light is the light of Jesus and His redemption. The light of love was radiating, the light of redemption, and it was giving, more than the sun; it was shinning especially on that day by eliminating the forces of darkness by trampling death by death. As it was shining with love, it was shinning too on the dead in hell through hope and He transferred them to paradise.

JESUS IS THE KING

Some believe that the greatest picture of Jesus as King is when He entered Jerusalem and the crowds surround Him with palm branches, crying out: "Hosanna! Blessed is He the Son of David." But in my opinion the greatest picture is Christ the King on the Cross. It fulfils the spirit of the words found in the Psalms: "The Lord reigns on a wood (the Cross)." It is because on the Cross, He bought us with His blood (Romans 5:9), so we became His own. He is the King. And so a spiritual Kingdom is started.

We see the King who bought us, and praise Him on this Good Friday with the hymn (Pek Ethronos) i.e "Your Throne, O God is forever and ever, a sceptre of righteousness is the sceptre of Your Kingdom." Then we say: "Gird Your sword upon Your thigh, O Mighty One, With Your glory and Your majesty. Gird the sword and be King." (Psalm 45).

How did He reign on a wood? The Lord owned us from the beginning; He created us and brought us from nothing. From our sins we became separated from the Kingdom of God, and with sins death reigned over us (Romans 5:17,14), so we were under His judgement. The Lord Jesus Christ was on the Cross and by death trampled death and saved us from the judgement of death and gave us life and we became His. He reigned over sin and death, but Satan also reigned and the Bible gives him many names, one of which is "The ruler of the world." (John 12: 31). That is the world was under sin and death.

On the Cross, the Lord Jesus overcame the kingdom of the devil and also on the Cross, He trample death by His death and paid the price of sin. The Lord said of the devil, "Because the ruler of this world is judged." (John 16:11). He also said: "I saw Satan fall like lightning from heaven." (Luke 10:18).

The Lord Jesus Christ defeated Satan in all his tricks and his wars but with the Cross, He destroyed his kingdom. Everything the devil gained over the past thousands of years, he lost when Jesus was on the Cross and He redeemed mankind from their sins. Satan is frightened from the Cross because it reminds him of his defeat. And so the sign of the Cross has power over Satan.

On the Cross, redemption is complete in which it destroyed the kingdom of Satan. Satan knows that redemption destroyed his kingdom and the Redeemer is the Son of God who offered unlimited redemption, which is sufficient for the remission of sins to all generations. Therefore, Satan shouted in the voice of his followers the famous verse: "If You are the Son of God, come down from the cross." (Matthew 27: 40; Mark 15:30). Come down from the Cross, so redemption is not fulfilled and so that the spiritual Kingdom can not be established.

Jesus was silent and He did not answer, because He is the Son of God, He rose on the Cross and He reigned. The thief on the Cross was admitted into Jesus' Kingdom. He said: "Remember me O Lord when You come into Your Kingdom." The thief may have been thinking of the coming Kingdom, in which He will come on a cloud, to gather the elect and take them to His Heavenly Kingdom. Our Lord alerted the thief of a very important point. He did not have to wait till He comes in the eternal heavenly kingdom, but there is a new Kingdom which began today on the Cross. Instead of the word "When I come", He said to him "Today" you will be with Me. Rejoice that today is the Kingdom of Jesus, you blessed thief. Gird Your sword upon Your thigh and lock Satan for a thousand years. And Satan fell like lightning from heaven.

Jesus on the Cross is more majestic and stunning than any king with a crown. We praise Him in the last Psalm of the sixth hour, which is especially for the crucifixion, saying: "The Lord reigns, He is clothed with majesty." (Psalm 92:1). He refused the kingdom which the Jews wanted for Him on Palm Sunday, and said: "My kingdom is not of this world." (John 18: 36). On the Cross He established the spiritual Kingdom. When we say to Him: "A scepter of righteousness is the scepter of Your kingdom" we mean that He reigned with righteousness and with justice, by paying the ransom of sins and with a divine justice. Blessed is He in His Kingdom.

JESUS' SUFFERING

The Lord's divine nature doesn't correspond with the sufferings, but He took our human nature and suffered instead of us. The humble and the meek, delivered Himself to the proud. "He gave His back to those who struck Him, and His cheeks to those who plucked out the beard; He did not hide His face from shame and spitting." (Isaiah 50:6). He bore all of these things from the weak human beings, who are made of dust. And if the grace of God leaves a person for one second, he will be lost. He bore with the false accusations and didn't say a word in defence of Himself.

If He defends Himself, He will contradict His actions and become innocent, and then we will be judged. He preferred to carry the judgement instead of us, and become guilty in order to be justified. He was charged with death in order to give us life. He didn't defend Himself, but instead was incarnated to offer Himself in order to fulfil the divine justice on behalf of our sins. Our sins don't need defending, they need redemption. It requires a sacrifice to die and to redeem. It requires a pure soul to die on behalf of evil souls; a Soul to die on behalf of other souls.

The only solution is to offer Himself as a sacrifice as a ransom for our sins. This means that He offers His pure Holy blood to be shed for many for the remission of sins. So the Father will smell the pleasing aroma, and say to all: "When I see the blood, I will pass over you." (Exodus 12:13).

Jesus' defence is not for Himself, but He defends us. It is not by words or by mouth, but by true work to please the divine justice, by His death on our behalf.

In the Garden of Gethsemane, He prepared Himself to carry the sins of the whole world; with all its cruelty and fornication. It was a cup full of bitterness. The Lord said: "My soul is exceedingly sorrowful, even to death." (Matthew 26: 38). He grieved over the whole of humanity, which reached the lowest level and lost its divine image in which we were created.

Although the Lord is the source of all comfort and joy, He said: "My soul is exceedingly sorrowful, even to death." This is due to the terrible images of human sin before His eyes, the hidden and the visible, with all their thoughts and feelings; all were before Him.

How can the Holy carry all these abominations? "O My Father, if this cup cannot pass away from Me unless I drink it, Your will be done." (Matthew 26:42). The righteous person can not bear to look at abominations and sin, how much more so can the complete Holy of

Holies be able to see and carry it all as though He were the unrighteous, on behalf of all, to die and stand before the Father?

My brethren, do not think that Jesus' sufferings were only of the body, but they were suffering of the soul and the spirit. The suffering of the flesh was seen by scourging, thorns, nails and crucifixion. Also they struck Him, spat on Him and He was made to carry the cross. More so He fell underneath the cross into the roughness of the road while He was carrying it. Not to mention He was thirsty and more and more.

There was a different kind of suffering which is revealed here: "My soul is exceedingly sorrowful, even to death", the pain of sadness on the fallen humanity, the pain that He encountered on the way from betrayal and cruelty and from ignorant people who screamed saying: "Crucify Him, crucify Him." Truly they did not know what they were doing. Also there was the pain towards His disciples, who were afraid, doubted, fled and hid and the Jewish leaders monitored them in order to destroy them.

The Lord was in the Garden and, "He knew that His hour had come." (John 13:1), "Knowing all things that would come upon Him." (John 18:4), He struggled till His sweat was drops of blood. "I have trodden the winepress alone." (Isaiah 63:3). Even His disciples, left Him in this critical hour; they couldn't stay awake for even one hour, although He asked them 3 times, "Watch and pray, lest you enter into temptation." (Matthew 26:41).

I want you to be awake for your sake and not for My sake. Keep awake, not to help me in my trouble, but watch and stay awake for your sake so you don't enter into temptation, because my enemy is near, the darkness is creeping with all its power and the devil wants to sift you as wheat. His aim is to knock the Shepherd down so the sheep will go astray.

Peter, wake up and watch before the rooster crows, stay awake with the Lord and struggle in prayer, so that you don't enter into tribulation if you are armed and protected. Peter, perhaps if you are awake, you will not deny! But the "heavy eyes" don't see the coming tribulation and don't even prepare for it. If one says to his teacher, "I put myself instead of You, even if it leads me to die with You." If you say all these things, shouldn't you be able to stay awake even for one hour?!

If you can't stay awake with Him, so how can you die with Him?! Watch yourself then and be prepared. How hard it is when it comes to the people and they are found asleep and their eyes are heavy! So that is how the Lord suffered for His disciples. If you can't do it, sleep now and rest. I will stay awake for you. I am not asleep nor resting like you, because I am awake and watching for your salvation.

The Lord Jesus Christ carried His own body, soul, peoples suffering and the whole of humanities sins. Of all these our sins are probably the heaviest, carried by Jesus for us; the One who is without sin, "to be sin for us." (2 Corinthians 5:21) "All we like sheep have gone astray; We have turned, every one, to his own way; And the Lord has laid on Him the iniquity of us all." (Isaiah 53:6). Because of the weight of all the sins, He expressed this great pain by saying to the Father: "Why have You forsaken Me." He was left to bear and carry all of humanities sin since Adam.

If repentance causes heaven to be joyful what about sin? The Bible said: "There will be more joy in heaven over one sinner who repents." In contrast there will be sadness for all who fall. Imagine then how much sadness the Lord had to bear, for it was the sin of every person. This encompasses millions upon millions of terrible pictures before the eyes of the Lord; to carry on our behalf.

The impurities that the Lord carried especially in our sins. Each sin, for each one of us, was a bitter drop in a bitter cup which the Lord was obliged to drink. Unless the Lord Himself erased all our sins with His blood, they would never been forgiven. That means that we hurt the Lord so much as we were a part of His agony on Good Friday.

Every time we sin, we should say to Him, against You only have I sinned and done this evil in Your sight. If we did hurt You Lord, don't allow us to hurt You again, and don't allow us to add further bitter drops in Your cup. Purge me with hyssop, and I shall be clean; wash me, and I shall be whiter than snow. Let Your joy be with our salvation, more than Your pain from our sins.

THE WORDS OF OUR LORD JESUS ON THE CROSS

There were seven words which the Lord said on the Cross during His suffering and they were all life-giving. He did not speak during the trial, during the torture, or the mockery. He rarely spoke. He was silent. He surrendered His own rights, His own dignity. "Love does not behave rudely, does not seek its own." (I Corinthians 13:5). But on the Cross He spoke, for our sake, for our benefit and for our salvation. Each word had a goal and a meaning; each word had its impact. We will look in depth at each word shortly; but first some general observations:

We noticed that each word of Christ on the Cross had the element of the giver. We wonder how it is that while He was on the Cross, with the image of weakness and defeat He was giving. He gave forgiveness to the people who crucified Him, He gave Paradise to the thief on the right, He gave to the Virgin St. Mary a spiritual, caring and attentive son. He gave to the beloved St. John the blessing of the Virgin in his house. He gave to the Father the ransom of the divine judgement. He gave to the whole of humanity the redemption and the remission of sins. He gave us also the contentment for the completion of salvation. He gave to everyone. He is the one who didn't receive anything from anyone. He offered everything and in return all He received was the bitterness of vinegar.

The first and the last words on the Cross were directed to the Father. The first word was directed to God the Father in saying: "Father, forgive them." The last word was directed to God the Father in saying: "Father, into Your hands I commit My spirit." In between the first and the last words, there were two words also directed to the Father: one of them "My God, My God, why have You forsaken Me" and the other "It is finished". Although it is a general declaration it carried a formal message to the Father; "The work that You gave Me to do, I finished it."

Then the majority of the words of Jesus or at least half of them were directed to the Father; this bears tranquillity to humanity. We noticed that when He speaks to the Father He used the words, "Father, My God." By using the word "Father", He was responding to those who said: "If You are the Son of God... come down from the Cross." He proved that He is the Son of God, but He didn't come down from the Cross, instead He was raised up to the highest heaven.

By using the word "Father", He proved His divinity and in the words "My God" He proved His humanity. God was made manifest in the flesh (I Timothy 3:16). The word "Father" answers the Arian Heresy which denied His divinity in the fourth Century. The word "My God" answers Eutychus, who denied Jesus' humanity in the fifth Century. In the first, He spoke as a Son to God, in the second, He spoke as a Son of Man, therefore He represents the whole of humanity. As He spoke He was not just addressing the Father only, but all of humanity; the Saints who were represented by the Virgin St. Mary and John the Beloved and the repentants in the thief on the right.

His words were blessing and grace. It was the time for salvation. He spoke words of forgiveness, salvation, paradise and blessing. He did not curse or punish anyone on the Cross. Although He suffered, He did not destroy the world, but he saved the world.

The sequence of the words spoke by Jesus on the Cross indicates His wisdom; others first, then Himself and Himself for the sake of others. He started first by asking forgiveness of the people; because He is on the Cross, the Holy Blood is actually doing the forgiveness. When He opened the door for forgiveness, the second word came especially to open Paradise; since He paid the ransom with His blood for forgiveness to open Paradise. We noticed also that Jesus Christ mentioned His enemies first and then His friends. His first word is specific to His Cross, then the thief, St. Mary the Virgin and St. John.

In His conversation with God the Father, He talked to Him as a

Father then as God. First as a loving Son, the only Begotten Son, who is in the bosom of the Father; He has declared Him (John 1:18), then as a Son of Man born in all ages.

The first three words were specifically for forgiveness and shepherding. His last four words were declaration the redemption and its completion. The words "My God, My God, why have You forsaken Me" means that the Father left Him to pay the ransom of redemption. They are also an expression of His psychological pain towards God's anger due to the sins of humanity. The words "I am thirsty" means the physical pain of the flesh for the sake of all people. Both words indicate that He will pay the ransom.

The words "It is finished" ensure that the ransom is paid. The words "In Your hands I commit My spirit" means death worthy of sin, and by Him salvation will be completed. All four words bear serenity to all humanity regarding the redemption. We noticed that the last two words have cheers of joy and victory. The Lord declares His redemption through suffering. And also declares His joy by completing the redemption.

The words "It is finished" mean that everything with regards to the redemption is finished. The Lord was happy to finish His work and He didn't allow anything to prevent its completion. The words "Into Your hands I commit My spirit" have the same meaning. With these words, He defeated Satan. The battle is finished and with His death the Lord wiped out the power of death... and declared joy and victory.

All of this gives us the idea that while He was on the Cross, He was working for our sake. It is not only redemption while He was on the Cross which He stressed; He was a teacher, He proclaimed His salvation.

In His first word, He put into practice His teachings on forgiveness and tolerance and the love of ones enemies. In the last word "In Your hands I commit My spirit" He educates us regarding the immortality of the soul and the transmission of the spirit after death to God. In His third word, He educates us on the genuine care for others with sincere effort and the practical application of the 5th commandment; He honoured His mother.

There is so much more to learn and to contemplate on these seven words. Note that the number seven is a symbol of perfection or completion. Let us now go deeply into each word one by one.

THE FIRST WORD:

"Father, forgive them, for they do not know what they do."

(Luke 23:34)

Our loving Lord Jesus, in His deep suffering on the Cross, thought of others not Himself. He forgot His pain, His sufferings, His wounds, He didn't worry about the lash on His back, nor the nails in His hands and feet, the tingling of the thorns in His forehead, nor His aching body. He put all these aside and all that He thought about was His love towards humanity. The first thing we need to remember is how He forgave His enemies and the people who crucified Him. And so was the first word on the cross "Father , forgive them, for they do not know what they do." (Luke 23: 34).

The Lord cared for his enemies first, before his friends and before Himself. He forgave those who persecuted Him, then forgave the thief who mocked Him first before believing. Then he cared for His mother and then, after all of that, He spoke of Himself. "Father, forgive them" He said these words when He was in the deepest agony and bodily pain. He suffered so much at the hands of these people and then He asks for their forgiveness! But He loved them far more than despising them.

Not only did He ask for their forgiveness, but He made excuses for them! These are the people who were not able to give excuses for themselves, and they shouted in audacity "His blood be on us and on our children." (Matthew 27:25). These are the people for whom the

Crucified Himself made excuses for by saying: "Because they don't know what they do." How great is the Lord's love; He did not pour on them the curse, He did not respond to them or think negatively about them, but His love was immensely positive. Instead He asked for their forgiveness and excused them, defending them before the heavenly Father, proclaiming that their sins were due to their ignorance.

As humans we blame these terrible acts of sin on envy, jealousy, hatred, the bad influence of the Jewish leaders, denial, sins of cruelty, swearing, mocking, attacking, scorn of the soldiers and the authorities, sin of injustice, fear, apathy from Pilate and in addition to all this murder, torture, lying, false witness during the trial. But our loving, crucified Lord, the gentle One never mentioned these sins, but instead excused them as ignorance, "They don't know what they do!" How great and immense is Your heart Lord and full of love; it is above our understanding.

In His forgiveness to them our Lord Jesus practically demonstrated how to implement His commandment of loving your enemy, "Love your enemies, bless those who curse you, do good to those who hate you, and pray for those who spitefully use you." (Matthew 5:44). Here He practised what He asked the people to do. The Lord does not give a commandment to others without practising it and implementing it Himself. Thus He was a role model for us in this deep and incredibly perfect way in which He implemented this commandment; He forgave His persecutors.

And you my blessed brothers and sisters, what is your position now from this verse: "Father, forgive them"? I wish for you that when you hear this verse on Good Friday and each time you remember it you say, "And me too Lord, I will do the same; all who hated me and whom I hated, all those who wore me down and persecute me, all who annoyed me, I will forgive them because they don't know what they do.

And so my brethren you join with Christ in His work and His love.

What do you benefit if the Lord forgives His enemies and you don't? What do you benefit if the Lord loves His enemies, while you do not love and have no tolerance? What do you benefit? Then you are not joining with Christ in His work and you don't follow in His footsteps.

We know now that the Lord forgave us so that we can forgive others and enjoy the blessings of forgiveness which come upon us when we forgive. When we remember those who have abused us, we think deeply about these words "Forgive them, for they don't know what they do", although it differs from the Lord Jesus' situation. He said: "Father, forgive them, because I paid the ransom of their sins."

Therefore, they don't owe anything anymore. I fulfilled the divine justice; I paid all that was owing so forgive them. Here I am, I will die for their sake. I will die for those who crucified Me and those who love Me and when I say "Forgive them", I didn't mean only these, but all who are under My cover in sharing My blood, all sinners who have repented from Adam till the end of all ages; forgive them, for that is why I came: "For this purpose I came to this hour." (John 12: 27).

One of those who fit into the description "They don't know what they do" is the great St Longenos, the soldier who pierced Christ's side with his spear. He pierced Jesus' side with a spear; he didn't know what he was doing so the Lord forgave him, and not just that, but He led him to His kingdom. This Saint believed and preached Christianity in Cappadocia and he was martyred during the time of Tiberius Caesar. The Lord honoured him with miracles after his death.

There was another saint who fits the description, "They don't know what they do". He was an immense advocate of torture and murder of the Christians. If we say that Emperor Diocletian was the most vicious of all people in his manner of torturing the Christians, there was another who assisted him in his torture, who was a terrifying giant and there was none like him in the whole of the Roman Empire. He was the one who the Christians were sent to for his different forms of merciless tortures.

This man was Saint Arianous, who was the governor of Ansena. He shed the blood of thousands and ten thousands of innocent Christians. Even he, who savagely murdered them, did not know what he was doing. He continued in his tortures until he drew closer to Jesus, believed and was martyred, in the name of Jesus, on 8th Baramhat by the hands of Emperor Diocletian. His name was written in the Synaxarium and the whole Church celebrates his feast day just like all the other great saints.

Saul of Tarsus also was another who did not know what he was doing. He made havoc for the Church, entering homes and dragging out men and women, committing them to prison (Acts 8:3). He watched on as St. Steven, the first deacon and the first Christian martyr, was being persecuted (Acts 7:58).

He was a terrifying and frightening person, but still he doesn't know what he is doing. He continued in this manner until the Lord appeared to him on his way to Damascus. He found him a good vessel and He drew him to Himself and then he believed, was baptised and his name became Paul. He preached in the name of Jesus Christ, worked harder than the rest of the disciples, was persecuted more than they were and received martyrdom at the hands of Emperor Nero. He became a pillar among the Christian pillars in the Church, and a light to ignite the lighthouse. He said: "But I obtained mercy because I did it ignorantly in unbelief." (I Timothy 1:13).

His life would have ended if not for the Lord Jesus, the soft hearted, who said "Father, forgive them, for they don't know what they do." "Father, forgive them", I don't want revenge; I don't want to treat them the same way they treated Me. Some of these people who crucified Me, "I am going to prepare a place for them, I will come again and receive you to Myself; that where I am, there you may be also." (John 14: 3).

The words of Jesus Christ "Father, forgive them", does not mean He forgave all who crucified Him without exception. Not anyone can enjoy forgiveness whether they crucified Him or didn't crucify Him. Forgiveness comes with two conditions: faith and repentance along with the rest of the Lord's commandments. This is essential for salvation because without these two no one can receive salvation or forgiveness.

Father, forgive them to whoever is a believer and a repentant and does good works deserving of repentance. The Bible says: "For God so loved the world that He gave His only begotten Son." He loves the whole world; He gave His only begotten Son for the sake of the whole world. Does the whole world enjoy this salvation? Definitely not! Jesus' salvation is given to "whoever believes in Him", so that the verse continues, "should not perish but have everlasting life." (John 3:16). This is the essence of belief, but the essence of repentance, the Lord says: "unless you repent you will all likewise perish." (Luke 13:3).

These words "Forgive them", does not apply to the Jews of today as they still live according to the Judaic beliefs, which is: denial of Christ, denial of the virginity of St. Mary and that Jesus of Nazareth, who was born 2000 years ago, had gone astray and was misguided and deserved to be crucified according to their forefathers. So they participate in the sin of their fathers, living in agreement of what they did and they are therefore deserving of judgement. If they, however, repent, believe and become Christians, then they will receive the Lord's forgiveness and so they will not be called Jews.

The Lord Jesus Christ offered His salvation to the whole world, but only to those who take pleasure in it, that is; to repent, to believe and follow His path and those who enjoy the work of the Holy Spirit through His sacraments.

To the believer and the repentant, the Lord offered forgiveness, but to the stubborn the Lord Jesus said about them, "Where I am you cannot come" (John 7: 34) and also, "You will die in your sins; for if you do not believe that I am He, you will die in your sins." (John 8:24). Three times in Chapter 8 in the Gospel of St. John the Apostle, Christ says: "If you do not believe in Me, you will die in Your sins.".

When Christ and His disciples entered a town in Samaria its people drove them out. His disciples, James and John asked the Lord, "Do You want us to command fire to come down from heaven and consume them," He turned and rebuked them, and said, "You do not know what manner of spirit you are of, for the Son of Man did not come to destroy men's lives, but to save them." (Luke 9: 52-56). This is how He answered His disciples, but to the Father, no doubt He said the words "Father, forgive them, for they don't know what they do." And so He waited patiently till they knew Him, they loved Him and believed in Him (John 4:42).

The words "Father, forgive them" carried a deep love and deep forgiveness and to understand its depth imagine that they are for yourself. You can forgive a person who annoys you, but to forgive a person who makes up false witness against you, judges you with injustice, aggravates people and leaders against you, mocks and hangs you on a cross, puts nails in your hands and feet and after all this, from the depth of your pain and suffering, you forgive them, pray for them and defend them; this requires a great love which is above normal boundaries and above natural ability.

Many people came to Christianity by this verse alone, "Father, forgive them." For this reason, I came, this is a consolation that pleases the heart in the midst of all the pain on the Cross, in the midst of the hurt of the mockery and all the pain of loneliness. They are defeated by their sins, defeated by the devil who worked in them, defeated also from low self esteem and ignorance. My feelings towards them are feelings of sympathy and compassion. I don't remember what they are doing to Me, because love doesn't seek its own (I Corinthians 13:50), but I look to their need for forgiveness.

Forgive them, because this makes Me happy as I fulfil My mission and achieve My goal. Truly, why was Jesus incarnated? Isn't it because the Father forgives these, the reason why He took the form of a bondservant, and came in the likeness of men (Philippians 2:7)? Isn't it in order to forgive them? Why did He carry our sins? Why was He crucified to the Cross? All of these, with no doubt, to forgive them and us.

These words are the beginning of the covenant of forgiveness, not the promise of forgiveness, but it is forgiveness by paying the ransom. It is a declaration of the divine justice that was fulfilled on the Cross, it is a breaking of the bonds of our sins, the evidence of the purchase of the one who paid the ransom.

He bought us with His blood so that we could enter Paradise with Him and enjoy the Kingdom of Heaven with Him. Wherever He is, we are too... and by these words, He says to the Father: "What do you want from these? What were their debts to You? Isn't death the wage of sin? Here I am, dying on their behalf. Here I am to free them from their debts. Free them from the death sentence. Now all Your rights are complete and after a while I will say to you "It is finished" so I forgive them.

The Lord Jesus Christ, with these words, proclaims victory over Satan. All of Satan's work is to take away people from God, away from forgiveness and to be in the way of salvation. The way of salvation is opened to the people and the wounded Lord is able to pour blood on the tabernacle for our sins to become Holy. His Love triumphed over hatred, "His humility was victorious over Satan's pride."

They said: "If You are the Son of God, come down from the Cross." But He declared that He is the Son by saying, "Father". He is the Son and He will remain on the Cross in order to forgive them. If

He came down from the Cross He would not be able to say "Forgive them". Now the sacrifice of Love is able to complete its work towards forgiveness.

All those who have died since the beginning of creation have been waiting and hoping to hear the words "Father, forgive them". If the Lord loved His persecutors, the people who crucified Him and He forgave them; how much then is His love towards His friends and followers and how much is His profound forgiveness and rewards. These were words which amazed the soldiers at the Cross and the thief on the right and now the second word, "Today, you will be with Me in Paradise".

THE SECOND WORD

Assuredly, I say to you, today you will be with Me in Paradise

(Luke 23:43).

This thief was the first one who spoke to the Lord on the Cross. He did not have a righteous life, but engaged in sins till the cross. He even reviled the Lord on the cross with the other robber (Matthew 27:44). Suddenly, his heart changed, he believed in Christ and became a defender instead of a reviler and turned from being a man of mockery to a man of prayer. How did he reach this faith? And how did he change? How did he believe in the Lord at a time when the Lord was in deep suffering and not in His glory, and with people mocking Him instead of seeking Him for blessings and healing?

Perhaps His forgiveness of those who crucified Him, deeply affected the thief's hardened heart. The kindness of the Lord's heart overcame the cruelty of the thief, or perhaps he changed because of the countenance of the face of Jesus, His expressions, His kindness and His gentle voice. The Lord's look at the thief may have softened his heart we don't know. Perhaps the thief's heart was ready to change and repent and it was good soil. He found the One who could clean it, extracting all the dirt and thorns and planting a good seed which will sprout goodness.

This thief was able to reach the Lord with those of the eleventh or the twelfth hour. He prayed a prayer and it was answered very quickly.

Many have long prayers, with vigilance, requests, supplications, sweating and tears, but this thief, with only one short, concentrated word, was able to receive everything. His prayers became a great contemplation for others, in which the whole Church repeats several times with him.

He is the only thief which the Lord Jesus answered rapidly, although many others did not even receive one word. Imagine the Lord not answering anyone during His trial, torture and crucifixion, "Yet He opened not His mouth, He was led as a lamb to the slaughter and as a sheep before its shearers is silent, so He opened not His mouth." (Isaiah 53: 7). He didn't answer Caiaphas the High Priest until he put Jesus under oath by the living God (Matthew 26: 63,64). Also Pilate the Governor marvelled greatly, "But He answered him not one word." (Matthew 27:14).

Many mocked and blasphemed Him yet He answered not a word. They challenged Him by saying: "If You are the Son of God, come down from the cross." (Matthew 27:40). Then one of the criminals who was hanging with Him, the thief on the left, blasphemed against Him saying: "If You are the Christ, save Yourself and us." But this thief on the right said: "Remember me when You come into Your kingdom" and he received the answer very quickly, "Assuredly, I say to you, today you will be with Me in Paradise." (Luke 23: 42,43).

How strange this friendship with the Lord! He was a friend at the Cross, a good friend!! The Lord extended this friendship to beyond the Cross, to be with Him in Paradise! He promised him saying, "Today, you will be with ME in Paradise". He said "With Me", that means, wherever the Lord is, he will be with Him. How happy and how lucky is that thief? He wasn't offended by the thief, but on the contrary, He found his heart full of virtues. He had a conversation with him on the cross and the Lord was happy to promise him and assured him of his fate before he died.

You will be with Me in Paradise, because your heart is with Me on the earth. You gave Me your heart, your fate on the cross and because you suffered with Me, so you will be glorified with Me, You were crucified with Me, and suffered with Me and you will live with Me.

How great is that meeting on the cross! So many meet with the Lord in Church and in prayer meetings. Others meet with Him in their locked rooms during the time of prayer. But to be able to meet with Him at the time of His crucifixion on the Cross, truly this is amazing! Did he ever think that one day he would repent and see the Lord this way?

The Kingdom of God does not come with observation, "The kingdom of God does not come with observation." (Luke 17: 20). We don't know when grace works in a person and how. The spirit, as the Lord said is like, "The wind blows where it wishes, so is everyone who is born of the Spirit." (John 3: 8). This thief lived all his life in sin and sin was attached to him until the cross when he blasphemed the Lord with his friend. Does this mean that grace was far from him? Or that the Lord forgot about him till the end? No, of course not, the Lord is merciful. He was waiting until the right time to work in him. It was at this point that He found him and He saved him, just a few moments from death.

We don't know who the elect are. Who would have imagined that this thief would be one of them! Who would have thought that within an hour he would receive what others have struggled to gain for tens of years? We are judging according to outer appearances, criticise some and lament others while they may be better off then we are. We say truly that this thief entered paradise with merit and deserving of it.

He was very unusual, truly unusual in all what he did. He confessed Jesus as the Lord, and he said, "Remember me O Lord." He confessed that He is a King by saying: "When You come into Your Kingdom." He confessed that He is a Saviour, able to take him to paradise. On the cross, he declared all his private sins and that he was deserving of death, and he scolded the other thief saying: "We indeed justly deserve, for we receive the due reward of our deeds." He rebuked his friend because he blasphemed Jesus Christ saying: "Do you not even fear God, seeing you are under the same condemnation? But this Man has done nothing wrong." (Luke 23: 40-41). And so He confessed Jesus' righteousness and that He was free from sin and so He should not be crucified for His own sin, but it is due to the sins of others that He is crucified.

It is amazing that of all the thousands of people who should defend Jesus, it was the thief on the cross! It was not one of the twelve disciples or even the seventy apostles, He was not defended by someone who had been healed by Him or raised from the dead. No one defended Him, He went alone.

He didn't allow anyone to say bad things about Jesus, he even rebuked his friend. Who would have thought of all His disciples and the believers that it would be the thief on the right that would be the only one to defend Him? Truly, as the Lord said: "Take heed that you do not despise one of these little ones." (Matthew 18: 10).

Don't think my brother that you are something, or you are better than someone else. Don't think that you are like one of the Apostles or one of those close to the Lord. All were silent, no one defended Jesus and the only one was the robber that no one would imagine and no one had heard of. The best thing about the thief, other than defending Jesus, was he looked for his eternity.

He was interested in his eternal fate. He wasn't concerned about his bodily pains, but about his fate after death. He shouted and asked for mercy and sought forgiveness, "Remember me O Lord." Remember me according to Your mercy and not according to our sins. David the Prophet said: "Remember, O Lord, Your tender mercies and Your loving kindnesses, for they are from of old. Do not remember the sins of my youth, nor my transgressions; according to Your mercy remember me, for Your goodness' sake, O Lord." (Psalm 25: 6,7). "Remember me," and do not include me amongst those whom You said: "I do not know you."

It was a memorable hour in my life when I was beside You on the cross. It was the most joyful hour of my life, enjoying Your suffering and I can boast in You, "I have been crucified with Christ." (Galatians 2:20); therefore remember me. I was crucified beside You, I am a shame for You, but I am proud eternally. It was enough for me, these joyful hours and I wanted to invest in them.

The words "Remember me" which I said to You mean that I knew You before and they also mean that I am well known to You. My name is written in Your book and is carved on Your palms. "He was numbered with the transgressors." (Isaiah 53:12), and crucified with sinners, it was counted shame to You, but it was a blessing and grace for me.

How sweet it is to be beside You. You made me forget all my pains, I don't feel them, but I feel Your spirit permeating inside my whole body, cleansing and purifying me and making me a different person. You are like a ray of sun which, when it stands beside a dirty body makes it pure and clean. I am happy with Your friendship, I wished I knew You before, so Remember me.

Let everyone cry with the thief saying, "Remember me, O Lord." Remember that you have a son in a far country, a prodigal slave. Remember me in my weakness, in my downfall, waiting for You to raise me up. Remember me because I am one of those who has no one to remember them, "I have no man to put me into the pool." (John 5:7).

The story of the thief on the right gives us something to contemplate on; that the time of death is different for each one of us. We shouldn't say that we will remember the Lord and repent at the last hour of our life, just as the thief did.

No, the other thief was at his last hour too, but the Bible says that he blasphemed Him and He did not fear God and eternal life was not important to him. He was only interested in getting rid of the cross (Luke 23: 39), in order to return to the world to enjoy his previous life and that he deserved to be rebuked by his friend. At the time of death, rather then repenting, he exceeded his number of sins with cruelty of heart! This thief on the left was close to Christ in body, he was beside Him on the cross, but his heart was far away, even at the time of death!! This time of death was not able to remind him of repentance or even to prepare him at all.

He wasn't affected by Christ's love in forgiving those who crucified Him, he wasn't even jealous of the promise that his friend received of entering Paradise, he didn't believe after he saw the earth quake, the rocks split and the darkness covering the whole land, he was busy not thinking of his eternity even at the last hour of his death. He still loved the world, he didn't want Jesus or His friendship, he just wanted to use Him as a way of getting down from the cross.

This is a very potent lesson to those who postpone their repentance believing that they need only repent in their last hour of life, in which they know not even the time!! Many are in the situation of the thief on the left, blaspheming and loving the world!!! Whoever is a slave to a habit will find it hard to break, even if his hands and feet are nailed and only have a few minutes to live! Unless one cooperates with the work of grace in their heart at the time of death, then they will also sin at the last hour.

Many people cry with heavy tears at the time of death, not crying because of their sins, but because death will prevent them from the pleasures of life! They cry because death will separate them from their friends and from their pleasures. The world is still in their heart even at the time of death. Don't think that death brings submission to the person!!! Not to all people. The thief on the right benefited from this last hour of his death, but the thief on the left did not. While the thief on the left blasphemed and mocked, the other was praying and asking for supplications saying: "Remember me when You come into Your Kingdom."

The Lord did not abandon this repentant thief, but his request was speedily answered more than he would have expected. In the thief's last hour of life, he didn't loose hope in God's mercy. The Lord also amplified his hope and confirmed it by saying to him, "Assuredly, I say to you, today you will be with Me in Paradise." You are now with Me. After a little moment, you will be with Me. As you were with Me in suffering and pain, you will be with Me "In paradise", you are now suffering, but over there you will have comfort.

The Lord says "In Paradise", he corrected the thief who said "In Your Kingdom" but He corrected him in a very gentle and soft way. The thief said, "Remember me O Lord when You come into Your Kingdom." That is good, he believed that Jesus has a spiritual Kingdom in heaven, and His Kingdom was not of this world, as the worldly people asked for. The heavenly Kingdom is where people will enter after the general resurrection, but straight after death they go to a waiting place for the righteous people, which is called "Paradise". So the Lord didn't say to the thief, "Today you will be in My Kingdom" but He said "in Paradise". The Lord initiated His work as a good teacher even on the Cross, with His usual soft and gentle way of teaching, explaining the mistakes of the people without telling them that they are wrong or sinful.

You will be with Me in Paradise, as a reassurance. You will come with Me on the cloud in the second coming, and you will be with Me on my right side on the day of judgement, as you are now on My right side on the cross which is a symbol of the righteous, and you will be with Me in My kingdom and you will be with Me in the eternal life which is never ending. I will be with you all the days till the end of ages.

Perhaps this promise made the thief wait happily to die, to be with Christ, which would be much better. Here we say how sweet is death?! "O Death, where is your sting?" (I Corinthians 15:55). Death is frightening to the wicked, but is joyful to those who die for hope, to whom received the promises, and saw the crowns, and calmed their fate after death and now they hear what Jesus said: "Today you will be with Me in paradise."

By saying, "you will be with Me in paradise", He didn't announce to the thief his mistake and his sins, but rather He announced the opening of the doors of Paradise for the first time since the sin of Adam. The thief was the first one Christ announced this truth. Paradise had been closed from this time and no one deserved to enter because of sin. These words which the Lord spoke are said during every farewell of a soul departing from this world. We say in the funeral prayers, "Open to him/her the door of Paradise as you did for the thief."

The remission of sins which the thief received was a divine work and the opening of Paradise was a divine work too. The Lord did two things on the Cross which reveals His divinity. He told the thief on the right, with all Power, "Today you will be with Me."

Now He the Righteous Judge; it is His right to issue a pardon for the eternity of a person. He made the judgment that the thief would enter into Paradise on that very day. No human being has this power! It is a divine power. Likewise, the command to open Paradise is one no one has the power to do, neither the leaders nor the prophets. Who did open the door of paradise or who was able to enter it? It is a divine action; it is also a declaration that the shedding of His blood is enough to open the door of Paradise.

Truly, He is the owner of this authority, " He who opens and no one shuts, and shuts and no one opens." (Revelation 3: 7; Isaiah 22:22). He holds the keys of Hades and of Death (Revelation 1:18). He holds the keys of heaven and of earth. He gave this power as a gift to His disciples; His agents on earth. He opened to the wise virgins and the foolish virgins pleaded with Him saying, "Lord, Lord, open for us." (Matthew 25:11). But He does not open His Paradise unless the heart was opened to Him before, like the thief on the right who deserved Christ saying to him: "Today, you will be in Paradise with Me."

The words "Today, you will be with Me" is a definite indicator that there is no Purgatory as some believe. The thief enters paradise on the same day of his death, without passing through Purgatory even for one hour!! Also the words "Today you will be with Me", refutes the idea that the soul of the dead person still comes into the place where it lived until the third day until the Church prays on the third day for the soul to leave the house! Did the soul of the thief stay until the third day or did it go to Paradise on the same day?! The Lord explains the fate of the person after death, and how Paradise is a waiting place for the righteous, and how they will be there with Jesus and enjoy His presence.

Today you will be with "Me", it is an enjoyable time to be with the Lord. The presence of the Lord is more beautiful than Paradise, it is the most joyful aspect of Paradise and the presence of the Lord is Paradise itself; it is the true Paradise to be with Him. This is what the Lord said and promised, "I will come again and receive you to Myself; that where I am, there you may be also." (John 14: 3). How beautiful is this promise, which is our dream to reach.

All of our spiritual life is to "Be with the Lord." With this promise the Lord pleased the heart of the thief; He didn't care about His own pain on the Cross and spoke to him in a calm and comforting manner. The Lord totally forgot about His pain, He forgot the nails and the thorns, the wounds and His aching body and instead He listened to the thief, talked to him and calmed and comforted him saying: "Love does not seek its own." (I Corinthians 13:5) but cares for others (ICorinthians 10:24).

There are so many times people come with their problems and agony to us for help, we got annoyed and say to them "Ok my brother, later, I am busy now, wait for a while." But the Lord Jesus, even on the Cross, even in His pain, He didn't say these words, but He gave His attention to the thief. He answered what he asked for, and He made him happy. The Lord Jesus shows us although He is on the Cross, He helped others. By this He showed us the importance of serving individuals as opposed to serving groups. In addition to the great redemption for the whole world, given to whoever believes in Him and His forgiveness on the Cross, there was an individual service with the thief, because one person, to Jesus, is not lost among the group. He is still important and worthy in the eyes of the Lord.

Therefore, the Lord Jesus Christ, in His entire earthy mission, worked in two fields: with individuals and with groups. The group work was among the crowd of five thousand who surrounded Him during His Sermon on the Mount and He fed them with five loaves and two fish. The individual work was among the twelve disciples, with Peter, James and John, with Nicodemus, in the house of Mary and Martha and with the Samaritan woman near the well. In the midst of His pain He didn't leave the individuals in order to work with the group. He never forgot the individual. He goes after the lost sheep while He is busy with the other ninety nine. He also saved the thief on the right while He was in the middle of taking care of the salvation of the rest of the world.

THE THIRD WORD

"Behold your son... Behold your mother"

(John 19:26, 27).

Caring for others was the most important issue for the Lord whilst on the Cross. Just as He cared for those who crucified Him by saying, "Father, forgive them" and He cared for the thief on the right by promising him Paradise, "Today, you will be with Me in Paradise," He cared also for His mother and promised her John the Beloved to care for her.

He promised the virgin to His celibate disciple. He promised His mother who often carried Him on her chest, to His disciple the beloved who often rested on His chest. He promised His mother who stood beside Him on the Cross, to the only disciple who followed Him until the Cross. He promised His mother who carried Him in her womb, to His disciple who later wrote a Gospel to emphasise His divinity. He said to her: "Behold your son" and He said to him, "Behold your mother." "And from that time, the disciple took her to his house." (John 19: 27).

Therefore, the Lord gave us an example of caring for our family members and our relatives in the flesh, especially the mother. He cared for the one who carried Him nine months. He cared for His mother and He lived His life giving her honour (Luke 2:51).

Usually people care for a person who is suffering, but Jesus in His pain and suffering, cares for others. Living a life of devotion, serving the Lord and keeping busy serving the big family, the Church, should be no excuse for you to neglect your family (I Timothy 5:8), or exempt you from honouring your parents and looking after your mother.

There was a link between Jesus Christ and His mother St. Mary. Her pure face was the first thing He saw when He came by flesh to the world and it was the last face He saw before His soul departed into the hands of the Father. It is the heart of the loving mother who always sought Him and followed Him wherever He went and was attached to Him in His suffering with love, saying to Him the impressive words, "But the world rejoices at the acceptance of salvation, while my heart burns when I look at your crucifixion, which You endured for the sake of all, O My Son and My God."

It is also the heart of the Son who cares for the mother in His severe pain and sufferings. And so the Lord Jesus Christ has to care for His mother during His sufferings by saying words of comfort to her even though a sword will pierce through her own soul (Luke 2:35). He shall comfort her during His sufferings by giving her a son suitable to look after her. He comforted her in 3 ways: by talking to her, by caring for her, by arranging her matters and giving her a spiritual son to comfort her and give her company.

The conversation on the Cross between the Lord and His mother is different from the conversation between Him and the thief on the right. The thief started first, but with Saint Mary, the Lord started first. She is His mother and He doesn't need to wait until she begins. He doesn't wait for her to complain, she never complained. St. Mary was always silent and never talked, even when she was next to the Cross. No one saw her crying or making even a sound, but she was quiet and strong in her sufferings. The Lord understood her silence and He heard it. He knows her feelings and her emotions. He talked to her without her asking Him. She obeyed His words and went with the beloved disciple to his house.

St. Mary was a blessing to John, blessing to his house, given from Jesus as a reward for His love. The disciple took her as a precious jewel, more expensive than the whole world. She stayed in his house as a costly deposit until she departed. It was said that John the disciple didn't leave Jerusalem until she departed. If John was able to reach such a level of love for the Lord to follow Him till the Cross and stay there, then he should receive a reward for that, here and in eternity. On earth he received the blessings of the Virgin in his house. Whoever followed Jesus benefited from His blessings and His grace.

The Virgin took John as her son; the Lord gave her the most gentle, loving, sincere and compassionate disciple. John the Beloved was the disciple which spoke the most about love. He is the one who said: "God is love." (I John 4:16). He is the disciple, "who lent on Jesus' bosom", He was loved by Jesus. He was the one who offered to St. Mary the closest picture of her Son.

It appeared that Jesus owned nothing on the Cross, even His clothes, they took it and divided it between them. But He owned John and He gave him His mother. John who offered His heart to Jesus, He took it and gave it as a gift to His mother, and so the Lord gathered all His beloved together. He also cared for His mother emotionally and materially. Who was then looking after who: the Virgin or John? The Virgin was in John's house, to fill him with grace and blessing and to grant him knowledge about Jesus, deeper and wider than the rest who knew Him.

This is a strong evidence to prove that St. Mary had no other children as the Protestants say. Because, if she had children, then they would ask for her and get her blessing by her presence in their home instead of a stranger. The Virgin was lonely at that time: she had no children, no Joseph the carpenter who had departed earlier, so He promised her to one of His disciples. The word "He is your son" gives us an idea about the spiritual sonship and also to honour the Virgin by all the disciples.

THE FOURTH WORD

"My God, My God, why have You forsaken Me?"

(Matthew 27:46).

These words don't mean His divinity departed from His humanity or that the Father left the Son. It does not mean separation, but it means that the Father left Him for suffering. His divinity never departed His humanity not even a single moment or a twinkle of an eye. We believe in this and we pray it in the Holy Liturgy.

His redemption is unlimited, giving unlimited salvation, required to forgive all sins in all ages. Then there is no separation between His humanity and His divinity. His relationship with the Father: He didn't leave Him, "Believe Me that I am in the Father and the Father in Me." (John 14: 11).

Then what do these words mean "Why have You forsaken Me"? They do not mean separation, but it means: You left Me for the suffering. You left Me to bear the divine anger over sins. This is from the side of the soul, but from the flesh side, so You left Me to feel the pain, the suffering. It would have been easy for Him to not feel the pain with His Divine power, if so it would have meant that the crucifixion was just a picture and not true suffering and so He would not have paid the ransom of sin and there would have been no redemption and no salvation.

But the Father left the Son to suffer, the Son accepted it and He suffered and that is why he came, it is leaving by an agreement. He left

Him by love, "Yet it pleased the Lord to bruise Him; He has put Him to grief."(Isaiah 53:10). Here is an example to help you understand better. Imagine a father taking his son for an operation. The father holds his son's hand and the doctor starts his work. The child screams calling his father saying, "Why have you left me?" Actually the father didn't leave his child, but was holding him tightly, although he left him for the pain and the suffering. He left him with love. This is a type of leaving without separation. This is just an example to make it easier to understand although there is a big difference between the two.

The words "Left Me" means that the suffering of the crucifixion was a real pain, and pain of the divine anger towards sins is so extensive. During this time of leaving, all the suffering and pain is concentrated and augmented, as well as, the pain for salvation. Here Jesus stood as a burnt offering and a sacrifice for sin, ignited by the divine fire until the offering becomes ashes in order to complete God's justice.

Many have interpreted these words saying that the Lord only mentioned these words to remind the Jews of Psalm 22 which started with these words. "You are mistaken, not knowing the Scriptures nor the power of God." (Matthew 22:29), although these books, as the Lord says "are they which testify of Me" (John 5:39). So the Lord gave them this particular Psalm to remind them, because it used to be known not by its number ,but by saying the first few words of it just as the monks do now a days.

What about this Psalm then? In this Psalm, "They pierced My hands and My feet; I can count all My bones. They look and stare at Me. They divided My garments among them, and for My clothing they cast lots." (Psalm 22:16-18). It was obvious that David, who wrote this Psalm, didn't have his hands or feet pierced, nor did anyone divide his garments or cast lots on his clothing. But this Psalm was inspired by prophecies about Jesus as Jesus said to them on the Cross: "Go, read the Psalm 'My God, My God, why have You forsaken Me?'", and see what has been said about Me. You will see that they were saying about

Me also: "A reproach of men, and despised by the people. All those who see Me ridicule Me; they shoot out the lip, they shake the head, saying, 'He trusted in the Lord, let Him rescue Him; Let Him deliver Him, since He delights in Him!'" (Psalm 22: 6-8).

We don't have the time to talk about the whole Psalm; it is a great image of the immense suffering of Jesus on the Cross. They face Him, "He opened their understanding, that they might comprehend the Scriptures." (Luke 24; 45). All that was written in the Psalms has been achieved. Therefore, He said in a little while "It is finished". But why didn't He say "It is finished" straight after "My God, My God, why have You forsaken Me?" because there was another word in the Psalms which wasn't yet fulfilled and that was, "My strength is dried up like a potsherd, and My tongue clings to My jaws" (verse 15). This will also be fulfilled in a little while when He says, "I am thirsty" and then He says afterward "It is finished."

Why did Jesus say "My God, My God"? He said it on behalf of the whole of humanity. He said it because He made Himself of no reputation, and took upon Himself the "form of a servant, and was made in the likeness of men" (Philippians 2:7,8). He said it because, "He humbled Himself, and became obedient unto death even the death of the Cross." (Philippians 2: 9). He spoke now as a son of man, He took on the human nature, He took his place, all the sins are put on Him, and He is paying the ransom on behalf of all of mankind.

Here we see all humanity speak on His mouth, because all the sins of the people are on Him. Sin is separation from God and it is the wrath of God. So the whole of humanity cries out saying: "My God, My God, why have You forsaken Me?" The Lord Jesus Christ represented the whole of humanity in several things if not all!

He represented us in fasting, on our behalf: Adam and Eve were not able to fast from the fruit which was prohibited; they cut it and ate it. He began His life by fasting from even the permitted food. He wasn't in need of fasting, but He fasted 40 days on our behalf as we chant in the praises at Church.

He represented us in the obedience to the Law: "The Lord looks down from heaven upon the children of men, to see if there are any who understand, who seek God. They have all turned aside, they have together become corrupt; there is none who does good, no, not one." (Psalm 14:2,3).

Jesus came, and on behalf of all humanity in the obedience to the Father and to the law, "To fulfil all righteousness" (Matthew 3:15) as when He was being baptised, and so He represented humanity by giving Himself a clean, pure life acceptable before the Father.

He also represented us in death and in paying the ransom of sins, "For He made Him who knew no sin to be sin for us." (2 Corinthians 5:21). He bore all the curses of the law, He bore also the wrath of God onto the sinner with all bitterness. So He represents the whole of humanity by saying, "My God , My God why have You forsaken Me."

He who helped everyone and never left anyone, they all deserted Him, even the Father. And so He paid the ransom for sin, and carried the wrath. He received the victory after He went through the suffering alone in flesh and soul. In order to be careful, He gave us a lesson from what He has gone through.

"See then that you walk circumspectly, not as fools but as wise." (Ephesians 5: 15). Be fearful to leave God otherwise He will leave us. The son Himself left, the pain of leaving was harsh. In all of this let us thank the Lord Jesus Christ and praise Him for all His love and His giving.

The words "Why have you forsaken Me" give us much comfort each time we experience tribulation. If God the Father allowed His Son to experience the pain, suffering and sadness, why do we then complain about the pain in which God the Father allows? The Father was pleased to allow His only Son to be crushed with sadness: "He is My beloved Son in whom I am well pleased." (Matthew 3: 17). We haven't been exposed to any of these pains although we deserve it, so why then do we complain about our tribulations?

The Son drank from the cup which was given by the Father; He said to Him: "According to Your will", He obeyed till death, the death of the Cross in all submissiveness. The words "Why have You forsaken Me", wasn't a type of protest or complaint, but a recording of His pain, proving its truth and proclaiming that the salvation process is on its way to completion.

THE FIFTH WORD

"I Thirst"

(John 19: 28).

Because of my sins, my brethren and because of your sins the mouth of our crucified Lord was dry: "My strength is dried up like a potsherd, And My tongue clings to My jaws." (Psalm 22:15). His body's water drained and bled from many causes. Some was due to the heavy sweat, falling like great drops of blood while He struggled for our sake in the Garden of Gethsemane (Luke 22:44). The sweat which fell down to the ground while carrying the Cross, and during the scorching hot weather, in the middle of the day and also the pain and the exhaustion of the trial, the beatings and the hitting, all contributed to His condition.

In addition to all of this, the great loss of blood is due to the crown of thorns and the nails. So His tongue clings to His jaws, He bears it all until He has no strength and says: "I am Thirsty." He proclaimed that the fire started to eat up the burnt sacrifice. He declared that the Divine Justice took its part, and the divinity, His covenant, did not interfere to reduce the pain of His humanity. It was a complete pain with the acceptable aroma that pleased the Father, and the Son expressed it by the words "I am thirsty". Let Eutychus be ashamed because he took away from the Lord's humanity. If His humanity was not complete, He would not say "I am thirsty".

It is strange that the fountain of water is thirsty. He who grants the everlasting water to all thirsty people (John 4:14). He who said to the Samaritan woman: "But whoever drinks of the water that I shall give him will never thirst. But the water that I shall give him will become in him a fountain of water springing up into everlasting life."

What did He mean by the words "I am thirsty"? No doubt, He was truly thirsty according to the flesh, but from the spiritual side He was thirsty for the salvation of the whole world. He was thirsty for the words "It is finished" which He will say later. As He said to the Samaritan woman "Give Me a drink", He didn't mean normal water, "Whoever drinks of this water will thirst again." (John 4:13), He didn't take the water from her, but He was thirsty for her salvation and for all of the city of Samaria.

He didn't say "I am thirsty" in order to take water from people for He knew that they would offer Him vinegar! (Matthew 27:48). He knew this by His divinity that reveals the unknown and the future. He knew that also from the prophecy which says: "For my thirst they gave me vinegar to drink." (Psalm 69:21).

He didn't say "I am Thirsty" for them to give Him water, the Lord doesn't need help from human beings. Also He meant to drink the cup of suffering until the end. They gave Him sour wine mingled with gall to drink, to anaesthetise Him to reduce His pain, "But when He had tasted it, He would not drink." (Matthew 27:34).

The Lord wanted to complete the prophecies about Him and to declare that the ransom is paid for, to reassure the people. The sinful human race mocked Him although He paid for its salvation. They gave Him vinegar for His thirst to increase the pain. We do this to Him also. Every time He asks to drink for our salvation, from the fruit of His vineyard which passes through our veins, do we offer Him vinegar of our sin, and our negligence?! My brother, put down this rod which you lifted up to Jesus' mouth, and take away this sponge filled with vinegar. You have wounded the One who loves you; do good deeds worth of repentance.

If you heard the Lord saying "I am thirsty", say to Him, "It is me Lord who dried Your mouth with my sins, I wish to give you my tears instead. I wish for You to hit this hard rock of mine, which is my heart, and blow water out of it so that it may flow.

THE SIXTH WORD

"It is finished."

(John 19: 30)

Jesus our Lord, the Righteous and complete in all things, the holy One who is without sin, who lived on earth a full life who pleased God the Father, He Himself fulfiled all this in His preaching, in His mission and in His service. He managed to fulfil His mission.

"I have finished the work which You have given Me to do." (John 17:4). He was able to complete all righteousness, fulfil all the law of righteousness, and cry out to all the people, "Which of you convicts Me of sin?" (John 8:46).

He also fulfils the prophecies regarding Himself and the related ones to the great redemption in a few years, around three years and a few months. He managed to do the work that nobody else could do before. He preached the annunciation of the Kingdom of God, He said to the Father, "I have glorified You on earth, I have manifested Your name to the men whom You have given Me out of the world. They were Yours, You gave them to Me, and they have kept Your word. For I have given to them the words which You have given Me; and they have received them, and all Mine are Yours, and Yours are Mine, and I am glorified in them. Those whom You gave Me I have kept; and none of them is lost, I have given them Your word, I know them." (John 17).

So He fulfilled the prophecies, the obedience, the righteousness, the mission, the preaching, the deeds and the love. "Having loved

His own who were in the world, He loved them to the end." (John 13:1). Then He was on the Cross to finish the work of sacrifice, the redemption and the salvation, to fulfil the reconciliation in which He reconciled heaven with earth.

On this Altar, the Lord put all our sins. He put all the sins of the people from all generations, from Adam till the end of ages, which includes all weakness, fornication, betrayal, adultery, lying, stealing, murdering, envy and arrogance; till the Son cried out loudly saying: "It is finished". Now we put our hands on this pure sacrifice and repent every day with new sins adding to His sufferings and pain in order for Him to delete them with His honoured blood.

He carried all the sins on His shoulders. He said about this, "I gave My back to those who struck Me, and My cheeks to those who plucked out the beard; I did not hide My face from shame and spitting." (Isaiah 50:6). He said also: "All those who see Me ridicule Me; a reproach of men, and despised by the people." (Psalm 22: 7,6). He was attacked by hitting, insults, beating, mocking, contempt, blasphemy and sarcasm.

They spat in His face and beat Him; and others struck Him saying: "Prophesy to us, Christ! Who is the one who struck You?" (Matthew 26: 67,68). "They stripped Him and put a scarlet robe on Him, twisted a crown of thorns, they crucified Him between two robbers to fulfil the prophecy which is written 'Cursed is everyone who hangs on a tree,'" (Galatians 3:13, Deuteronomy 21:23) and so He became "a curse for our sake". On the tree, they filled Him with insults and mockery, He looked at all of these and said: "It is finished."

As He fulfilled His curse, His sufferings were complete, as well as the wrath and the ransom and He offered Himself as a sacrifice. The fire burnt the burnt offering until it became ashes (Leviticus 6:10). When the Lord saw that the work of redemption and salvation was finished and gave the divine judge all that He asked for, He cried out saying: "It is finished."

The salvation for all is finished; the redemption is complete, able now for the woman's Descendant to crush the head of the serpent. The Lord was able to destroy the kingdom of Satan and, as psalm 93 says, "The Lord reigns." Now the redemption is completed in full, enough for all. Now the veil is torn in two, the way to the holy of the holies is open, reconciliation is finished, the hope for the sleeping Saints who departed. The only thing left is for the Lord God to ride prosperously "Gird Your sword upon Your thigh, O Mighty One, With Your glory and Your majesty." (Psalm 45:3). The Lord says with joy: "It is finished."

The words "It is finished" are filled with cheers of joy and victory. The Lord cheers those who struggle and reign. He was able to buy us with a ransom, build a spiritual foundation, destroy Satan's kingdom in which he used to be called, "the ruler of the world." (John 14:30).

Are you able my brother to succeed like the Lord? Are you able to be on the cross and crush the head of the serpent? Are you able to see your works in which the Lord gave you and you say "It is finished"? I wish that you will always put these beautiful words before you, "The work that You gave me to do, I finished it." Always put the image of Jesus, who finished His work, in front of you.

THE SEVENTH WORD

"Father, into Your hands I commit My spirit"

(Luke 23:46)

The Lord finished His work on the Cross. He also finished the work before the Cross. There is still extra work left to do after He submits His Spirit on the Cross. "He led captivity captive, and gave gifts to men." (Ephesians 4: 8). He needed to go down to Hades and preach to the dead for hope and to move these sleeping saints, who departed, from Hades to Paradise thereby opening the doors of Paradise which were closed since the first sin.

Once he finished the work of redemption, there was no time to delay. He needed to get out of the flesh to continue the salvation necessary for those who departed too. He yielded up His Spirit in the Hands of the Father, so He will be able to do the work that is required to be done after death. So He cried out loudly, "Father, in Your hands I commit My spirit."

In Your hands I committed it and in no other hands, but Yours, "The ruler of the world is coming and he has nothing in Me." (John 14:30), "I came forth from the Father and have come into the world. Again, I leave the world and go to the Father." (John 16:28).

How much the ruler of this world needs this soul; to capture like he did with other souls in prison? But he wasn't able to take this special soul in which the Father will take in His Hands, this soul no one else is able to take. "I have power to lay it down; I have power to take it again."

(John 10: 18). Lazarus the beggar died, and was carried by the angels to Abraham's bosom (Luke 16:22). The soul of St. Mary was carried by Jesus, but the soul of Jesus was carried by the Lord God the father.

The Apostle Matthew said that Jesus, "Cried out with a loud voice." (Matthew 27:50), and yielded up His spirit. So what do we understand from this word, "Cried out with a loud voice"?

There was no doubt He was very exhausted and worn out in the flesh. After all this pain, He carried the Cross even though He fell underneath it, after the whipping, spitting and beating, after the blood and the water flowed from His flesh, after His mouth dried and He said: "I am thirsty." How could He cry with a loud voice with His tongue clinging to His jaws?!

His crying out at the time of death "with a loud voice" indicates that He had another power over the power of humanity; which is His Divinity. His crying with a loud voice indicates His victory. With death, He trampled and conquered death; this loud voice threatened and conquered Satan. Truly, in Christ's death there is victory; the victory of the redeemer who is able to save the whole world and crush the head of the serpent.

These words "In Your hands I commit My spirit" assures us and show us the immortality of the spirit. It doesn't end in death. Death is like a passing over or transition from life to life. The most important matter is where the spirit will end up after its death? If one is assured of this point, then he will accept death with joy and happiness, saying I am delighted to leave.

And you, my brother: Are you calmed about the fate of your spirit? Will you commit it into the hands of Jesus, and the angels will carry it like Lazarus' spirit, or will Satan capture it and say: "This is mine, it is from my army, it was living under my obedience and so I will take it to be with me." Oh what a terrifying thing!!! So calm yourself my brother, where will your spirit go? Also, put this beautiful hymn before you: "Let me die the death of the righteous, and let my end be like his!" (Numbers 23:10).

Commit yourself into His hands from now on. Stay away from all evil things and be close to the Lord. Be like the angel of the seven churches in which the Lord holds His hands with them. Put yourself also in the hands of Jesus and be sure that He will let you hear His beautiful voice saying: "I give them eternal life, and they shall never perish; neither shall anyone snatch them out of My hand." (John 10:28). Every time a sin comes by thought or desire, ask yourself explicitly: "Is my spirit with the Lord, with the Father?"

THE EFFECTS OF THESE WORDS IN OUR LIFE

These precious words in which the Lord spoke on the Cross; let us put them in our heart, let them work in our life. Read each word with meditation and respond to them. We are going to give two examples on how the heart responds with these two words:

"My Father, forgive them." The Lord taught us to pray in the Lord 's Prayer, "Forgive us our trespasses as we forgive those who trespass against us." Then the words, "My Father, forgive them," must be a condition we must follow for the remission or forgiveness of our sins. We can not think that forgiveness is granted to others when we say, "My Father, forgive them"; in reality, he is taking this forgiveness for himself, because the condition that you take, is to forgive others, "Forgive and you will be forgiven." (Luke 6: 37).

When the Lord Jesus Christ taught us the Lord's Prayer, He didn't comment on any other supplication other than this one. So He said: "For if you forgive men their trespasses, your heavenly Father will also forgive you. But if you do not forgive men their trespasses, neither will your Father forgive your trespasses." (Matthew 6:14,5).

Therefore, if you don't forgive others, you will prevent forgiveness for yourself and not for others. If you say, "Father, forgive them", He will answer you saying, "And also I will forgive you." So then, your forgiveness to others is a must; you have to do it in order to receive forgiveness. Perhaps this forgiveness makes you troubled from within, and it is not easy on your heart. How could I forgive those who did such and such to me; they humiliated me, troubled me and crushed me into the dust! I say to you, when you grant this person forgiveness, you give it to yourself. Forgive so the Lord will forgive you. I say to you, forgive with love, and not by force.

The Lord Jesus Christ came on the Cross to take forgiveness from the Father for all the sins of all of humanity. He forgave those who crucified Him first. He was saying to the Father: "I will forgive them all that they did to Me, so that in order You Forgive Me." Not for Him to forgive His sins, because Jesus is with no sin (John 8:46). But to forgive the sins that He carried as He is "The Lamb of God who takes away the sin of the world!" (John 1:29), "And the Lord has laid on Him the iniquity of us all." (Isaiah 53: 6).

You may say: "How can I forgive what they did to me? It is enough for me to be silent, not answer evil for evil." No, my brother, this silence is not enough. In order to triumph yourself from within you have to forgive. When you have triumphed from within and forgive, you will then be raised to the Cross.

When you reach the Cross, you will be able to say: "that I may know Him and the power of His resurrection, and the fellowship of His sufferings." (Philippians 3:10). I entered in His fellowship, reached the Cross and have received forgiveness of my trespasses because they do not know what they are doing.

Today you will be with Me in the paradise. Tell yourself: "In order to hear this promise from Jesus, I have to say like the thief, 'we receive justly, for we receive the due reward of our deeds.'" The thief on the right did not complain of his sufferings, but he asks for forgiveness in eternal life. So be like him, and don't be like the other thief who asked Jesus to go down from the Cross and take him with Him: "Save Yourself and us."

This poor ignorant person; when Jesus goes down from the Cross He will destroy the whole world. This thief could have sought to be saved. He could have said: "Wait for a while on the Cross, for my sake, so I am not destroyed... Please Lord, bear it for my sake, bear it to pay the ransom of my sins till death.

My brother, be in the spirit like the thief on the right who was thinking of his eternal life, and was not in the flesh like the thief on the left who only thought of his own salvation. Try not to escape from tribulation when it comes upon you, but in every problem say these words which the thief on the right said: "We indeed justly deserve, for we receive the due reward of our deeds."

As you want the Lord to remember you in His kingdom, then remember Him on earth and let your heart be filled with His love. Don't ask the Lord to remember you only on earth, but ask Him also in His kingdom. If there are nails and crosses on the earth, don't worry, the important thing is your fate in the Kingdom. It is nothing if you lived your earthly life on the cross, but it is important to be with Him in His paradise.

Don't think to go down from the cross, but bear and have patience. The Lord said to the thief, "Today, you will be with Me in Paradise", because Christ accepted his faith, his confession and his repentance. And you, did you offer the Lord your confession, repentance and faith in order to deserve to be with Him in Paradise? If you haven't, then start from now. Join with Him in the sufferings so as to be glorified also with Him.

Remember the words, "Today, you will be with Me in Paradise" are very encouraging words which grant hope. If the thief received the promise of Paradise in spite of all his sins and his evil deeds you should not despair whatever your sins are. If the thief's repentance was accepted while it was the last hour of his life, then do not despair if your old life was eaten by locusts and was completely wasted

The words "Today, you will be with Me in Paradise" gives us a practical example for speedy answers to prayers. As soon as the thief said, "Remember me O Lord", the Lord answered quickly, "Today, you will be with Me in Paradise". Then don't get bored from prayers and supplications, and don't let the words "Remember me Lord" leave your mouth, saying all the time, from deep within your heart, with faith and trust that He will answer.

Don't let the devil fight you with embarrassment so you don't ask. The Tax Collector, in his deep shame said, "Lord, have mercy". The thief knew his sins and said, "Remember me O Lord." And so all of us, although there is shame covering our faces because of our sins, and we are not able to raise our face to the Lord, but it is only because of His mercy, His love and His forgiveness that we can still say the words, "Remember me O Lord" until we receive the promise from Him to be in Paradise.

The Lord didn't stop by just giving the thief a promise to Paradise, but more, he received a promise that He will be with Him, because the most important thing in Paradise is to be with the Lord. Yes, Paradise without the Lord is nothing, no pleasure, no value and not even worth the word Paradise. True pleasure is to be with the Lord, the presence of the Lord with His people, enjoying His presence, His love, His company, His light, His Fatherhood and His gentleness.

Then don't ask for Paradise , but ask for the Lord Himself. Ask to be with Him, meditate on His smile and His joyful face, as David said: "To You, Lord, Do not hide Your face from me." It is strange that the thief received the promise to be with the Lord in Paradise, although he was beside the Lord on earth.

Although, it was a very little time he spent with the Lord, he was able to be granted continuous company with the Lord, forever. It was a very intense hour which reached to the depth of our Lord's heart. It is therefore, not by increasing the time spent with the Lord, but by the depth. One word uttered in depth is worth a great deal. Say this word, live with this deep relationship, so you can reach the depth with the Lord.

CPSIA information can be obtained
at www.ICGtesting.com
Printed in the USA
FFOW03n1054240317
33649FF